THE STORY
of
BISHOP'S CASTLE

THE STORY

of

BISHOP'S CASTLE

Edited by

David Preshous,
George Baugh, John Leonard,
Gavin Watson & Andrew Wigley

Logaston Press

LOGASTON PRESS
Little Logaston Woonton Almeley
Herefordshire HR3 6QH
logastonpress.co.uk

First published by Logaston Press 2016

ISBN 978 1 9010839 08 9

Typeset by Logaston Press
and printed and bound in Poland by
www.lfbookservices.co.uk

Front cover: Bishop's Castle from Middle Bailey
Rear cover: Eaton railway station (B.C. Railway); House on Crutches;
View down High Street; Blunden Hall.

CONTENTS

ACKNOWLEDGEMENTS

This book is the product of much research by a team of authors pursuing their subjects with enthusiasm to offer a survey of Bishop's Castle's history and character in an accessible style.

Thanks are offered in the first place for generous financial support from the Shropshire Archaeological and Historical Society's Pagett Fund, the Walker Trust, Bishop's Castle Town Council and Bishop's Castle Civic Society. The South-West Shropshire Historical and Archaeological Society (S.W.S.H.A.S.) is thanked for support and for acting as banker.

Bishop's Castle Heritage Forum has backed the publication, and much practical assistance has been received from the Bishop's Castle Heritage Resource Centre (B.C.H.R.C.). The Centre provided a meeting place and made its impressive range of local resources available, while the volunteers, responsive to all inquiries, have offered guidance and expertise. Similarly, Mary McKenzie, the county archivist, and Shropshire Archives staff have been very helpful on many occasions, as have Hereford Cathedral and the Diocesan Office, and the Bishop's Castle Railway Society and Museum. Enterprise South-West, the town's IT, Computer and Business Centre, has given valuable help and advice on technical matters.

It is especially pleasing that James Lawson, well acquainted with local historical research, agreed to write the Foreword.

The authors have had access to much published documentary material but were also able to consult many local people with special interests in the town's history and development. It is impossible to name all who have shared their knowledge, but grateful thanks are offered to them, particularly by the author of Chapter 13. Mark Hutton expressed an early interest in the book and is thanked for advice in connexion with Chapter 6. The author of Chapters 4 and 8 acknowledges the late Anne Lawrence's work on the castle's history and John Bennett's on local bus operators; the authors of Chapters 11 and 12 wish to add their thanks to the House on Crutches Museum Collection Trust and Mrs Janet Preshous and to acknowledge the work of the late Mrs Margot Daniel and the late Mrs Ivy Evans, long-standing members of the S.W.S.H.A.S. Research Group.

Many of the illustrations have been provided by the authors and editors; others come from the S.W.S.H.A.S. Collection or from the resources of B.C.H.R.C.; and wherever possible photographers, or the owners of photographs, are named under the captions. Acknowledgement of permissions is also offered to Emmanuel Beddoes (for illustration 13.2), the Bishop's Castle Railway Society (9.4), Marion Blockley (for the map facing page 1), the British Museum (11.1), the Clwyd-Powys Archaeological Trust (4.1), Nigel Gaspar (6.2), Mrs Humphries (13:9), M. Jukes (10.5), the Alan Keef Collection (9.5), Colin Love (4.5), Ken Lucas (9.4), Jean North/ Henry Hand (10.1), the Omnibus Society (8:5), Keith Ritherdon (4:2), Scenesetters (1.1-2, 4, and 6-9), Shropshire Archives (6.1, 7.1) Shropshire Council (14.6), Shropshire Museum Service (2.3 (figurine), 3.2, 4), the *Shropshire Star* (11.4, 13.7), Peter Toghill (1.3, 5), the Town Council (6:2), the *Wellington Journal* (13.7), Basil Wood (9:3) and K. Woodward (9:6).

It was a particular pleasure that Andy and Karen Johnson, of Logaston Press, agreed to undertake this publication. They have a tremendous reputation in local-history publishing, which is due in no small part to their patience, good humour and understanding.

The Editors

FOREWORD

The Story of Bishop's Castle guides the reader from geological time through to the 21st century. A Norman planted town, the borough was carved out of the manor of Lydbury North in the early 12th century by a bishop of Hereford. The linear town plan stretches from the castle at the top of the hill to the church at the bottom. The castle began to decay in the Elizabethan period and effectively nothing remains, the site having been colonized by buildings. The backsides of the burgage plots have now been developed, but the town plan remains basically intact. Some have claimed that the town is no more than a village, and in 2001 its population was still below 2,000 despite peripheral new housing since the Second World War. The town remains a border town serving the needs of an isolated pastoral area. By the end of the Middle Ages it had a Friday market and annual fairs. These were confirmed in a royal charter acquired in 1573, and in 1584 forty-odd burgesses elected two Members of Parliament for the first time. The town became a notoriously rotten borough in the early 18th century until Robert Clive, a rich nabob, created a pocket borough by buying out all those whose property gave them a political interest in it.

Until the early 17th century there were separate marketing places for different products, but in 1619 the lord of the manor, the Earl of Northampton, built a market hall, part of which survives as the Bishop's Castle Railway Museum. This was superseded by the present Town Hall in the middle of the street built probably in the 1750s. It dominates the town from the steepest part of the street with its clock and cupola with bells striking the hours and quarters. A Market Hall, embellished with the Clive arms, was provided in 1781.

The medieval town bell was in the church tower and summoned the burgesses to suppress affrays; traders coming to the fair were forbidden to carry arms as late as the 1570s.

The isolated town's communications have been principally with Shrewsbury. The main route originally ran between the Stiperstones and the Long Mynd via Norbury and Bridges over Cothercott Hill to Pulverbatch and Longden and so down to Shrewsbury A more westerly route, from Lydham along the Hope Valley to Minsterley, was turnpiked in the 1830s. More excitingly, the mid-19th century spawned a railway from Craven Arms, an ambitious project, which only once paid a dividend and was more or less bankrupt from the start. A remarkable and crazy railway, it survived in a receiver's hands until 1935. Nevertheless it benefited the town and the surrounding area by providing a source of coal and an outlet for timber and some livestock more reliably than anything the town had had before.

The victualling trade has always been prominent; pubs abounded and despite more straightened times there are still six, including the Castle Hotel. At a time in the 1950s when country breweries almost disappeared the Three Tuns continued brewing in its fine Victorian tower brewery. Hostelries exploited the era of the rotten borough submitting bloated bills for 'treating'. All this was not new: the puritan vicar, Walter Stephens (1576-1629), inveighed against the 'Friday Devil' – drunkenness on market day – though to little effect.

My own interest in the town was kindled in the late 1950s when as a post-graduate I was working on 18th-century politics – writing up Bishop's Castle elections in the rotten borough's most corrupt, early 18th-century, phase. That story is re-told later in this book, but there is one individual who spans the transition from 'rotten' to 'pocket' borough – Corbyn Morris (1710-79), the son of Edmund Morris. Edmund was tenant of Blunden Hall under the Charltons of Ludford and a burgess and freeholder in the town. He was worth a few votes in hard-fought elections. Corbyn was a bright boy, and his father was anxious to provide him with a good education. Edmund's support of the Duke of Chandos was thus conditional on providing a place for the boy in the Charterhouse; that depended on a vacancy, and until one was available Chandos paid the fees. The boy next appears at Queens' College, Cambridge, in 1727 as a pensioner on the recommendation of Robert More of Linley. After Corbyn graduated More sought a 'job' for the 'ingenious and industrious young man', telling Sir Robert Walpole of the family's support for the Whig interest at Bishop's Castle. It was forthcoming, and subsequent promotion in the Treasury and customs administration all exploited the family support for the Whigs. The *Oxford Dictionary of National Biography* notes that he was a political hack for successive Whig administrations and an economic theorist but states nothing of his Bishop's Castle background beyond his birth there. When Lord Clive was turning Bishop's Castle into a pocket borough the Morris interest was duly acquired – at a price.

In the 21st century the town continues to be a hub for the surrounding area. It provides health services to remote communities – G.P. surgery, old people's home at Stone House, G.P. hospital with facilities for audiology and physiotherapy. Within the town there is a pharmacy, opticians and chiropodist. The town has a strong sense of community especially in defence of its hospital. A trust recently raised the money needed to restore and re-equip the 18th-century Town Hall and now administers it. Voluntary effort supports the Railway Museum and the House on Crutches Museum. There is an active Historical Research Group in association with the South-West Shropshire Archaeological and Historical Society, which publishes an annual *Journal*. The present book bears witness to much of the work that has been done in recent years and provides a much needed history of the town.

James Lawson
1st June 2016

ABBREVIATIONS

B.C.H.R.C.	Bishop's Castle Historical Resource Centre
Jnl	Journal
S.A.	Shropshire Archives, Shrewsbury
S.W.S.H.A.S.	South-West Shropshire Historical and Archaeological Society
T.S.A.S.	Transactions of the Shropshire Archaeological and Historical Society
V.C.H.	Victoria County History followed by the abbreviated county name

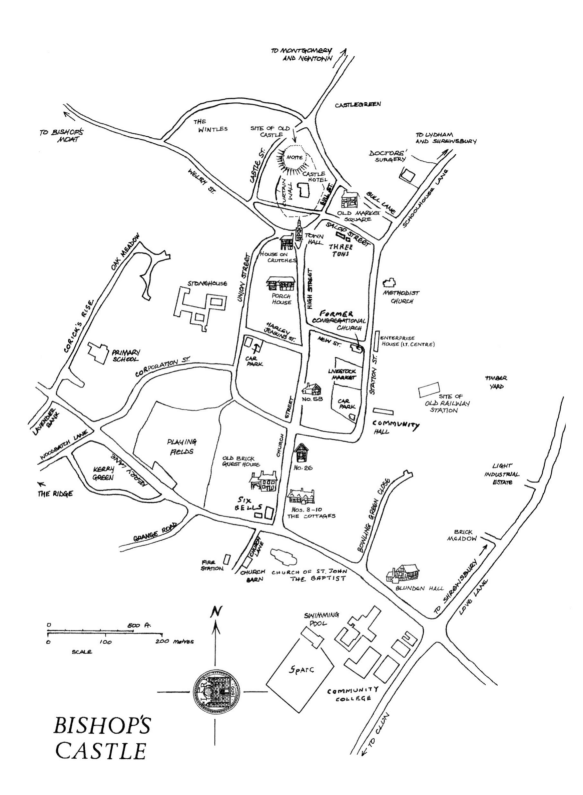

TO MONTGOMERY AND NEWTOWN

CASTLEGREEN

THE WINTLES

SITE OF OLD CASTLE

TO BISHOP'S MOAT

TO LYDHAM AND SHREWSBURY

DOCTORS' SURGERY

WELSH ST.

CASTLE ST.

MOTTE

CASTLE HOTEL

CURTAIN WALL

BULL LANE

SCHOOLHOUSE LANE

OLD MARKET SQUARE

SALOP STREET

THREE TONS

TOWN HALL

HOUSE ON CRUTCHES

STONEHOUSE

OAK MEADOW

CORICK'S RISE

UNION STREET

PORCH HOUSE

HIGH STREET

METHODIST CHURCH

FORMER CONGREGATIONAL CHURCH

HARLEY JENKINS ST.

NEW ST.

ENTERPRISE HOUSE (I.T. CENTRE)

PRIMARY SCHOOL

CORPORATION ST.

CAR PARK

TIMBER YARD

LIVESTOCK MARKET

STATION ST.

LAVENDER BANK

WOODBATCH LANE

STREET

NO. 58

CAR PARK

SITE OF OLD RAILWAY STATION

COMMUNITY HALL

PLAYING FIELDS

CHURCH STREET

LIGHT INDUSTRIAL ESTATE

KERRY GREEN

KERRY LANE

OLD BRICK GUEST HOUSE

NO. 26

THE RIDGE

SIX BELLS

NOS. 8-10 THE COTTAGES

BOWLING GREEN CLOSE

BRICK MEADOW

GRANGE ROAD

FIRE STATION

CHURCH LANE

CHURCH BARN

CHURCH OF ST. JOHN THE BAPTIST

BLUNDEN HALL

TO SHREWSBURY

LOVE LANE

N

500 Ft.

100   200 metres

SCALE

SWIMMING POOL

SPARC

COMMUNITY COLLEGE

TO CLUN

BISHOP'S CASTLE

1   A Landscape Shaped by Rock, Ice and Water

Today the weekly stories of Bishop's Castle can be read in both the *Powys County Times* and the *South Shropshire Journal*, a reflection of the fact that Bishop's Castle is a border town near the administrative boundary between England and Wales. Thirteen centuries ago the border was defined by Offa's Dyke just four miles further west, separating the Anglo-Saxon kingdom of Mercia from the Welsh lordship of Powys. But really the boundary is defined by the nature of the landscape in which the town developed. This region, known as the Marches, a word which itself means 'border', straddles the significant scenic transition between lowland and upland Britain. This is seen historically in the lowland pattern of villages such as Lydbury North, Lydham and More – a cluster of farmhouses and cottages around the central church surrounded by cultivable land which could be worked on the traditional Anglo-Saxon pattern of a centralised village with (usually) three open fields cultivated by the villagers 'in common'. Further west across the Clun Forest this gives way to a scatter of farmsteads, isolated or in small hamlets, each farmer cultivating as best he could the poorer soils on steeper slopes and leaving large areas of unenclosed hillside as common land, typical of the ancient Celtic farming pattern.

Fig. 1.1 The border landscape around Bishop's Castle,
seen from the flank of the Long Mynd above Myndtown

Fig. 1.2 Late Precambrian volcanic scenery would have looked much like that of Galapagos today (above): mostly extinct volcanoes eroding rapidly into the sea – but without the vegetation and onlooker!

The town sits on the eastern end of the Kerry Ridge in a defensive position, once dominated by its castle, initially a motte-and-bailey structure built by a bishop of Hereford around 1100, hence its name. As the rest of this book reveals, the border history continues. This is as far west as the railway was built (before it ran out of money), and the market still sells the hardy stock of Welsh upland farms to English farmers for fattening on lowland pastures.

There is a tendency to think of the surrounding landscape as being naturally immutable and threatened only by our own human activity. It is now designated as an Area of Outstanding Natural Beauty. But to understand the origins and evolution of that border landscape, and hence the significance of the town today, we must cast our minds back, metaphorically speaking, 570 million years to the time when the oldest rock that can be seen in the area was formed.

At that time (Precambrian) the piece of the Earth's continental crust which underlies the Marches lay south of the Antarctic Circle. It was a time before creatures had evolved with hard enough skeletons to be fossilized and life had yet to colonize the land. The surrounding landscape was one of intense volcanic activity, as it had been for several million years, with two plates of the Earth's crust grinding together. The very rapid erosion of the volcanoes carried sediment into an extensive shallow basin where it accumulated, layer upon layer, to a depth of as much as seven kilometres. Movement between the plates squashed this sediment into a vast U-shaped fold, the much eroded remains of which are now seen between the Stiperstones and Church Stretton, most notably as the Long Mynd.

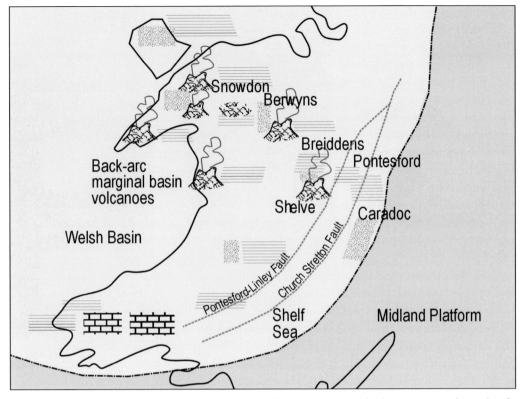

Fig. 1.3 The main geographical features 450 million years ago, which gave rise to the rocks of today's border landscape. (© Peter Toghill)

But clearly much more happened before this area finished up in the temperate latitudes of the northern hemisphere. After the end of a Precambrian Ice Age, the new continental mountains were rapidly eroded and disappeared under the waves of a rising sea. In this sea life started to evolve more rapidly with the appearance of several different groups of animals with hard external skeletons, but there were still no land plants, so the land remained vulnerable to rapid erosion.

Meanwhile our piece of continental crust, 'Avalonia', was drifting northwards through the southern tropics, narrowing the ocean to the north. About 450 million years ago it collided with another continent, 'Baltica'. This resulted in a folding of the strata which we see today in the area to the north of Bishop's Castle, centred around the small village of Shelve. A few million years later, renewed rise in sea levels caused a beach to form around the 'Long Mynd', which became an island in a shallow sea. Fossilized remains of shelly creatures can be found in the rock formed from this beach at several points around the southern end of the Long Mynd from Minton to More.

To the south and west of the Long Mynd a continental slope descended into a deeper ocean. Sediment periodically slumped off the edge of the shelf into deeper water to the west, each slump depositing a layer (bed) from several millimetres up to 15cm in thickness. Most beds were made up of very fine particles solidifying later to mudstone and siltstone, though some were coarser sandstones. These rocks split easily along the planes of their bedding, and are often cracked – 'joined' – at a steep angle to the bedding, caused by their having been squeezed following burial and then released as the overburden was eroded away. The result is a shaley stone with a tendency to weather into fragments. It is this rock, today named by geologists the Bailey Hill Formation after its exposure around Bailey Hill west of Knighton, which underlies the Kerry Ridge and is the very foundation of the top of the town. Wander up Bull Lane and to your right you will see that in places the walls built of thin flat slabs of this rock rest directly on a foundation of the solid rock dipping noticeably to the east (Fig. 1.4).

Fig. 1.4 Wall in Bull Lane of rock from the nearby quarry, sitting directly on dipping beds of the Bailey Hill Formation.

Further compression of the ocean-floor sediments between the continents of Avalonia/ Baltica and Laurentia 420 million years ago led to the final closure of the Iapetus Ocean, and the Caledonian mountain building with the uplift of a whole new mountain range across the north and west of Britain, the residual roots of which are seen in Snowdonia, the Lake District and Scotland (Fig. 1.5).

During these periods of folding and uplift, two intrusions of molten magma rose through cracks in the Earth's crust close to 'Bishop's Castle' and solidified as stronger rock within the sedimentary beds. The older is a coarsely crystalline rock, known as gabbro. It was extensively quarried in the past at More (Squilver) Quarry three miles north of Bishop's Castle. Whilst today that is now a large man-made gash in the hillside, it is believed that the gabbro was a molten lava feeder for a volcano that rose high above More Quarry 445 million years ago. About 20 million years later the second

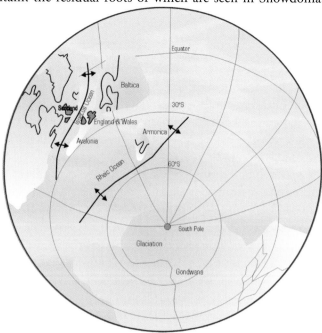

Fig. 1.5 Map of the world 450 million years ago with Avalonia/Baltica about to collide with Laurentia.
(© Peter Toghill)

4

intrusion was at Upper Heblands, to the north of the town. Again it is a crystalline rock, but much finer grained and known as microgranite, indicative of its high silica content. It was never quarried for use in more than a few local buildings, but it does produce a noticeable hummock in the landscape.

As a result of this Caledonian mountain building, the whole geography of the Marches was reversed as the new mountains to the north and west eroded rapidly. Huge quantities of silt, sand and pebbles were swept southwards in rivers that spread their load over a vast delta, the remnants of which we now see as the Old Red Sandstone of the Clee Hills and the Brecon Beacons. But this, and other great crustal movements that continued as our continent drifted northwards over the next 150 million years, across the equator and into the northern tropics, has left no visible evidence in the immediate surroundings of Bishop's Castle.

During this Old Red Sandstone (or Devonian) Period land plants evolved, and by 330 million years ago vast equatorial swamps were buried by influxes of sea which gave rise to our coal seams and hence the name of the Carboniferous Period given to this time. Then another continental collision, bringing together all the Earth's main continental plates into one super continent known as Pangea, left 'the Marches' land-locked amidst the development of great sandy deserts. Across a much eroded and subdued landscape shallow seas covered much of Britain. In these clear warm waters shelly creatures flourished and died, their skeletons accumulating as limestone, now seen in the 180-million-year-old Jurassic limestone of the Cotswolds. After a brief period of lower sea levels, an almost levelled British Isles was covered by a vast shallow sea in which a thick deposit of chalk accumulated from the skeletons of microscopic plants and animals settling in clear waters far from land.

Only about 80 million years ago did continued movements of the Earth's crust start to put into place the landscape which was to evolve gradually into the Marches countryside seen today. A rift appeared in the crust to the west of the European plate as the crust was pushed up by movement of the molten magma deep beneath. This rift gradually opened up to become the Atlantic Ocean, with the ocean crusts on which Britain and America sit being pulled apart by the currents in the semi-fluid mantle. The creation of a new ocean floor spreading out from the mid-Atlantic ridge is a process that continues to the present day. The stresses caused by this, and younger continental collisions (Alpine) to the south, warped the north-west corner of the European continent.

As the northern part of Wales rose up, so the younger rocks such as the chalk and Jurassic limestones eroded to expose the rocks that had formed 350 million years earlier. Thus the essential elements of today's landscape were revealed. The strongest of the ancient rocks locally, the Longmyndian, the Stiperstones Quartzite and the Bailey Hill Formation, remained as upstanding hill country, whilst the much weaker rocks formed from the finer muddy sediments of the old ocean floors were eroded away.

Then as recently as two-and-a-half million years ago the world climate started to cool down again. The Earth entered its most recent ice age, a period during which there were at least four intensely cold spells with warmer spells (inter-glacials) between them. Each glacial period modified the earlier landscape as huge ice sheets blanketed even the higher ground, and valley glaciers scraped away material in their path and deposited it at their snouts or beneath the ice as they melted.

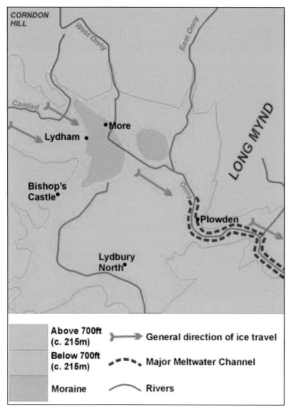

The most recent of these glacial periods started about 35,000 years ago and finished as recently as 13,000 years ago. The south-eastern margin of this glaciation was roughly through the heart of the South Shropshire Hills; and it was this that left us with the overall shape of the landscape around Bishop's Castle seen today (Fig. 1.6).

Most notable is the fact that ice flowing off the high ground of mid-Wales split into two separate valley glaciers west of Churchstoke. One branch flowed west of the Corndon and Shelve uplands on a northerly course, deepening the Rea Valley towards Shrewsbury. The other flowed eastwards following lower ground and deepening the valley that runs south of Corndon and the Stiperstones and north of Bishop's Castle, with a deep and narrow meltwater channel at Plowden. The resulting post-glacial drainage pattern has left the area immediately around Bishop's Castle with only rather small streams, instead of the rivers which might be expected to occupy such wide valleys.

Fig. 1.6 Map summarizing this last glaciation's main features, which are still visible in today's landscape. Much of the land below 700ft (215m) has some degree of glacial deposit on it, with the flanks of the streams having more recent alluvial flood plains.

Fig. 1.7 Terminal moraine of a Spitsbergen glacier. Note the huge mixture of particle size from boulders to clay. The flat-topped patches are dead ice, which will melt to give 'kettle holes'.

As the glaciers finally melted away they left behind a number of features that can be seen in the landscape and which have influenced settlement in the surrounding villages. In particular, the village of More sits on the hummocky ground of a terminal moraine: the point at which the retreating ice front deposited irregular mounds of glacial debris. Isolated patches of ice within this glacial debris melted later and left steep-sided depressions, known as kettle holes, which are noticeable around Lydham.

Building the Town

The foregoing summary of the geological setting of Bishop's Castle is reflected in the building materials used in the town, although this might not be as immediately obvious as it is for example in the Cotswolds. Many of the older stone buildings are rendered, because the local stone is of relatively poor quality. Also we tend now to think of the ubiquitous brick buildings as being of imported materials, but for a long period the town had its local brick works.

The stronger beds of rock within the ridge of the Bailey Hill Formation, which gave the town the ideal dominating position for its original motte-and-bailey castle, were used for rebuilding the castle in stone c.1100. The stone was quarried alongside the castle's foundations as can be glimpsed behind the houses of Welsh Street. Also close by, the Shropshire Way footpath leaves Castle Green and leads to a much in-filled old quarry which almost certainly provided further stone for the castle and other buildings in the town, and continued to do so as recently as 2007 for facing new housing on the adjacent Wintles development (Fig. 1.8).

From the 18th century onwards, many of the town's buildings were constructed of brick, which, like the stone, was locally sourced before the coming of the railway, and which contributes to the distinctive physical character of the town. Sources are often reflected in the field and street names, a very recent one being Brick Meadow close to the former railway station, and in visible remains at the Roveries. The locally made bricks used glacial till, deposited by the glaciers. This comprises small pebbles set in a matrix of mud and sand dragged along by the glacial ice and in part ground down by its movement. Before making the bricks, by hand in wooden moulds, it was the practice to 'pug' the mud and separate out the larger stones and gravel. The success of this process varied considerably, as can be seen in several of

Fig. 1.8 At the entrance to the quarry behind the Wintles a rubble stone wall abuts the natural outcrop of the Bailey Hill Formation.

the older brick walls around the town, for instance down Bull Street opposite the Clive memorial. The inclusion of large pebbles can cause serious weaknesses and in time lead to more rapid disintegration of the bricks (Fig. 1.9).

So it is that this gallop through the evolution of the physical foundations of Bishop's Castle and its surrounding landscape sets the scene for the more conventional history of the town discussed in the following

Fig. 1.9 A badly pugged local brick in Bull Street.

chapters. Moreover some of the geological factors remain with us, but well hidden. As recently as 1990 further movement on the Pontesford-Linley fault caused the so-called Bishop's Castle or Clun earthquake: a stark reminder that the earth still moves.

Further reading

P. Toghill, *Geology of Shropshire* (2nd edn. Crowood Press, Marlborough, 2006).
A. Jenkinson, 'The building stones of Bishop's Castle', *Jnl. of S.W.S.H.A.S.* **25**, pp.41-9.
B.C.H.R.C., geology files.

2 THE PREHISTORY OF BISHOP'S CASTLE

Introduction

Writing a prehistory of Bishop's Castle presents a problem, as there was no prehistoric Bishop's Castle. To the best of our knowledge the future site of the town is not known to have been occupied before the late 11th century AD. However, the town's location within the landscape of south Shropshire has a story of human colonization and settlement, extending from the end of the last ice age to the establishment of Roman authority, that can be reconstructed by archaeology.

The natural environment shapes human settlement and the development of culture and society. It was modified by human exploitation, as successive generations altered their surroundings, from the extensive woodlands that developed after the ice age to the agrarian and pastoral landscape similar to that seen today. An important factor in the development of the landscape around Bishop's Castle has been the relative isolation of the Shropshire hills.

The Holocene – from 10000 BC

In the immediate hinterland of Bishop's Castle there is evidence for human activity in the Kemp valley (see Fig. 2.1) revealed in the pollen from core samples taken from alluvial sediments on the valley floor. The pollen from each plant species is distinctive, enabling them to be identified from the shape, size and surface structure. Pollen is often preserved when sealed within floodplain silts and clays and by analysing sample cores taken from these sediments past patterns of vegetation cover can be reconstructed. Material from within these cores can also be radiocarbon-dated to provide an absolute chronology. The variation in plant species over time indicates how the environment changed as a result of both natural processes and cultural activity.

Analysis of the pollen in the core samples from the Kemp valley provided significant data about the environmental conditions from the end of the ice age (*c*.10000 BC). By this time the improving climate enabled a diversity of plant species to colonize the fertile sediments deposited by post-glacial rivers and lakes. Grasses were initially dominant, although birch (*Betula*) and dwarf species such as juniper (*Juniperus*) were present by *c*.10300 BC. These were followed by the development of a deciduous forest of hazel (*Corylus avellana*), pine (*Pinus*), elm (*Ulmus*) and oak (*Quercus*) between 9500 and 7000 BC. Alder (*Alnus*) arrived and spread on the wet floodplains in the river valleys from 6200 BC. A warmer climate is indicated by the arrival of lime (*Tilia*) at *c*.5600 BC, with mean summer temperatures up to two degrees centigrade higher than today. The first evidence for human activity dates from around 6000 BC.

The Hunter-Foragers of the Mesolithic – 6000-4000 BC

During the Mesolithic the source of the Kemp brook, close to the site where Bishop's Castle was later established, and the other valleys in the area offered rich wetlands that were surrounded by wooded hills. This area supported freshwater fish, shellfish and wildfowl, while the surrounding forests were a source of game and an array of seasonal plant foods. As a result, the Mesolithic hunter-foragers adopted a highly mobile lifestyle, moving through the landscape between ephemeral camps at locations where such foodstuffs were known to abound.

By 6000 BC Britain had become an island, concentrating the population and limiting their hunting and foraging ranges. This would have been a gradual process as sea levels rose and the fertile plain of Doggerland was inundated, becoming the bed of the North Sea. In the later Mesolithic, people began to modify their environment by using fire to create limited clearings within the forests. This would have created enhanced grazing for game, making hunting easier and reducing the need for an extensive annual round.

The first indications of a later Mesolithic presence in the Bishop's Castle area come from flints, such as those that have been found south-east of More (**25**) and on the slopes of Oakeley Mynd. These belong to a technological tradition that was limited in its range but sophisticated in its function. They include small, geometric, finely made points and blades known as microliths (Fig. 2.3), several of which would have been hafted together to create composite tools. Analysis indicates that the flint from which they were made was obtained from the glacial gravel deposits, rather than the chalk lands of southern England. Other materials in use at the time would have included wood, antler, horn, bone and sinew, leather and a range of other types of stone.

Agriculture and Settlement – *c.*4000-2500 BC

The introduction of agriculture changed human society and culture, although in north-western Europe this was a prolonged process as the mobile communities that existed at the end of the Mesolithic gradually began to keep domesticated cattle and pigs and cultivate crops such as wheat and barley. In the pollen sequence from the Kemp valley at the beginning of this new period, known as the Neolithic, there is a marked increase in woodland clearance and the first appearance of cereal pollen and herb species that indicate more open grazing land. Despite this, game and wild plant foods from the woodlands would have remained an important component of the diet, and the wetlands on the floors of the valleys in the Bishop's Castle area would have continued to be exploited for fish and wildfowl.

The first significant monuments began to be constructed in some places, particularly burial mounds such as long barrows and mortuary enclosures, which often contain the remains of several individuals. It is thought that these sites may have been perceived as the homes of the ancestors, acting as a form of territorial marker, enabling communities to establish their claims to the areas in which they lived and farmed. The flint scrapers and blades that have been found on Oakeley Mynd and the hills around Clun provide evidence for the wider use of the landscape.

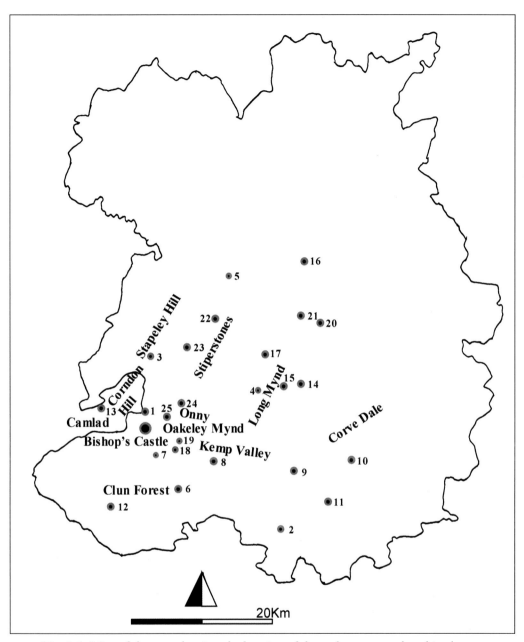

Fig. 2.1 Map of the area showing the location of those places as numbered in the text.
1 Roveries hillfort; 2 Rocks Green; 3 Mitchell's Fold; 4 Robin Hood's Butts;
5 Walleybourne brook nr. Pontesbury; 6 Broadward Hall; 7 Bury Ditches; 8 Burrow Hill;
9 Norton Camp; 10 Brown Clee hill; 11 Titterstone Clee hill; 12 Caer Caradoc, Chapel Lawn;
13 Roundton Hill (Montgomeryshire) nr. Churchstoke; 14 Caer Caradoc over the Stretton Gap;
15 Bodbury Ring; 16 Weeping Cross; 17 Wilderley Hill; 18 Lower Down; 19 Lydbury North; 20
Wrekin hillfort; 21 Viroconium Cornoviorum (Wroxeter); 22 Snailbeach Farm;
23 Gravels (Roman Gravels); 24 Linley Hall; 25 More.

The Neolithic period also saw the first use of pottery, and archaeologists use the shape and decoration of the vessels to identify different craft traditions. Early Neolithic (*c.*4400-3300 BC) pottery of a style similar to that found elsewhere in western Britain was found at two locations on the Roveries hillfort during excavations in the early 1960s. This indicates that the summit of the hill was inhabited for a time about 4,000 years before the Iron Age hillfort was constructed. It has been suggested that this early use of the hill may have been associated with a 'causewayed enclosure', a type of site best known from the chalk lands of southern England and comprising one or more circuits of 'segmented' ditches (i.e. lines of pits that provided material for a more continuous bank). This may not have been a permanent settlement but rather a focal point in the landscape for a mobile population to gather at certain times of the year.

The Stratification of Society and the coming of Bronze – 2500-600 BC
Whilst the beginning of the period known as the Bronze Age is marked by the introduction of the first use of metals, it also saw wider changes in society. The readily apparent remains forming the Early Bronze Age (2500-1500 BC) are ceremonial monuments such as stone circles like Mitchell's Fold (**3**) (Fig. 2.2), the funerary monuments such as Robin Hood's Butts (**4**), and other barrows and cairns on the Long Mynd, Stapeley Hill and the

Fig. 2.2 Long Meg at Mitchell's Fold Bronze Age stone circle; Bury Ditches hillfort, nr. Bishop's Castle; and prehistoric linear banks on Stapeley Common.

Stiperstones. The appearance of these monuments suggests that society had become more consolidated and hierarchical, with an increasing emphasis on individual status and display and control over the landscape. Agriculture became more firmly established within the landscape, and communities appear to have become more sedentary. However, few settlements from this period have been identified in Shropshire apart from a possible transient site at Rocks Green (**2**) near Ludlow.

Evidence for bronze working comes from the Early Bronze Age flat axe mould found in the Walleybourne brook near Pontesbury (**5**). It might be noted that copper-bearing rocks outcrop at Westcott, near Cothercott, and were mined historically. However, stone tools also continued to be made and used. In the Bishop's Castle area, for instance, distinctive types of massive perforated stone axe-hammers and battle-axes were made using a stone known as picrite, which outcrops near Corndon Hill. The items date to the Early Bronze Age, rather than the preceding Neolithic, and are thought to have had a different function from the earlier polished stone axes. Investigations around the hill found evidence for prehistoric stone extraction by small workings on the south-eastern side, near Hyssington, and some tentative evidence for axe production.

The Neolithic to Bronze Age transition coincided with a climatic optimum, when average temperatures were higher than today. After this point the climate gradually began to cool and become wetter. People adapted their agricultural practices to suit the new conditions, increasingly using the higher land for grazing. The linear earth banks and ditches that surround Mitchell's Fold on Stapeley Hill (Fig. 2.2) might date to this period, possibly providing evidence of Bronze Age transhumance (i.e. seasonal movements of animals to summer pastures). Other evidence from this period comes in the form of the numerous Middle Bronze Age (1500-1000 BC) 'palstaves' (i.e. axe-heads that had flanges to make them easier to haft) which have been found in the Shropshire Hills.

As the period progressed an expanding population and continued cultivation of increasingly exhausted soils placed a greater demand on diminishing resources, creating the conditions for further social change. This seemed to have more of an effect in the uplands and highlands of western Britain, including the south Shropshire Hills, where the first enclosed hilltop settlement began to emerge. Whether these were intended for security, or for storing resources and other forms of wealth, remains unknown. However, the Late Bronze Age (1000-600 BC) did see the use of ever growing numbers of increasingly sophisticated weapons, including the sword. Finds from this period from the Bishop's Castle area include the Bloody Romans hoard of bronze spearheads and a sword fragments. This was found in 1862 on the Oakeley estate in a field which has acquired this fanciful local name. The finds belong to a wider metalworking tradition focused on the Thames and Severn valleys, which archaeologists refer to as the Wilburton complex, after the primary hoard from this location. Other hoards of this type were found in 1867 near Broadward Hall (**6**) in the Clun valley and comprised two to three hundred socketed and barbed bronze spearheads, and numerous sword fragments.

It is likely that bronze weaponry of this type was produced for a social élite, who were able to support specialist metalworkers. Such items would have been used for conspicuous display of status and imply increased élite control of resources. This indicates that society was becoming structurally more complex and sophisticated, with endemic warfare. Together with the development of fine craftsmanship, a society can be seen emerging that prefigures the Iron Age.

Hillforts, tribes and the Age of Iron – 600 BC-AD 43

Hillforts represent the most impressive prehistoric monuments in the Bishop's Castle area and date to the period known as the Iron Age. They have traditionally been seen as the product of a warrior society, albeit one in which most people continued to live as farmers in enclosed farmsteads. This period also saw the emergence of regional tribal identities, which in Shropshire and Cheshire comprised the group which in the Roman period became known as the *Cornovii*.

The Iron Age is so named because the period saw the first use of iron. Whilst bronze and even stone remained in use, iron became the dominant material for making tools, weapons and armour. Because of both its novelty and superior material properties, it would have been considered prestigious and thus initially only available to the élite to display their status, wealth and power. These factors are central to understanding society in Iron Age Britain.

Relatively lightly defended hilltop enclosures had first appeared the later Bronze Age, and their gradual enlargement and embellishment over the course of the Iron Age produced the large and impressive hillforts found near Bishop's Castle and elsewhere in Shropshire. Locally these include the Roveries (**1**); Roundton Hill (**13**); Billings Ring near Plowden; Bury Ditches (**7**) overlooking the Kemp valley and visible from Bishop's Castle (Fig. 2.2); Burrow Hill (**8**) above Aston on Clun; Norton Camp (**9**) at Craven Arms. Further east are the four hillforts on Brown Clee (**10**) and Titterstone Clee (**11**); to the south are Caer Caradoc (**12**) at Chapel Lawn, and to the north Bodbury Ring (**15**) on the Long Mynd and another Caer Caradoc (**14**) east of Church Stretton. They range in size from 1 to 28 hectares and some have evidence of internal hut platforms. Recent research suggests that hillforts may have had a range of uses beyond communal defence, including domestic, economic, manufacturing and ritual functions. The degree to which these monuments were permanently occupied requires further research, but almost certainly it varied over time and from site to site.

Despite these uncertainties, it is clear that they represent the ability of an organized society to mobilize and maintain a sufficient labour force to construct such massive hilltop enclosures. They are located in prominent positions, with ramparts that follow the contours, and are places from which to see and be seen in the surrounding landscape. The number of ramparts varies; some had one (univallate) or two (bivallate) banks and ditches, while others had more (multivallate), probably indicating status. Excavation has shown that many developed from earlier timber box-framed ramparts, and some, such as the Roveries, show signs of drystone walling. Later rampart structures comprised continuous steep slopes from the top of the bank to the bottom of the ditch, called a glacis. These would have been topped with a timber palisade, and the entrance ways often consisted of an inturned passageway that ended with imposing wooden gates.

Control of the land and protection of the predominantly agrarian population would have been vital to the élite's economic success and the maintenance of their wealth and status. Inter-tribal warfare and local conflict was endemic, and the élite would also have controlled other resources such as the salt that was traded from the brine springs around Nantwich in the Cheshire plain to the north. The basic economic unit was the farmstead enclosure comprising a single bank and ditch that enclosed half a hectare. These were located throughout the landscape and many have now been located as cropmarks or parch marks in dry weather on the lower ground in Shropshire. Housing, in common with the interior of the hillforts, would have comprised timber roundhouses with an open central hearth. The fire in this hearth would have produced heat and light for all domestic activities. The roundhouses would have been occupied by family groups who were largely self-sufficient, obtaining such items as they could not make themselves by trade. Examples of these settlements are at Weeping Cross (**16**) south of Shrewsbury, Wilderley Hill bank (**17**) near Church Stretton and Lower Down (**18**) above the Kemp valley near Lydbury North (**19**). A number of sites have been identified from cropmarks along the Kemp valley which, although not necessarily contemporaneous, provide some indication of the extent of settlement (fig. 2.2).

Two significant features of Cornovian society were that they did not issue coinage, as the tribes of the south and south-east did, and they do not appear to have produced their own pottery. They did, however, produce a type of ceramic container for transporting and storing salt, which archaeologists term briquetage, and what pottery they did use came from beyond the tribal territory and was acquired through trade. It therefore seems likely that most vessels were of turned or carved wood, horn, or leather, which tend not to survive in the archaeological record. However, Cornovian metalwork shows a high degree of skill.

The Authority of Rome – AD 43

Although there had been contact and trade since at least the Neolithic period, the Roman conquest in 43 AD brought Britain under the direct control of a Mediterranean power whose territories extended from the Rhine to the Sahara and from Spain to Syria. The empire had a population estimated at about fifty million, with two million in Britain. The consequences of the initial invasion, and the following four decades of military campaigning until control was fully established, had profound effects on Iron Age societies. Based on the estimates of the effects of the Roman conquest of Gaul, some now think that as many as one million people may have been killed or enslaved, as land and territory were appropriated through the brutal application of raw military power.

In Shropshire, the establishment of Roman forts, especially the legionary fort of *Legio XIV* at Wroxeter, removed the power of the Iron Age élite. However, although there is some evidence for a military action at the Wrekin hillfort (**20**), there is little other sign of conflict. This may indicate that the Cornovian élite opted to submit rather than fight, adopting a pragmatic approach to maintain their wealth, status and power. By co-operating in the administration of their tribal territory and people on behalf of Rome they may have secured a degree of continuity. The subsequent establishment of the tribal capital of *Viroconium Cornoviorum* (Wroxeter) (**21**) provided a central location that enabled them to gain access to the wider economy of the Roman Empire, and from which they could both rule and be ruled.

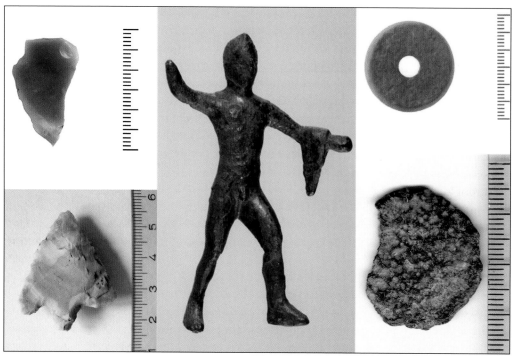

Fig. 2.3 A Mesolithic microlith; a Bronze Age flint barbed-and-tanged arrowhead from Lydbury North; a silvered-bronze Hercules figurine from Lydbury North; a spindle whorl, possibly Iron Age, from Lydbury North; and a Roman dupondius coin from Lower Down. (The figurine is in the Shrewsbury Museum and Art Gallery)

For the 360 or so years when Britain was dominated by Rome, little seems to have changed for the rural agrarian population of the hinterland of *Viroconium* (**21**), especially in the Shropshire Hills. For the inhabitants of the Bishop's Castle area the rhythms of the agricultural cycle and their local customs would have continued much as before. On rural sites Roman pottery and other items become rapidly scarcer the further one gets from *Viroconium* and other urban centres. Where Roman material is found it is probable that it was procured through trade, and pottery vessels may simply have been used as incidental packaging for the contents. Investigation of an enclosure at Lower Down (**18**) near Lydbury North (**19**) yielded a *dupondius* Roman coin (a lower denomination brass coin) (Fig. 2.3), Severn Valley Ware Roman pottery and Malvernian pottery from Worcestershire, while in Lydbury North a silvered-bronze Hercules statuette has been found (Fig. 2.3). However, there is no suggestion that the occupants were Roman or indeed Romanized British. Further, the Celtic languages of the Iron Age southern British survived as Welsh, which suggests that the majority of the rural population was relatively unaffected by Roman culture after nearly four centuries.

There is, however, some evidence for Roman exploitation of the lead deposits in the Shropshire Hills. This includes the lead ingots that have been found in the area, such as the ingot or pig of lead found north-west of Bishop's Castle in 1767. Another ingot was discovered near Snailbeach Farm (**22**) in 1796, and a third in the Roveries hillfort (**1**) in

1851. The identity of these ingots was facilitated by the cast inscription IMP. HADRIAN. AVG, which dates them to the reign of the Emperor Hadrian (AD 117-38) and indicates state, and most likely military, involvement in the mining operations. Mining activity has been identified at the Gravels (Roman Gravels) (**23**), where further Roman ingots are said to have been found, together with candles and spades. The Roman buildings that were discovered at Linley Hall (**24**), two miles north of Bishop's Castle, are thought by some to represent a centre for controlling and administering the lead mines in the area. Since 1856 fragmentary walls suggesting a large domestic building, gravel floors, drains, a channel of flue-tiles, and a stone aqueduct have been discovered. There is also a mosaic in the church at More (**25**) which may be from this site.

Throughout prehistory the landscape of the area around Bishop's Castle was occupied and constantly modified by human activity. An ever increasing population sought to control their environment, resulting in changes that were social, cultural, economic, political and technological. The surviving evidence, as summarized in this chapter, is fragmentary, but it provides us with a perspective on these communities.

Bibliography

Primary Sources:
Historic Environments Record, Shropshire, HER PRN 03177 – MSA2056.
Historic Environments Record, Shropshire, HER PRN 00746.
Plutarch, *The Fall of the Roman Republic*, transl. R. Warner (Penguin, 1972).

Secondary Sources:
C. Burgess, D. Coombs, and D.G. Davies, 'The Broadward Complex and Barbed Spearheads', in *Prehistoric Man in Wales and the West: Essays in Honour of L.F. Chitty*, ed. F. Lynch and C. Burgess (Adams & Dart, Bath, 1972).

B. Cunliffe, *Iron Age Communities in Britain* (4th edn. 2005, Routledge, Abingdon).

V.L. Gaffney, R.H. White, and H. Goodchild, *Wroxeter, the Cornovii and the Urban Process*, **1**: *Researching the Hinterland* (Jnl. of Roman Archaeology, Suppl. Series No. 68; Portsmouth, Rhode Island, 2007.)

M.J. Greene, *The Making of the Lydbury Landscape – six thousand years of human intervention* (The Lydbury Field Group, Lydbury North, 2009).

M.J. Greene, 'Beyond the hinterland: understanding late Iron-Age transitional rural settlement and society in S. Shropshire' (Birmingham Univ. M.Sc. thesis, 2016).

A.F. Harding, *European Societies in the Bronze Age* (Cambridge Univ. Press, 2000).

C.C. Haselgrove, 'Wealth, prestige and power: the dynamics of late Iron Age political centralisation in south-east England', in *Ranking, Resource and Exchange*, ed. C. Renfrew and S. Shennan (Cambridge Univ. Press, 1982), pp.79-88.

R. Hingley, *Rural Settlement in Roman Britain* (Seaby, London, 1989).

T. Ingold, 'Territoriality and tenure: the appropriation of space in hunting and gathering societies', in *The Appropriation of Nature: Essays on Human Ecology and Social Relations*, ed. T. Ingold (Manchester Univ. Press, 1986), pp.130-64.

N.W. Jones and S. Burrow, *A Potential Axe Factory near Hyssington, Powys: Survey and excavation 2007-8* (Report for Cadw, Welshpool; Clwyd-Powys Archaeological Trust, 2009).

D. Mattingly, *An Imperial Possession: Britain in the Roman Empire* (Penguin, 2007).

M. Millett, *The Romanization of Britain, An Essay in Archaeological Interpretation* (Cambridge Univ. Press, 1990).

N. Morley, *The Roman Empire: Roots of Imperialism* (Pluto Press, London, 2010).

M. Shaw, *The Lead, Copper and Barytes Mines of Shropshire* (Logaston Press, Woonton 2009).

J. Thomas, *Understanding the Neolithic* (Routledge, London, 1990).

M. Todd, *Roman Britain 55 BC–AD 400* (Fontana Press, London, 1981).

A. Wigley, 'Rooted to the Spot: the "smaller enclosures" of the later first millennium BC in the central Welsh Marches', in *The Later Iron Age in Britain and Beyond*, ed. C. Haselgrove and T. Moore (Oxbow, Oxford, 2007).

3   SOUTH SHROPSHIRE 410-1066: THE ANGLO-SAXONS

According to a persistent folk memory, the beginnings of the town of Bishop's Castle can be traced back to a land grant made by a landowner after a miracle cure in Anglo-Saxon times. The story goes that Egwin Shakehead, an Anglo-Saxon landowner in the area of south Shropshire, went on a pilgrimage to the shrine of St Æthelbert of East Anglia, king and martyr, in Hereford cathedral. There he was miraculously cured of his palsy. In gratitude he gave his large estate of Lydbury North to the bishop of Hereford. Later, the bishop built a castle here: Bishop's Castle. We have, however, no real information about Egwin, and cannot even be sure to which century he belonged – or even if he existed at all.

There are virtually no contemporary written records for this area so there is little in the way of specific names, dates or events and archaeology has so far yielded only limited help. The Anglo-Saxon Chronicle gives 792 as the date of the murder of King Æthelbert, so any gift must have been later than that. And the first castle in England, at Richard's Castle in Herefordshire, was not built until 1050. So at the end of the Anglo-Saxon kingdom in 1066, there may have been nothing more than a few scattered farmsteads in the area now occupied by Bishop's Castle.

Nevertheless, the six and a half centuries between the Romans' departure and the arrival of the Normans are important. During those 'Dark Ages' (dark to us, not necessarily to those who lived through them) tribalism and the rivalry of local warlords seem gradually to have given way to a relatively orderly society sharing customs and, crucially, laws and a legal system which fostered regional and national identities. Thus by the 11th century England was arguably the best administered state in Europe. Domesday Book[1] is unique, and the speed with which it was prepared and the comprehensiveness of its account of the country's wealth and resources testify to a well established and highly effective administrative system. This chapter aims to shed some light on this period and to show how the area fared between the Roman and Norman conquests.

The native British peoples of what is now south-west Shropshire had experienced some Romanization before the withdrawal of official contact in 410. Roman roads crossed the region between major towns and carried traffic to and from the lead mines at Shelve. Roman administrators and soldiers must have been seen. Wroxeter was near enough for local people to visit. New buildings continued to arise there as late as the 6th century. The Romans withdrew, but for many people life probably went on as it had done for centuries.

Gildas, a British monk living c.500-70, recorded that Germanic mercenaries were invited to Britain,[2] and Bede, 'the father of English history', writing in Monkwearmouth at the beginning of the 8th century, reported that between 449 and 456 Germanic tribes had been recruited to help to resist incursions by the Picts and Scots.[3]

These Germanic peoples – Angles, Saxons and Jutes – settled and gradually advanced westwards across Britain. Old theories of mass killings of native British peoples by Germanic invaders have long been thought to be false. They do not seem to have wiped out the established British people; there is no archaeological evidence for such massacres. The pattern seems to have been that a small Anglo-Saxon ruling group defeated and replaced established leaders, intermarrying with local people, so that within a few generations they had melded into one community. Modern DNA research supports this idea. A detailed study of the genetic make-up of the peoples of the British Isles, published in 2013 and claimed to be 'the most exciting discovery in Anglo-Saxon history in the past ten years',[4] shows that most people in Britain share a genetic inheritance from both Anglo-Saxon and native British forebears. By contrast, earlier Roman and later Norman conquerors have left little DNA evidence of their presence.

Place-names also point to a mixing of the local populations. Celtic names, such as Clun, Pentre, Bettws-y-crwyn and Llanfair Waterdine are densest south-west of Bishop's Castle, but Anglo-Saxon names, such as Churchstoke, Leighton, Forden and Welshpool spread beyond Offa's Dyke. A possible 5th-century Anglo-Saxon 'palace' at Forden Gaer near Welshpool has been revealed by excavation.[5] In the early Anglo-Saxon period there was no firm boundary between what have become England and Wales.[6]

The Anglo-Saxons brought their pagan religious beliefs and practices with them from their homelands east of the Rhine, never conquered by the Romans. They found themselves among peoples who had lived in an empire where the official religion was Christianity, a system of belief which imposed on its adherents the duty – strange to polytheists – to convert unbelievers to the 'one true faith'. Celtic Christianity, which had struck deep roots in Wales and the western seaboard of Scotland, was based on tribal groupings, with travelling priests or teachers making regular visits to their scattered followers, and it has been plausibly suggested that early Christians in the Marches shared this tradition.[7] A 7th- to 8th-century Saxon cemetery excavated at Bromfield, near Ludlow, contains 31 graves, with signs that most of their occupants were Christian, although three had grave goods, normal in pagan Saxon burial rites.[8] This suggests that conversion happened gradually.

The Anglo-Saxon kingdoms have left documentary evidence in both Latin and in their own Germanic dialects. The writings include practical legal and administrative documents

---

The Tribal Hidage[9]

The Tribal Hidage is a good example of the thoroughness of Anglo-Saxon taxation records. These were based on the 'hide', a measure of land which seems to take account of productivity, as well as area. Scholars believe that, broadly, a hide would yield enough to feed a household and its dependants. The Westerna, or Magonsæte (in what became Herefordshire and south Shropshire), were taxed at 7,000 hides, the same as the Wreocensæte (around the Wrekin and Wroxeter), the Hwicce (Worcester), the East Saxons (Essex), the South Saxons (Sussex) and the people around Lincoln.

– charters, laws and wills – but also literature: poems, riddles, stories and a surprisingly rich vein of historical material.

Overwhelmingly the scribes of documents which have come down to us were churchmen, so it is not surprising that tales of conversions from paganism, the doings of saints, accounts of miracles, the establishment of new churches, appointments of bishops, and grants of land to monasteries and churches figure largely.

They also tell of the gradual diminishing of the Celtic church as the different traditions of the southern and eastern areas of Britain came to predominate, based on the more centralized practices of Rome. In 597 Pope Gregory the Great, allegedly inspired by the boyish beauty of Northumbrian children on sale in the slave market in Rome ('Not Angles but Angels'), dispatched St Augustine to Canterbury to launch a conversion campaign. Organization and discipline won the day. At the Synod of Whitby in 664, arbitration between Roman and Celtic priests about calculating the date of Easter and other matters brought victory for the Roman rite, and the Celtic church was pushed back into the western fringes of Wales and of Scotland.

In 669 Theodore of Tarsus was sent from Rome to Canterbury to organize the lands of the Angles and Saxons into dioceses. He did not challenge the Celts head-on, but in 676 he created the diocese of Hereford for a people called the Magonsætan, whose territory included what is now south-west Shropshire and where there may have been some continuity from Celtic Christianity.[10] Unfortunately very few genuine Anglo-Saxon charters survived repeated Welsh attacks on Hereford,[11] though there are plenty of later forgeries asserting the property claims of bishops and abbots. By contrast, the neighbouring diocese of the Hwicce (Worcester) has genuine early charters, from which some of their tribal boundaries can be plotted; their royal family granted lands to found religious houses, and parishes were established. Similar processes probably operated in Shropshire.

Against this background, a long succession of changing rivalries, battles and alliances between local kings occurred between the start of Anglo-Saxon settlement in the 5th century and the establishment of a unified kingdom of England in the 10th. Eventually it was the

---

The Magonsætan royal family c.650-c.725[12]

According to Asser the Britons in what became Herefordshire and south-west Shropshire were governed by a family descended from Merewalh, third son of Penda, king of Mercia. Because few charters survive there are few references to the Magonsætan but we know that Merewalh became a Christian. He already had two sons when he sought a Christian wife from Kent. Intermarriage between Germanic royal families was a common political device to cement alliances and secure peace.

Merewalh gave lands and money to found several religious centres, the best known of which was in Wenlock, where his daughter Mildburg became abbess. As was often the case in Anglo-Saxon religious houses, a woman from a powerful family ruled a mixed establishment of monks and nuns.

Merewalh died c.685. He was succeeded by his sons Merchelm and Mildfrith. Mildfrith and his family were buried in Hereford cathedral, probably in the 720s.

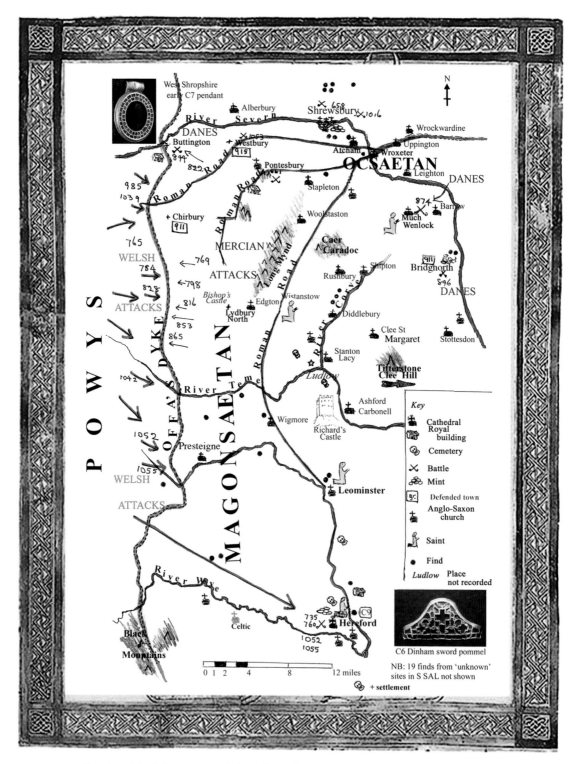

Fig. 3.1 The Magonsæte sub-kingdom of Mercia. (Drawn by Margaret Wilson)

royal house of Wessex which became dominant, but there were important periods when this area of the Marches, under the kings of Mercia, played a crucial role in events. A hoard of Saxon coins, found at Watlington (Oxon.) in 2015, reveals that Alfred 'the Great', king of Wessex, and Ceolwulf II, king of Mercia, ruled as equals.[13] Ceolwulf probably controlled more lands than Alfred, but because Alfred outlived him the importance of the Mercians could be 'air brushed' from historic records.

The early history of the kingdom is uncertain, but Mercian monarchs included in their 'authentic' pedigree Icel, son of Eomer, who is mentioned in the great Anglo-Saxon poem Beowulf. He is credited with leading his Angles from the north German plain to East Anglia and the Trent Valley, where he ruled for perhaps 20 years from c.515. There is no directly traceable line of descent from the Iclingas to Penda, the king who started Mercia's rise to major importance, but eventually even European royal families liked to claim kinship with Mercian rulers, often through the female line.

Penda was a remarkable man. He took control of the kingdom from Cearl (perhaps a

kinsman) c.626. Shrewd in making alliances, he was equally ruthless in breaking them when it suited his expansionist ambition. He won the kingdom of the Hwicce from Wessex in 628. In the 630s he joined forces with Cadwallon, king of Gwynedd, who had a fortified camp on Long Mountain near Welshpool, to recapture territory from Northumbria. In 633 the allies took the fight to Northumbria itself, and laid waste the country. The Northumbrians returned under King Oswald in 642 but were defeated, possibly at Oswestry (Oswald's Tree), leaving Penda the most formidable ruler in England.[14] Despite this success, no Mercian king is recorded as chief king, or Bretwalda, of the Anglo-Saxons, but in reality Penda was that.[15] Political bias may explain this omission from written sources: Anglo-Saxon historiography was dominated by Northumbria and Wessex and Penda had defeated both. Moreover, he retained his paganism while the monkish scribes were seeking to celebrate the triumph of Christianity.

Fig. 3.2 This pendant was found in west Shropshire in 2004. The border consists of small rectangular cloisonné garnets set over a patterned gold foil. It dates to the early 7th century and measures 3.4cm x 2.5cm. (Shropshire Museum Service)

Perhaps, however, a glimpse of the splendour of Penda's kingship can be seen in the richness of the 'Staffordshire Hoard' of Anglo-Saxon artefacts. Michael

23

Wood suggests that they might have been Penda's.[16] Welsh poems may preserve a tradition that Cynddylan, the last prince of Powys, who ruled parts of modern Shropshire, turned on his former allies and defeated the Mercians c.655 at Wall, near Lichfield and the site of the hoard. The garnet and gold pendant recently discovered in west Shropshire is of a similar date.

Penda's reign ended in 655 when he was killed at an unknown site near Leeds, leading an expedition against Oswiu of Northumbria. For three years Mercia became a Northumbrian province, but a Mercian revolt put Penda's son Wulfhere on the throne in 658 and gradually he rebuilt the kingdom's fortunes. Cenwealh, king of Wessex, fought at Posentesbyrig at Easter 661.[17] If that can be identified with Pontesbury (as local efforts have attempted), it could indicate some Wessex intervention in Mercia during King Wulfhere's early years. But the persistence of the identification owes more to the locally nursed legend of the Golden Arrow (and to Mary Webb's novel of that name) than to historically verifiable fact.

Mercian supremacy ebbed again after Wulfhere's death in 674, but a century later Offa, king of Mercia 757-96, re-established the kingdom as a major force. He arranged marriage links with other kings to secure peace. He developed market towns, controlled the currency and introduced the silver sceatta or 'penny', possibly named after Penda. He fostered trade links with Charlemagne's continental empire and was 'the only ruler in western Europe who could attempt to deal on equal terms with Charlemagne'.[18] Between 781 and 796 Offa enjoyed the hegemony of the whole of England south of the Humber and east of the Tamar. In 787 his influence was powerful enough to persuade the pope to create a new archbishopric at Lichfield, with control over the Mercian dioceses, including Hereford. After his death Mercian civil authority faded and the new archbishopric lasted only another seven years until 803. Nevertheless, his achievement was an important step towards the ultimate unification of the Anglo-Saxon kingdoms.

Offa's most famous memorial may be Offa's Dyke, which is the longest linear earthwork in Britain and one of the longest in Europe. Most of it lies on or near the modern border between England and Wales. It is over 150 miles long, up to about 65 feet wide, and in places 8 feet high. The ditch is on the Welsh side, and the bank on the eastern (Mercian) side. The sections in south-west Shropshire, especially near Llanfair Waterdine, are among the best preserved.

Attribution of the work to Offa was long accepted. It has the support of Asser, the Welsh monk and historian writing in the early 9th century: 'There was in Mercia in fairly recent time a certain vigorous king called Offa, who terrified all the neighbouring kings and provinces around him, and who had a great dyke built between Wales and Mercia from sea to sea.'[19]

None of the many digs on different parts of the Dyke, however, has produced reliable dating evidence. A section of the Dyke near Chirk was excavated in 2013. Material from an ancient layer of redeposited turf underneath the bank, probably from the original construction, was radio-carbon dated to the second half of the 6th century, in a range between 430 and 652[20] – two centuries before Offa. This result needs to be tested in other locations, but suggests that the Dyke might well have been built over a long period. Smaller, earlier, ditches and dykes may already have existed, and Offa could have united them into the one bearing his name. Its precise purpose remains obscure. There is no real evidence that it ever saw significant military occupation or use. It could have been constructed between Mercia and Powys by mutual consent, to define their territories; or it could have had a political purpose, to demonstrate the power and authority of its builder(s). Gaps may have permitted controlled movement between the kingdoms. No indications have been found of any worksites, but we can be sure its construction needed a large, well organized workforce.

During the 860s and 870s Danish invasions and conquests of large areas of southern and eastern Anglo-Saxon territories pushed Mercia back from most of its eastern lands, including London, and the Danes destroyed Wenlock Priory in 874. When Æthelred II became ruler of Mercia in 883 (or a few years earlier) he looked to Alfred 'the Great', king of Wessex, as an ally to help him regain control of his eastern lands and to safeguard his western territory, including Shropshire. Together they regained London in 885, but Æthelred had to acknowledge Wessex's supremacy while Alfred in turn relied heavily on Mercian support to resist the Danes.

In 893 a Danish army followed the Thames and then the Severn until Æthelred's forces of Mercians, West Saxons and Welsh stopped them at the Battle of Buttington (Mont.). Very few Danes survived the battle after being besieged for several weeks in the fortification they had built. Æthelred spent the next three years fighting the Danes alongside Alfred's son, the future King Edward the Elder. The Danes returned to the region in 895 and built a fort at Quatford, near the site of the future town of Bridgnorth. They were routed by King Alfred's pursuing forces.

Æthelred married Alfred's eldest child Æthelflæd, who had been well educated at her father's court and had absorbed the sense of a united Anglo-Saxon England, the importance of efficient administration and a unifying common religion, and the need for strong trade and effective taxation. She had also learned much about tactical warfare and understood the value of well-fortified towns. When Æthelred was killed in battle in 911, she continued to rule in his place, taking an active part in planning campaigns and organizing the establishment of defensive *burhs* along Mercia's frontiers. She continued fighting in former northern parts of Mercia, defeating Vikings at their great stronghold of York, where she was due to receive the city from them in 918, had she not died 48 hours before the appointed day. In the Anglo-Saxon Chronicle she is known as the 'Lady of the Mercians'. The Irish, Celts, Picts, Danes and Vikings greatly respected her. The Annals of Ulster refer to her as *Famosissima Regina Saxonum*, 'the most renowned Queen of the Saxons'.[21]

Mercian defended towns (see Fig. 3.1)

After Æthelred II was killed in battle in 911 his wife Æthelflæd continued to rule in his place. She organized the defence of nine towns in Mercia, putting timber palisades around them, including a new Saxon *burh*, or town, at Chester (907). Others were at Bridgnorth (912) and Chirbury (915), both of which were fortified against the Danes and Welsh. The place name Westbury may preserve a *burh* on the Roman road from Wroxeter to Forden Gaer near Welshpool.

By 918 Shropshire, with the rest of Mercia, had become part of the kingdom of Wessex, ruled by King Edward the Elder. In 927 his son, Æthelstan, whom Æthelflæd had fostered when his mother died *c*.899, and whose claim to the throne she had supported, declared himself King of the English. Altogether, Æthelflaed's political and military skills ensured that her reign was crucial in the creation of a unified kingdom of England.

In 1006 further Danish raids in many parts of England brought the Anglo-Saxon Chronicle's first mentions of Shropshire. King Æthelred II of England spent Christmas in the county, and it was then, it seems, that he was advised to buy off the Danes with the enormous 'tribute' that was paid early next year. Such decisions helped to earn him the unenviable nickname *Unræd* – 'ill counselled'. It is in Æthelred's reign that the recorded history of the sheriff begins – now distinct from the king's reeve and identifiable as normally the leading lay official in the shire mote. Æthelred's kingdom was efficiently divided into shires administered by a sheriff on his behalf. The sheriff was responsible for raising armies, collecting taxes, and enforcing law and order in his shire. In Shropshire's case, the western boundary was not settled for another five hundred years and the hundred of Leintwardine in the south included much territory now in Herefordshire.

During Edward the Confessor's reign (1042-66) the principal landowners in this area were the king himself, the bishop of Hereford and 'Eadric'. King Edward was lord of Minsterley and surrounding lands, including Chirbury. From this base he could keep control of the borderlands of the March. The bishop of Hereford held Lydbury North, where – probably long before 1066 – there was a church whose large parish would have included the area in which the new town of Bishop's Castle was to be planted. It is hard to be sure who 'Eadric', the third landowner, actually was. Eadric was a common name in late Anglo-Saxon England, and many manors were owned by an ealdorman of that name. However, some places were distinguished in Domesday Book as belonging in 1066 to Eadric Silvaticus – Eadric the Wild or Savage Eadric. At that time he and his cousin Siward, two of the richest thegns in England, held manors in many counties.[22] He was a nephew of Eadric Streona, a Mercian ealdorman, is reputed to have owned more than 56 manors in 1066, and could tax about 3,500 people. His annual rents yielded nearly £600,000 in today's money.

Notwithstanding the problem of identifying all Eadric's lands, it is claimed that he may have held 115½ hides in Shropshire, valued at £98 1s 7d. That was 7.9% of the Shropshire hidage and 9.41% of Shropshire's total value. His cousin Siward may have held 71⅓ hides in Shropshire, valued at £48 2s. Eadric does not seem to have fought at Hastings, but even so William the Conqueror, whose initial demands had sought the surrender of lands only from those who 'had stood against me in battle and were killed there', attempted to confiscate his lands throughout England. Eadric responded like Hereward the Wake in the east by leading guerrilla attacks on the Normans. He managed to hold onto his Shropshire manors for a while.

The information about land ownership is provided in the Domesday Book.[23] The Anglo-Saxon Chronicle records that in 1085 William the Conqueror held his Christmas court in Gloucester. He wanted important information about his realm and ordered what became known as the Domesday survey to be made. By Easter 1086 it was complete. The Anglo-Saxon administrative structure had enabled William to send a standard list of questions to

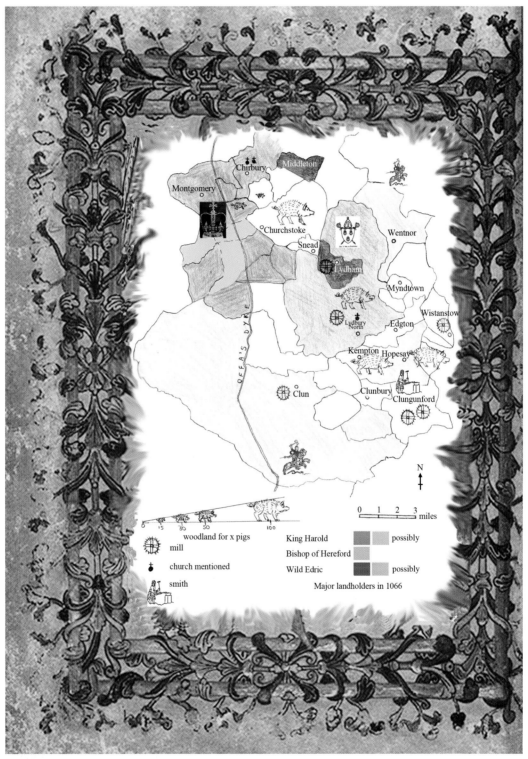

Fig. 3.3 South-west Shropshire, 1066. (Drawn by Margaret Wilson)

nearly every county in England. There were no Welsh shires, but along the borders information was collected from some places now in Wales. Questions included who held the land 'on the day when King Edward was alive and dead'. William wanted to know how land values had changed between 1066 and 1086 and how much he could collect in taxes. The information collected is not always in a standard form, but what was recorded helps to give a detailed account of south-west Shropshire before the Norman Conquest.

The Domesday Book records churches either as landowners or as priests endowed with peasant-standard shares of a vill's lands – but not otherwise: beyond their landholdings churches were of no interest to the survey's compilers, and in Shropshire a few seem not to have been recorded. Priests from the well-staffed portionary churches at Bromfield, Chirbury, Pontesbury or Westbury may have been called to minister to churchless people in south-west Shropshire.

Domesday Book also gives us an idea of how people managed the land around what was to become Bishop's Castle by 1066. It tells us how many mills there were, but not their exact locations. Many would have been water-powered, with a wheel set either horizontally or vertically, often on artificial watercourses. Others would have been powered by animals, usually oxen. There were no windmills, which used later technologies and were in any case always less reliable and less controllable than the alternatives. Fisheries may have accompanied flour mills to take advantage of mill ponds and watercourses, and piggeries would have consumed the husks produced by the milling. Woodland was also an important resource and therefore included in the record; different ways of quantifying it were used. Most commonly in south-west Shropshire it was the number of pigs which could be pannaged (supported) in the woods, but we do not know if those were the actual numbers being farmed or estimates of the potential.

In Anglo-Saxon England smiths were essential workers, repairing and making indispensable items of metal.[25] They were held in great esteem, but surprisingly few are mentioned in south-west Shropshire. Needing lots of wood or charcoal for their fires, some travelled between settlements. Swords were made of iron but needed to be both flexible and strong. Pattern welded blades, a technique perfected by the Anglo-Saxons where strips of iron were

Fig. 3.4 The Saxon sword pommel found at Dinham, near Ludlow, made from gold and garnet. It measures 3cm by 2cm and has been dated to 600-700AD. (Shropshire Museum Service)

plaited then beaten together to form the core of the blade, had sharp steel edges added to both sides. Swords thus produced were the finest in the world for more than a thousand years. For the wealthiest men pommels made by goldsmiths would have been added, like the garnet and gold example found at Dinham, near Ludlow (Fig. 3.4). Although the smith recorded at Hopesay may not have made swords, he would certainly have made sharp cutting tools.

All this adds up to a thriving society, operating under an established code of law, self-sufficient in most of the necessities of life, capable of trading with a reliable system of currency to get what it could not provide for itself, conscious of its own history, and supporting fine craftsmanship, as well as sophisticated achievements in art and literature. During the Anglo-Saxon period south-west Shropshire had developed from a localized tribal community to a people living under a centralized national government. Ecclesiastical and civic administration had been established for centuries to come. The Anglo-Saxon legacy we have long enjoyed includes church organization (dioceses, parishes, churches, preaching crosses); the calendar system (B.C. and A.D. introduced by Bede in the 7th century, whence our current system of dates originates); the legal system (the common law and juries); the local government structure (counties, hundreds and parishes); and the military system (army, local levies and the navy). The monetary system established at this time lasted until 1971 and the structure and basic vocabulary of the English tongue derives directly from the dialects spoken by the tribes who arrived here as the Romans left. In a pleasing irony, this marvellously flexible language has replaced Latin as the world's most-used means of communication between people of different nations.

As Shrewsbury had a mint, it must also have been a *burh*, as mints were only in important market towns. Moneyers were working in Shrewsbury and Hereford from the reign of Æthelstan (925-39) onwards, and in Bridgnorth from 979 onwards. Both Shrewsbury and Hereford continued to have mints until 1066. Some mints had several moneyers, each known from his coins. Finds, however, give a very limited record of the mints' activity as, by law, coins had to be melted and reissued very frequently in an attempt to keep a high quality coinage. New coins were issued whenever there was a change of ruler.

Further reading

Gildas. The standard edition of his *De Excidio Britanniae et Conquestu*, probably written in the 540s, is by T. Mommsen. For Gildas ('the only authority who was in any sense contemporary with the period of the Anglo-Saxon invasions') and his work see A. Gransden, *Historical Writing in England c.550 to c.1307* (1974), pp.1-5.

Bede's *Historia Ecclesiastica Gentis Anglorum* was completed in 731. The classic edition is by C. Plummer (1896, reprinted 1961), but L. Sherley-Price's edition for Penguin Classics (1962) is easily accessible. See Gransden, op. cit. pp.13-28.

The Anglo-Saxon Chronicles, originating in the 8th century or earlier, were continued until the 12th century; there are many accessible texts, e.g. G.N. Garmonsway's edition for Everyman's Library (1955) or *The Anglo-Saxon Chronicles*, ed. A. Savage (Bramley Books, 1997). The historiographical background to the Chronicles is summarized by Gransden, op. cit. pp.30-41.

Mercia and the Tribal Hidage. The earliest and most complete of the seven surviving MSS. of the Tribal Hidage is in British Library MS. Harley 3271, f. 6v. A digitized image of it can be seen at www.bl.uk/manuscripts/Viewer.aspx?ref=harley_ms_3271_f006v. For informative discussions see S. Zaluckyj, *Mercia: The Anglo-Saxon Kingdom of Central England* (2001), pp.16-21, 25, and *Mercia: An Anglo-Saxon kingdom in Europe*, ed. M.P. Brown and C.A. Farr (2001), pp.23-34.

Asser's *Life of King Alfred* was purportedly written in 793, six years before Alfred's death. Scholarly controversy surrounding the work is summarized in Gransden, op. cit. pp.46-53. R.H. Hodgkin's two-volume *A History of the Anglo-Saxons*, a wide ranging study of a rich and aristocratic society down to King Alfred's death in 899, has remained essential reading through successive editions between 1935 and 1959. F.M. Stenton, *Anglo-Saxon England* (3rd edn. 1971 and reprints) remains the best account of the Anglo-Saxons down to 1066; but see also James Campbell's stimulating essays in *The Anglo-Saxon State* (2000).

Domesday Book. In addition to the good, and handy, Phillimore edition of the Shropshire Domesday folios by F. and C. Thorne there is an edited text and commentary in *V.C.H. Salop.* **1**, pp.279-349 (indexed ibid. **2**), which should be used in light of the text and essential up-to-date commentary published in *The Shropshire Domesday* by Alecto Historical Editions (1990).

For the rich pre-Conquest aristocratic kinsmen Edric *Silvaticus* and Siward see also C.P. Lewis, 'English and Norman government and lordship in the Welsh borders 1039-87' (Oxford Univ. D.Phil. thesis, 1985), pp.82-5, 105-6, 112-13, 171-5.

4   FROM PLANTED TOWN TO INCORPORATED BOROUGH

In 1066 Duke William II of Normandy, claiming his right to the English throne by conces-
sion of Edward the Confessor,[1] landed on the south coast with an army of French and
Breton soldiers. Having defeated and killed King Harold on 14th October at the battle of
Hastings, he quickly overran much of the country. To maintain his conquest he gave his
followers lands confiscated from the old English nobility and those who opposed him. The
Normans built many castles to defend their new lands. Most of Shropshire was entrusted
to the Conqueror's cousin, Roger of Montgomery, Earl of Shrewsbury.

Many of the early Norman castles were of a standard pattern – an earth mound (motte),
topped by a timber tower, and an enclosure with a ditch and earth rampart (bailey). Many
are still visible in the Welsh Marches – notably Hên Domen (near Montgomery, built by
Earl Roger to defend the ford over the Severn at Rhydwhyman), Lydham, More, Hardwick,
Colebatch and Churchstoke. They were positioned to defend vulnerable areas such as river
valleys, as refuges for the local population, and to act as jumping-off points for incursions
into Wales.

Much earlier, perhaps around the end of the 8th century, a bishop of Hereford had
acquired – persistent legend suggests as the gift of the thegn Egwin Shakehead – the vast
estate of Lydbury, some 18,000 acres of valuable land, close to what became the Welsh
border. In 1086 Domesday Book records that the estate had 28 ploughlands (four of them
in the lord's hands, one belonging to the church and 23 tenanted) and 'there might be 92
more'.[2] The bishops, who retained their possessions after the Conquest, were numbered
among the most powerful landowners of the Welsh March, and would certainly want to
ensure that such an asset was properly defended. Medieval bishops were very different from
their present-day successors: they were men of substantial power and authority and often
warlike and ruthless in maintaining their status.

Around 1080 a motte and bailey castle, Bishop's Moat, was built on high ground two
miles west of the present town. It stood on the Kerry Ridgeway, an ancient east-west
trackway, and overlooked the Camlad valley. Its well-preserved site on a commanding position is still imposing. The motte stands about 9 metres high, and the bailey encloses an area
90 by 60 metres. The site, however, is in a very exposed position, and it may have served as
a watch tower and a temporary, rather than a permanent, settlement (Fig. 4.1).

After 1080 a second motte and bailey was established at a lower level, at the top of a
steep slope above the small river Pennel. This was to become 'the bishop's castle'. It was
probably built by a predecessor of Bishop Béthune and so before 1127. It was at first

Fig. 4.1 Bishop's Moat from the air. (Photo. Clwyd-Powys Archaeological Trust)

referred to as the 'New Castle' or *Lindebia* (Lydbury) Castle. In 1255 the bishop was found to have one castle within his manor of Lydbury North – and that was Bishop's Castle. The Welsh called the place *Y Trefesgob*, 'the Bishop's Town'.[3]

A regular Norman policy was to follow the foundation of castles with adjacent civilian settlements, which would confirm and strengthen the occupation and enable the surrounding land to be kept under cultivation. These 'planted' towns sprang up in many places – Bridgnorth, Clun, Ludlow and Oswestry are examples. Settlers or burgesses would have been attracted by the offer of housing with land and privileged tenures.

Bishop's Castle followed a traditional grid pattern.[4] From the castle a main street (now High Street and Church Street) led down the hill, lined by houses with frontages between 55 and 70 feet wide, and with strips of land (burgage plots) behind them extending to two 'back lanes' (now Union Street and Station Street) parallel to the main street. The first development of 32 plots ended where Union Street and Station Street now meet, but the town was later extended by a further 14 to reach the church. Remarkably, the shape of this first town remains virtually intact today, though most of the burgage plots were later divided up and built on (Fig. 4.2).

The castle remained the focal point of the settlement, and a clue as to how the castle was manned is afforded by a mid-12th-century charter of Bishop Gilbert Foliot granting land for a money rent and the service of finding a sergeant to serve 40 days a year in the castle: his charter is one of the earliest examples of a rare type, and if one supposes another eight such grants to have been made, then the bishop would have had a sergeant in his castle all year round. In 1154 the castle passed briefly into the hands of Hugh de Mortimer, of Wigmore Castle, but it was restored to the bishop next year.[5] An uneasy pattern of changing

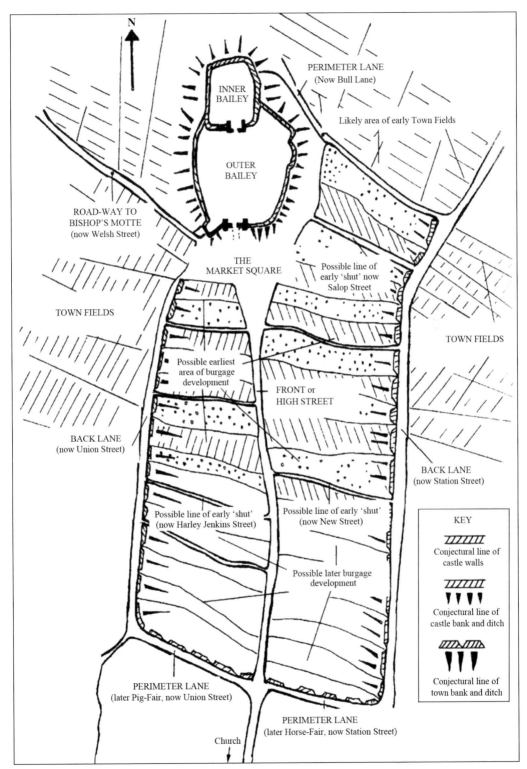

N

INNER
BAILEY

OUTER
BAILEY

PERIMETER LANE
(Now Bull Lane)

Likely area of early Town Fields

ROAD-WAY TO
BISHOP'S MOTTE
(now Welsh Street)

THE
MARKET SQUARE

Possible line of
early 'shut' now
Salop Street

TOWN FIELDS

TOWN FIELDS

Possible earliest
area of burgage
development

FRONT or
HIGH STREET

BACK LANE
(now Union Street)

BACK LANE
(now Station Street)

Possible line of early 'shut'
(now Harley Jenkins Street)

Possible line of early 'shut'
(now New Street)

KEY

Possible later burgage
development

Conjectural line of
castle walls

Conjectural line of
castle bank and ditch

Conjectural line of
town bank and ditch

PERIMETER LANE
(later Pig-Fair, now Union Street)

PERIMETER LANE
(later Horse-Fair, now Station Street)

Church

Fig. 4.2 Plan of the 'planted' town

33

ownership and control was to be a feature of the town, largely owing to its position in the heart of the unsettled and volatile Welsh March.

Within a hundred years of its foundation the town had 46 burgess plots and was clearly thriving. In 1167 a rent roll of the episcopal estate (then in the king's hands) recorded Lydbury North as producing an annual income of £124 – over a third of the total income of the see of Hereford. That same year Geoffrey de Vere, sheriff of Shropshire, was made keeper of the manor and castle of *Lindebia* (Lydbury) and was allocated 20 marks (£13 6s 8d) to fortify 'the Castle of *Lindebia-nort* by order of the King'. As keeper, de Vere received an annual salary of £20 or £21.[6]

This was almost certainly the point at which the earth and timber motte and bailey castle was replaced by a stone structure. Owing to the almost complete disappearance of the castle building in the 17th and 18th centuries, it is difficult to give a confident description. Several pictures exist from Elizabethan and later times, but they are probably somewhat romanticized! Nevertheless the extent of the castle can be traced today. Its outer limit is preserved in the circular street pattern – Bull Street, Bull Lane and Castle Street, with the walls running behind the present properties in Welsh Street and Market Square. The original motte was replaced by a stone keep, located on the present bowling green. Like its counterparts in Clun and Hopton Castle, it was intended more as a fortified dwelling than a military fortress.

The bishop of Hereford had another 'tower keep' at Lea, about 1½ miles east of the town. Its first recorded tenant was Robert Corbet in the 1320s, and the family retained possession until 1645, when, during the Civil War, Parliament ordered a Royalist garrison stationed there to be removed and the castle destroyed.[7] A farmhouse was built on the site soon after, and today the castle ruins are incorporated into the farm buildings.

It has been suggested that the building erected in Bishop's Castle had an egg-shaped outer bailey and a circular shell keep,[8] but a more recent view is that the keep was more likely to have been rectangular,[9] perhaps resembling the tower at Hopton Castle. The outer wall had towers and a gatehouse facing directly down the present High Street and opening onto a market area (today filled in by gradual encroachment so that, although still called 'Market Square', it now has the character of a narrow street).

Although by no means grand, the new structure must have been commodious enough to accommodate visiting bishops, and even royalty. The 19-year-old Henry III visited Lydbury North – and so perhaps Bishop's Castle – in 1226 on his way to Shrewsbury.[10] The keep probably had three floors – the lowest for storage, and the upper storeys for accommodation and entertainment. To ensure a degree of self-sufficiency, the castle would have contained a bakery, brewery, stabling and possibly a forge. It is believed that there was a well beneath the Bowling Green, to provide a water supply.

Bishop's Castle was now beginning to assume a prominent position in this area of the March, and in due course the townspeople would receive some benefit from the jurisdictional and economic privileges which King John granted to their lord, Bishop Braose (or Briouze), the son of a powerful Marcher lord, in his charter of 1203.[11] The bishop's new privileges were expressed – as had long been the practice – in a long and conventional litany of obsolete words, some dating from Anglo-Saxon times and whose precise meaning was no longer clear to anyone.[12] Even so, what was in fact being assured to the bishop throughout his estates would have been well understood. The grant of sac, tallage and toll and team, would have authorized his manorial courts to sit as courts leet (or great courts) twice a year, around Easter and Michaelmas, to deal with matters reserved for the manors of less privileged lords in courts held at the same two seasons of the year by the sheriff in his 'tourn' – his judicial journey – around the county.[13] Infangthief and outfangthief, originally the right to have a manorial gallows and hang thieves caught red-handed,[14] had probably dwindled (as royal justice expanded) to the right to receive the chattels of executed felons. Other words in the charter conveyed fiscal privilege: hideage or carucage presumably exempted the bishop's manors from the tax invented in 1194 to replace the old geld or Danegeld and to ransom King Richard I from captivity in Germany;[15] stretward probably exempted the bishop's manors from contributing to the cost of policing Shropshire's roads during the cattle-droving season between Michaelmas and Martinmas (i.e. October).[16] Yet other words – carriage, passage, portage, stallage, for example – must indicate powers to ease trade and travel in various ways.

In what proportions the bishop and his manorial tenants shared the benefits of such privileges must remain speculative. But the privileges remained with succeeding bishops even after King John turned against the Briouze family to destroy them;[17] the privileges were confirmed in 1241 to Bishop Peter d'Aigueblanche, the Savoyard nobleman newly appointed Bishop of Hereford. And in the long run Bishop's Castle stood to gain: when, for example, incorporation came in 1573 (see below) the twice yearly great court became the borough's court and was held in the castle.[18]

Other charters to later bishops brought more immediate benefits to the locality. In 1249 Henry III granted Bishop d'Aigueblanche a Friday market and an annual fair on the vigil, feast, and morrow of the Decollation (beheading) of St John the Baptist (23rd-25th June) in Lydbury North,[19] and that may have benefited the bishop's new town at the Castle. Indeed by 1292 that market and at least one of the fairs may have been held in Bishop's Castle; at any rate they then survived a royal inquiry[20] into the rights and privileges exercised by lords.

Markets and fairs were very important in giving a community new status and promoting its economy. Thus Bishop's Castle flourished whilst some new towns failed. The lord of nearby Lydham was granted a market and two annual fairs there in 1267 and given other privileges going with a 'free borough' in 1270,[21] but little success followed. Caus castle and borough, near Westbury, was built and developed by the Corbets, and in 1349 there was a market and 58 burgage plots; but it failed economically and was eventually abandoned.[22]

Markets and fairs may have attracted trade with the Welsh, reducing some of the tensions of the border. Nevertheless the March remained an unsettled area, with threats of Welsh incursions as well as feuds between English barons. In 1223 the king had allowed Bishop Gilbert Foliot to summon all the knights and tenants of his fee to defend Bishop's Castle and the lands there against the king's enemies. The families owing castle guard included the Plowdens, the Oakeleys and the Walcots.[23]

Bishop d'Aigueblanche was involved with the town's fortunes during the civil war of Henry III's reign. In 1262 he wrote to inform the king that the Marches were in turmoil, with raids from the Welsh prince Llewelyn, who was warring against the king (and was soon to give his backing to Simon de Montfort). The bishop had left Hereford inadequately defended, needing 'at least 40 of the King's horse-soldiers' to make the city secure. Having retired to Gloucester, he was detained there by infirmity and fear of certain 'malevolents' (opponents of the king) thirsting for his life. In 1263 Henry dispatched Prince Edward, Earl of Chester, to assess the situation, and Edward requested that d'Aigueblanche be instructed to return at once to Lydbury Castle to take part in the defence of the March.[24] But the bishop was arrested by some lords of the baronial party and imprisoned briefly at Eardisley, Herefordshire before being released in 1263.[25]

That same year, in what may have been an episode of private strife, Bishop's Castle was attacked and captured by John Fitzalan II, lord of Clun, Oswestry and Arundel (Sussex). The victor made an inventory of stores taken in the castle and grange; they included 13 oxen, 2 waggons, 2 carts, 32 horse loads of corn, and a year's supply of the agricultural produce from two ox teams, as well as the bishop's white mare and iron surcoat. Armaments in the castle consisted of 6 hauberks (shirts of mail), 6 *chapels de fer* (broad-rimmed iron helmets) and 6 *balistae* (catapults), suggesting a permanent garrison of just six. That would have been augmented when necessary by local conscripts. The only man killed in the attack was the constable. Fitzalan held the castle for 16 weeks during which houses, other buildings and timber suffered great damage.[26]

During the attack and subsequent occupation, the castle building fell into disrepair. The damages amounted to the enormous sum of 1,060 marks (£706 13s 4d), perhaps equivalent to half a million pounds today.[27] The work of repair fell to Thomas Cantilupe, one of the most famous bishops of Hereford – canonized as St Thomas of Hereford in 1320.

Cantilupe, like his predecessors and successors, visited the town regularly to carry out their pastoral and other duties and to check on the running of their castle and estate. In 1290 Bishop Swinfield arrived for a four-day stay over Rogationtide and Ascension Day – 11th May that year. His visit gives some idea of the scale of the necessary arrangements. He arrived with 34 horses, and his household consumed 2 quarters of bread baked from flour from the manor (6s 8d), 1 carcass of beef (6s 1½d), 1 roe deer, 11 kids and 2 bacons from the manor, 2 calves (12d), 13 geese (4d), 3 fowls (12d), 28 capons, 12 fowls – a present, eggs (10½d), milk (3½d) and

Fig. 4.3 St Thomas Becket and St Thomas Cantilupe as depicted in a window in Credenhill church (Herefs.)

36

bread (3d). Cod, salmon and plaice are also included in the list, and charcoal cost 3d.[28] Bishop Swinfield was doubtless satisfied with his reception.

By 1291 – and probably well before this episcopal visit – there was a parish church at the southern end of the town. The vicar's annual stipend was £4 13s 4d, just over half of what Wigmore Abbey received from the parish's appropriated rectorial tithes. The story of St John the Baptist's church is told in Chapter 7.

In the 14th century the Welsh border remained an unsettled part of the kingdom. From 1322 Bishop Orleton opposed Edward II and became a partisan of Queen Isabella, the Mortimers, and other insurgent Marcher barons. In 1324 his lands were seized by the king, who appointed a constable of Bishop's Castle. Eventually, however, in 1327 – in the new reign dominated by Queen Isabella and Roger Mortimer, Earl of March – Orleton had the temporalities (secular possessions) of his see restored.[29]

There was friction too between neighbouring castles – Bishop's Castle and the king's castle of Montgomery. In 1383 John Says of Montgomery petitioned that a certain Ieuan, a tenant of Bishop's Castle, had, with a number of men-at-arms, taken him and imprisoned him for eight days in Clun castle. In the same year, there was a complaint that tenants of the lordship of Bishop's Castle feloniously killed William ap Howell, tenant of the king. Petitions and counter-petitions concerning incidents like these were not infrequent.

Between 1315 and 1322 there was widespread famine in Europe caused by extreme weather conditions and crop failure, and the effects of this would have been felt keenly even in remote corners of the Welsh border. A tax assessment made in 1341 showed the value of the estates of Lydbury and Bishop's Castle greatly reduced: upwards of a third of the land was no longer being tilled owing to lack of manpower.[30] The coming of the Black Death 1349-50 would have caused further hardship.

When, in 1356, Bishop Trilleck and his cathedral chapter decided to reduce the number of manor houses to be maintained and kept in repair from 24 to just 6 – a drastic measure of retrenchment – Bishop's Castle was one of those retained.[31] The reasons for its retention must have included the quality of its rebuilt castle, its strategic position, and perhaps its rate of recovery from the ravages of the Black Death.

The bishop's residences, whatever their number, and along with the whole episcopal estate, fell to the Crown during vacancies in the see, as is shown by the king's appointment of the Shropshire escheator, John ate Wode, as constable of the castle during the year-long vacancy of 1361-2: he was granted a salary of £10 per annum and was charged to find 40 men from the town and surrounding area for the wars in France. He had a robe such as 'esquires of a Lord' wear (or 20d in lieu) and was paid 4d for every brewing of ale made in the castle, 6d a day for keeping a brace of horses in livery, and 2d a day for a porter. Normally, however, the bishop appointed all his estate officials, sometimes to more than one job, as in 1449, when his receiver-general of Bishop's Castle was also appointed constable of the castle.[32]

Economic growth of the town was further promoted when, in September 1394, a royal charter to the bishop specified a market in Bishop's Castle. Richard II granted Bishop Trefnant a Wednesday market and an annual fair on All Souls' Day and the two following days (2nd-4th November) – a good time for selling fattened pigs and surplus livestock for slaughter.[33]

Fig. 4.4 The Castle: watercolour of unknown provenance, and perhaps imaginative since Leland's eye-witness account describes the castle as 'not veri hy'.
(Photo. Keith Ritherdon)

Early in the next century conflicts of national importance came to the Marches with the battles of Bryn Glas (Pilleth) in 1402 and Shrewsbury in 1403, when Hotspur and Owain Glyn Dwr attempted to overthrow King Henry IV. Late in 1404, at one of the most dangerous periods of the revolt and notwithstanding the fact that Bishop's Castle was a private castle (granted to the newly appointed Bishop Mascall just a few weeks earlier with the rest of his temporalities), Bishop's Castle and Welshpool were substantially garrisoned for the king. (National emergencies as well as vacancies in the see could see the Crown taking control of the bishop's castle.) Command of the garrisons was given to John Talbot, as deputy for his stepfather, Lord Furnival; it marks the beginning of the military career of one who, as Earl of Shrewsbury and the 'English Achilles', was to spend the last years of his life in the vain defence of Henry VI's French possessions and claim to be king of France.[34] But Bishop's Castle was also, and perhaps more particularly, affected by the outbreaks of local lawlessness which attended the uncertainties of the early 15th century. The breakdown of law and order was widespread. In 1406 Bishop Mascall reported 52 churches in his diocese badly damaged, with the loss of glebe land in Bishop's Castle and the bishop's *temporalia* (worldly possessions). Indictments before magistrates tell the same story. Howell ap Cadwaladour and Howell ap Madogyn were accused of having feloniously murdered William Shery and John Yope of Asterton at Bishop's Castle in 1403 and of burning several houses at Norbury – 'they are common thieves and despoilers of fields'. And Yewekes Duy of Bishop's Castle was to be produced in the King's Bench at Westminster at Michaelmas 1415, accused of giving food and other necessities to three men who were Welsh rebels, knowing that they had broken into houses at Hardwick and stolen items of bedding.[35]

Later that century, during the Wars of the Roses between the houses of York and Lancaster, there were engagements at Ludford Bridge (1459) and Mortimer's Cross (1461). Two local families, the Walcots of Walcot (Lancastrian) and the Plowdens of Plowden (Yorkist), are said to have clashed during this latter conflict, resulting in the death of a Walcot from a halberd wound.[36]

An event of great significance for the town and region therefore was Edward IV's creation of the Council in the Marches of Wales in 1472. This body, responsible for the government of Wales and the Border counties, reduced the tensions and conflicts which had been regular and debilitating features of life over a wide area. However, a consequence of this positive development was a lessening of the importance of the border castles. Bishop's Castle would now gradually move from being a town focused on its castle, to asserting its other role as an important market centre for the rural economy.

About 1539 the antiquary John Leland, commissioned by Henry VIII to travel around England to report on the monastic libraries, wrote: 'the Bishop of Heref orde hath a castel of good strenketh yn the marches toward Shreuisbyri-shire cawlled Bisshops Castel, and ther to lieth a town cawlled Bisshopes Town, wher is wekely kept a very good market.' 'Bishops Castel [he added] well maintenid is set on a stronge rokke, but not veri hy'.[37]

In 1559 Elizabeth I decided to acquire Bishop's Castle, and by a forced exchange the town passed out of Bishop Scory's hands and became Crown property. A survey carried out for the Crown recorded a castle still habitable, with 13 rooms covered with lead, a tower on the eastern wall containing a stable, two rooms covered with tiles, two further rooms in the 'new buyldinge' between the building over the gate and 'le prison tower', a dovecote, garden, forest and park.[38]

Elizabeth I's interest in Bishop's Castle did not end there. On 16th July 1573 she granted the town its most important charter, incorporating it in the name of the bailiff and burgesses. The 'free borough' was now self-governing, no longer dependent upon powers devolved by the bishops. Robert Mason was named as the first bailiff, and Edmund Plowden, Charles Walcot, Matthew Lloid, Andrew Blunden, John Thomas the elder, John Thomas the younger, Edward Jones, Thomas Harrington, Robert Mason, Roger Bowen, Hugh Mason, Edward Bowen, David Rowland and John Tanlyns named as chief burgesses. They would elect a new bailiff annually, before Michaelmas, and appoint a recorder, clerk, constable and two sergeants-at-mace[39] to carry silver maces before the bailiff. Maces are still carried today at mayoral functions, the present ones dating from 1698.

The name heading the list of chief burgesses, that of Edmund Plowden, is of special interest. Plowden's ancestral home was Plowden Hall, some five miles east of Bishop's Castle, but he was probably born in 1519/20 at Blunden Hall on the southern edge of the town. This was the residence of his uncle, Robert Blunden, who took the Plowden family in while repairs were being carried out to Plowden Hall.

Plowden distinguished himself as a lawyer and was an M.P. during Mary I's reign and a member of the Council in the Marches. He also protested against heresy laws proposed against Protestants. He was a man of high principle, a devout Roman Catholic, and a staunch and outspoken opponent of religious prejudice. The story is told that Elizabeth I offered him the Lord Chancellorship and that he asked to be excused: 'Your Majesty well knows I find no reason to swerve from the Catholic Faith in which you and I were brought up ... I should not have in charge your Majesty's conscience for one week before I should incur your displeasure, if it be your Majesty's intent to continue the system of persecuting the retainers of the Catholic Faith.' Elizabeth, it is said, accepted his bold refusal. The story is probably unfounded, but it is likely that by the 1570s he enjoyed the queen's confidence. When he died in 1585 he was buried in a fine tomb in the Temple Church, London.

Edmund Plowden's appearance heading the list of Bishops Castle's first burgesses has led to the suggestion that he may have been in some way instrumental in persuading the queen to take the unusual step of granting an important charter of incorporation to a very small and remote community. There is, however, no direct evidence for that,[40] and it has been pointed out that, as a Roman Catholic, his public influence would have been limited.

The 1573 charter was followed by another in 1617 from King James I, confirming and enlarging the burgesses' powers.

The bailiff and burgesses now had significant control over the town. The bailiff was justice of the peace, coroner and keeper of the town gaol. As clerk of the market he was responsible *inter alia* for checking the common-law offences of regrating (buying up provisions in the market in order to re-sell them locally at a higher price) and forestalling (buying provisions before they came to market, or preventing their coming to market, in order to mark up their eventual price). Within the borough he controlled the quality of bread, wine, ale and other victuals offered for sale, inspected the weights and measures used, and checked the work of bakers, butchers, brewers, taverners, victuallers, tanners, craftsmen and other tradesmen. The corporation enjoyed all the privileges and tax exemptions that

Fig. 4.5 Charter celebrations 1973. (Photo. Colin Love)

had been granted in earlier (episcopal) charters. It had a court of record to be held on alternate Saturdays and was entitled to the forfeited goods of felons and fugitives, the fines and amercements from royal courts, deodands (chattels or animals which had caused a person's death), waifs (stolen items discarded by a thief), and strays.

The new governing body took its responsibilities seriously. It ordered the building of a town hall and a gaol, took steps to pave the streets and clean the gutters, and prevented the pollution of the water conduit. Like any other community Bishop's Castle had its rough side, so the bailiff and burgesses attempted to raise the standards of behaviour in the town. They restricted the sale of ale 'to avoid the syn of drunckenes which here among us of this town bringeth a slander to the ghospel'. A less attractive sense of self-importance shows in an edict of 1613 which said that 'persons of inferior place and condicion lyveing within this borough shall hensfourth geve cyvile reverence to the bailiff and fifteen head burgesses and shall not presume to talk to them in publick having their heads covered'![41]

The charters of Elizabeth I and James I dramatically altered the status of the town. The castle, which had for centuries been the focal point of the community and indeed the main reason for the town's existence, lost its importance, became ruinous, and all but disappeared. But, as will appear, the borough had been empowered to embark on a new and vigorous political and economic life.

Bibliography

J.C. Anderson, *Shropshire – its Early History and Antiquities* (1864; reprinted Morten, 1972).

[E.G. Griffiths,] *History of Bishop's Castle* (A. Hughes, 1901) – copy in S.A.

B. Trinder, *History of Shropshire* (Phillimore, 1983).

M. Cheesewright, *Bishop's Castle Town Guide* (Bishop's Castle Chamber of Trade, 1986).

M. Jackson, *Castles of Shropshire* (Shropshire Libraries, 1988).

A. Lawrence, *The Bishop's Castle* (House on Crutches Museum, 1995).

The Gale of Life: Two Thousand Years in South-West Shropshire, ed. J. Leonard *et al.* (Logaston Press, 2000).

P. and A. Duckers, *Castles of Shropshire* (Tempus, 2006).

5   Bishop's Castle in the Civil Wars

In September 1645 the town of Bishop's Castle was in flames, and its church with it. We do not know how many died (if any) – the church registers of births, deaths and marriages for 1642–51 are lost. Nor do we know precisely which buildings were destroyed, though by 1648 the whole of the church (except for the tower) had to be entirely rebuilt. This deliberate firing of the town by Sir William Vaughan, the Royalist commander at Ludlow, was the last serious throw against Bishop's Castle as the four years of the First Civil War dragged towards its end.

It is thus obvious that by the final stages of the conflict the Royalist forces in Shropshire were sure that Bishop's Castle was committed to the Parliamentary side, but it was not always so. As the tides of the war ebbed and flowed, families and town administrations faced changing circumstances and uncertain choices, which most citizens of England would much rather have avoided.

This chapter charts the shifting positions of some of the leading families in Bishop's Castle over the four years from 1642 to 1646, and notes the development, among the middling people of the town, of organized protection against the misbehaviour of soldiers of both sides, a development in which Bishop's Castle may have led the way and provided a model for towns in other parts of England. Of the poorest folk in the area, we have no direct record, so we cannot hear their individual voices, but we can make some educated guesses about how war on their doorsteps made a hard life harder still.

First, however, we need a national context for the local picture. Looking at the underlying political and religious arguments, it must be remembered that in post-medieval Europe power politics and organized religion were never very far apart. Charles I's view was that he was 'the Lord's anointed', king by divine right, confirmed by the religious ceremony of his coronation. He therefore saw no need to seek consent of his subjects; as he declared to his parliament in 1628, 'I allow [owe] account of my actions to God alone'. The established church, of which he was Supreme Governor, was an essential buttress of his authority. To preserve the legitimacy of his kingship, the archbishops and bishops he appointed had a duty to exercise doctrinal discipline in churches throughout the land. Prayers for the king were required at every service; preachers were personally licensed by their bishops; and texts for their sermons were prescribed.

Ritual was an important psychological tool in this attempt to use religion to prop up civil authority. William Laud, appointed Archbishop of Canterbury in 1635, reintroduced altar rails, vestments, copes and other 'Popish' paraphernalia which had fallen out of favour in Elizabeth I's reign; and he tried to use the episcopal hierarchy to force often unwilling clergy to adopt them. We are fortunate in Bishop's Castle to be able to see nearby contemporary physical evidence of those liturgical squabbles. At Lydbury North the candlesticks Laud prescribed are still displayed, a rare survival in an English parish church, while at the other end of the Anglican spectrum, not too far away in Langley Chapel a few miles east of Church Stretton, is an almost unique example of a complete Puritan interior, virtually untouched since the 16th century.

Unfortunately Charles I's authoritarianism in both civil administration and Church government raised serious difficulties in both matters. First, on the civil side, a succession of expensive foreign policy failures drained the king's exchequer while Parliament, jealous of its power to control taxation, insisted on trying to hold his government to account for any supply they might grant him. Charles was thus constantly short of funds, and was forced to resort to obscure precedents of doubtful legality to extort money from increasingly reluctant landowners and merchants – just the class of citizens who would otherwise be the strongest supporters of legal authority.

Secondly, as theology developed along lines opened up by Luther and Calvin to reduce the importance of priests as intermediaries between God and men, and as increasing literacy broadened access to the scriptures in English rather than Latin, established doctrines were questioned and strict orthodoxy became impossible to maintain. Recusants, those who failed to attend worship in their parish church, were liable to fines, but even so defiant Puritans held their own services while determined Catholics worshipped in private houses, which sometimes had secret chapels and hiding places for visiting priests, as at nearby Plowden Hall.

Charles I's two immediate predecessors, Elizabeth I and James I, had managed by subtlety and compromise to prevent these tensions bursting out into open strife, but Charles was not a man for subtlety and was too stiff to recognize when compromise was necessary. He made armed struggle almost inevitable when, in a botched attempt at a *coup d'état* on 4th January 1642, he sent armed soldiers into the House of Commons to arrest the 'Five members' he saw as ringleaders of opposition.

Historians distinguish three stages in the conflict generally known as 'The English Civil War', but only the first, crucial, stage affected Shropshire directly. It began in September 1642, when King Charles I raised his standard in Nottingham, formally challenging the rebellious subjects who were resisting his attempts to rule without Parliament. This English Civil War – or the 'Great Rebellion', or the 'War of the Three Kingdoms' – was altogether an untidy business, as the uncertainty of its very title demonstrates. It was not a simple matter of cavaliers against roundheads, or Catholics against Protestants; plotting its battles and sieges on a map would not give any sense of a unifying strategy; and even Oliver Cromwell, the ultimate victor, was conscious of an uncertainty of purpose: 'Religion was not the thing at first contested for, but God brought it to that issue at last.'

To make sense of the war in the particular circumstances of Bishop's Castle, two questions need to be considered: 'What were the objectives of the generals on each side?' and 'What were the concerns of the people around whom the campaigns were waged?'

It is significant that, after despatching Prince Rupert to London with a small cavalry force, the king's first move was to head for Derby and then, after some hesitation, Shrewsbury. At that moment Charles had probably no more than 800 horse and 300 foot soldiers at his command, so the essential priority was to develop military capacity. He therefore sought territory where he might find reliable friends, aiming to bolster support and build up his forces. Wales was securely for the king, the English midlands more doubtful, and thus the Shropshire Marches had strategic importance.

The key to the military effort was the need to secure control of territory, and if possible extend it. In the mid 17th century there was precious little machinery of government as we understand it today, and everything, including law and order, operated at local level. Anyone, king or parliamentary commissioner, had to have enough influence over the traditional sources of authority in each parish or county – usually the great families, the squires and the senior burgesses – to get them to do what was wanted. In the last resort this authority rested on the capacity to use force, but there was no permanent army, and troops were raised and paid through these same local mechanisms. Armies were expensive, needing food, drink, lodging, weapons, ammunition, horses and recruits to fill the places of soldiers lost to injury, death or desertion. The first imperative for any military commander was, therefore, to keep a firm grip on the territory he occupied, in order to control its resources and to stop the enemy getting their hands on them.

For the overwhelming majority of the inhabitants of the territories thus controlled, the principal concern would be survival: just to keep themselves and their families alive, and to preserve what they could of their homes and their property, if they were lucky enough to have any. Further up the social scale, the aristocracy, greater and lesser gentry, the clergy and the rising commercial classes, all facing demands for support in cash and in kind from both of the belligerent parties, could not entirely avoid concerning themselves with the more abstract constitutional and religious arguments which had led to the outbreak of war in 1642. And hanging over them throughout the whole four years of struggle was the question 'Who is going to win?' No-one who was not a zealot wanted to finish up on the losing side. In what follows, it can be seen that zealotry was not much in evidence in Bishop's Castle.

This is not to deny that locally, popular feeling could run high. In a letter of June 1642 Lady Brilliana Harley at Brampton Bryan Castle wrote to her husband Sir Robert Harley in London that William Littleton, a Puritan from Bishop's Castle 'being in Ludlow last week, as he came out of the church, a man came to him and looked him in the face and cried "Roundhead"; he gave the fellow a good box of the ear and stepped to one that had a cudgel and took it from him and beat him soundly'. The Harleys were strongly Parliamentarian, and Lady Brilliana would later defend her castle against a Royalist siege.

The castle in the town saw no action during the Civil War. The last constable had been appointed in 1610, and within 30 years the castle was described as derelict, with the lead stripped from its roofs and serviceable timbers and masonry incorporated in the houses of the town. Nevertheless it was by no means unusual for abandoned fortifications to be repaired and put to use, even if only to solve a problem of finding somewhere to lodge soldiers, so it is worth asking why this did not happen here. Elsewhere in Shropshire, at High Ercall, for example, not only did the Royalists fortify and garrison the manor house but they demolished an entire village to deprive possible attacking forces of cover. Perhaps part of the answer lies in the difference in agricultural potential between the even, well watered acres of north Shropshire and the stony, hilly south-west. Here was less corn and fewer horses and cattle, so less to requisition or plunder. Perhaps, also, the broader strategic picture at the beginning of the war in 1642 needs to be considered. The Royalists' first actions in Shropshire were to secure Shrewsbury and Ludlow, where considerable repairs to the existing medieval fortifications were carried out and new earthworks raised, better able to withstand the shells and cannonballs discharged by increasingly effective 17th-century ordnance. These two strong points controlled the north-south route along the middle Marches, so had great strategic importance. Bishop's Castle, at the end of a ridge running east-west, was well placed to control incursions from Wales, but otherwise was not on any route to anywhere of military significance. At the beginning of the war Royalist commanders had no doubt about the loyalty of Wales, so there was no need to worry about the western flank, whose protection was the only useful role for a significant garrison at Bishop's Castle. Later, in 1644, a small cavalry unit was stationed at Lea Castle, a mile east of the town. This proved a great nuisance to local inhabitants, but made no militarily important contribution to the Royalists' war effort.

Even so, the local gentry faced hard decisions. Among landowners there was a natural tendency to defend property and the hereditary principle, but that did not mean universal enthusiasm for the king's cause. Loyalty to the office of king often struggled with unhappiness at the kingly person's policy.

In Bishop's Castle, the town's two Members of Parliament took different sides. Richard More of Linley (1576-1643) was returned for the two Parliaments of 1640 – the 'Short' and the 'Long' Parliaments. He was high sheriff of Shropshire in 1617 and had been bailiff of Bishop's Castle in 1637. He was a staunch Parliamentarian and his son Samuel became a colonel in the Parliamentary army. In contrast, his fellow M.P. for the borough was Sir Robert Howard, who had inherited the manors of Clun and Bishop's Castle and had represented Bishop's Castle in all six Parliaments since 1624. He was not an active member, though he claimed parliamentary privilege when brought before Star Chamber for adultery with the estranged wife of Sir John Villiers. He led a regiment of Dragoons for the king and was 'disabled' from the House of Commons in 1644 as a Royalist. Commander of the Bridgnorth garrison when it was besieged by Parliamentary troops in 1644–5, he surrendered and was allowed to return to his estates on payment of a fine of £942 and a promise to fight no more.

At county level Humphrey Walcot of Lydbury North (1586-1650) had been sheriff of Shropshire in 1631. His brother William had been a page to the king, so it was not surprising that Charles, in Shrewsbury in 1642, turned to him for a financial contribution. Walcot obliged with the very significant sum of £5,000. In 1646, however, he was imprisoned in Ludlow castle for 'disaffection to the King's cause'. It is possible that by that date he had realized that the Royalists were going to lose the war and was therefore seeking to establish his credentials with the likely victors; but a sympathy for 'Puritan' forms of worship seems to have been genuine. His son John was a Presbyterian and a close friend of the Parliamentarian Robert Harley of Brampton Bryan. It is hard, therefore, to avoid the conclusion that Walcots were at best reluctant Royalists.

Active at borough level in the corporation of Bishop's Castle during the war were Richard Oakeley (1592-1653) and William Blunden (1602-1643?). Oakeley was receiver general (treasurer) and solicitor to Westminster Abbey, and had started to buy land around Bishop's Castle in 1622. He represented the borough in the Parliament of 1624. He purchased the manor of Lydham in 1628 and in 1625 had secured the office of recorder in Bishop's Castle, a legal post of some prestige and patronage. From 1642 he worked as a Royalist commissioner but by 1645 was distancing himself from that cause.

Blunden was a churchwarden in Bishop's Castle in 1634-5 and bailiff in 1642-3. On the outbreak of the war in 1642 he lost no time in declaring his position, signing a petition of local gentry promising 'to adventure their lives and fortunes in defence of his Royal and Sacred person'. He recruited dragoons (troops equipped with horse, musket and short sword who could fight either as cavalry or dismounted as musketeers) for the Shropshire regiment commanded by Sir Vincent Corbet, but disappeared from the historical record in 1643. His estate was never seized by Parliament so it seems likely that he was killed in action.

It is noteworthy – and at first glance surprising – that there is no evidence that the Plowdens, owners of extensive estates in the Onny valley and the area's principal Catholic family, took any public position on the tumultuous events of the Civil War. Plowden Hall contains 'priest holes', and there is no doubt that the family retained their loyalty to the 'old religion', but they took no part in raising troops for the king, and there is no record of their funding his efforts. Their policy of keeping a low profile seems to have served them well, and the apparent modesty of their secluded home, which has grown by accretion but has never undergone major rebuilding in the pursuit of changing architectural fashion, shows that they have continued to avoid drawing attention to themselves by any sort of ostentation. The north transept of the parish church at Lydbury North, known to this day as the Plowden Chapel, is an ancient Roman Catholic chapel where mass is still said once a year.

The corporation of Bishop's Castle faced obvious difficulties when they looked at the divided opinions of these leading personalities who were effectively responsible for public administration in the area. Wisely they began by addressing concerns which were common to all citizens: the safety of their families and the security of their property. On 6th December 1642 the corporation decreed that, 'by reason of the soldiers remaining in the County, all householders should keep watch through the night and all persons keeping horses and mares should be ready to ride to such places as the Bailiff appoints'. Householders had to provide themselves at their own cost with suitable weapons for safeguarding their own person. The corporation was thus setting up its own local defence against marauders from either side.

On 24th December the corporation made a further order: 'Whereas an association has been formed throughout the county of Salop for the preservation of every particular person from plundering, of late too much exercised, and whereas it has been concluded by the several Justices of the Peace for the allotments of Clun and Purslow and most of the inhabitants, gentry and freeholders of the same, that eight horses with able riders ... shall be instantly provided within every allotment, William Blunden Esq. [the town bailiff] shall have the power to nominate four able and sufficient inhabitants of the town of Bishop's Castle to provide four horses with riders etc. at the general charge of the town'. The 'Association' comprised 80 landowners who signed an 'Engagement and resolution of the principal gentlemen of the County of Salop for the raising and maintaining of forces at their own charge, for the defence of his Majesty, their country, and more particularly the fortunes, persons and estates of the Subscribers'. It is worth noting that, although the Association at this stage of the war declared its loyalty to the king, it was frank in admitting that its first concern was the preservation of its subscribers' own property and families. Richard Oakeley was one of the signatories, and in January 1643 and again in March 1643 his accounts show that he paid a 'levy for the raising of a dragoon and part of his arms and pay'.

Despite the efforts of Oakeley and his fellow subscribers, the king's commanders were not satisfied. In January 1643 Sir Thomas Scriven, annoyed at having had no response from the constable of the Purslow hundred to his warrants requiring money to be collected to maintain Royalist troops, ordered all the militia of the hundred to muster at Ludlow 'by nine in the morning with their arms complete, and that gentlemen and other inhabitants of the hundred who are contributors to maintenance also be there, to see them well furnished and to satisfy me and others why their monies were not sent in according to warrants'. It is not clear how many responded to the summons, but we can guess that it was not a great success because Richard Oakeley, Walter Waring, William Blunden and H. Bromley, acting for the borough corporation, sent out further warrants to the high constable demanding that 'all able bodied men between the ages of 16 and 60, with such horses and weapons that they possessed, should assemble at Bishop's Castle Town Hall on the 23rd by 9am'. In spite of threats of fines and imprisonment for those who failed to obey, the warrants had little effect. A reissued warrant of 9th February also met with a poor response.

On the Parliamentary side steps were being taken to secure finance and manpower for their armies. In February 1643 a Shropshire Committee was established (with More of Linley a member), but it made little headway until September that year when a proper fortified base was established in Wem.

Meanwhile in Bishop's Castle ordinary civic business had to be managed and expenses met. The burgesses were faced with a levy of £10 each to repair the town hall and tower and £5 each to repair Church Bridge and the town conduit. There is some mystery about these levies: what was the 'tower' that wanted repair if it was not the castle? The church tower was no concern of the corporation and there is no evidence that the old market hall of 1618/19 had a tower. Perhaps the castle was not as completely ruinous as has been assumed? Or perhaps it was a matter of public safety, and something had to be done to prevent the abandoned structure falling into the road? The 'church bridge' is also an unidentified feature in a town without any significant water to be crossed. No great engineering structure could have been required to cover the gutter carrying the Pennal stream past the church, but there may have been some legalistic argument about the burgesses' powers to raise 'pontage' dues for anything that was not dignified with the name of 'bridge'.

In May Richard Oakeley and his kinsman Ambrose King, with other local burgesses, met to protest about continuing disorder. As a result Henry Wall, who as sergeant of Bishop's Castle was responsible for law enforcement, was replaced by Edward Broughton. Despite the new sergeant the problem continued and in March 1644 the corporation ordered that all inhabitants of the town, 'on hearing of a musket or other public notice, shall repair to the aid of any particular house or village, with their best arms, for the defence of the same from plundering or any other violent or wilful breach of His Majesty's peace'. It is probably unwise to imagine that this reference to 'His Majesty' implied royalist enthusiasms; 'The King's Peace' was a standard legal formula meaning public order.

So far, the war had been a trouble to the people of Bishop's Castle, but they had seen no actual fighting. In 1644, however, matters started to change as the better-organized Parliamentary interests began to loosen the Royalists' grip on the county. February saw the first significant military action in south Shropshire. Control of the corridor between Shrewsbury and Ludlow was vital and the Royalists judged that a fortified and garrisoned Hopton Castle would help to protect it. Hearing of this intention (telling evidence of the effectiveness of the Parliamentarians' local intelligence network), Colonel Samuel More moved in with a score of men to defend the position. They held out against Royalist besiegers for a fortnight but, after refusing two offers of parley, More was forced to surrender when the Royalists forced an entry through a garderobe shaft. There was no promise of safe conduct for the men, who were stripped naked, driven into a swamp and drowned or brutally clubbed to death. More himself had value as a tradeable prisoner and was taken to Ludlow where he was held until exchanged for a captive Royalist.

Hopton was only a fleeting success for the king's party. Oswestry fell to Parliament in June, Montgomery in September. This was a major turning point, both militarily and in the loyalty of the population. The Royalists began to look insecure, and the Ludlow garrison found it harder to provision itself from the surrounding countryside. The consequences for Bishop's Castle were serious. In October Sir Michael Woodhouse, governor at Ludlow, ordered Colonel Vangeris, a Dutch mercenary commanding a troop of horse, to garrison Lea Castle, the medieval tower house a mile east of Bishop's Castle. Woodhouse complained to Prince Rupert about Vangeris's unreliability, but the colonel was efficient enough to make himself thoroughly unpopular with local people by his demands (with menaces) for provisions.

Fig. 5.1 Hopton Castle. (Photo. Gavin Watson)

In 1644 there were more than 1,000 men in arms around the district and by February 1645 about 1,600. The pressures thus placed on struggling civilians contributed to the emergence of bodies of citizens dubbed 'clubmen'. These were rosters of burgesses who banded together to protect women against rape, men against forcible conscription, and crops, livestock and property against theft and damage. Their name came from their improvised weapons – cudgels and assorted agricultural implements fastened to long poles. They did not take sides in the war but were ready to go to the relief of any property under attack. The earliest reference to 'clubmen' was printed in *Mercurius Britannicus*, a Parliamentary propaganda sheet, in January 1645, citing a report of 18th December 1644 from Wem, naming Bishop's Castle as their origin: 'Out of Shropshire we hear there are above a thousand in arms about Clun and Bishop's Castle standing out against both sides, neither for the King nor for the Parliament, but standing upon their own guard for the preservation

Fig. 5.2 A carving in the south-west corner of the south transept of Bishop's Castle church said to be of Gervase Needham, vicar of Bishop's Castle 1629-46, a leader of the local clubmen. (Photo. Gavin Watson)

of their own lives and fortunes.' The idea spread, and other groups sprang up, especially in the south-western counties. Some were accused of indiscipline to the point of plunder, but the Bishop's Castle clubmen seem to have been well organized and controlled. Their main concern was the behaviour of Royalist soldiers and they particularly demanded that Colonel Vangeris be posted elsewhere and that the garrisons at Lea Castle and at Stokesay Castle be evacuated. Vangeris was indeed posted away and was killed in Gloucestershire two months later.

The clubmen's leaders were the Revd Gervase Needham, vicar of Bishop's Castle, Jeremy Powell and Francis Harris, members of the minor gentry, and Richard Heath, possibly the curate in Clunbury. The careers of Needham and Heath illustrate some of the difficulties facing clergy during the Civil Wars. In 1642 Needham signed the 'Loyal Address of the Shropshire Clergy' in support of the king. In 1644 he was leading the clubmen and protesting to the Royalist governor in Ludlow about the activities of Vangeris. Two years later, in 1646, with Parliament in control in Shropshire, he was ejected from his living and his house and goods were burned. He was then prevented from keeping the school with which he was trying to support his family and he died in 1649, three days before King Charles was beheaded. There is a brass plate and a stone bust thought to be of him in the south transept of Bishop's Castle church. Richard Heath advanced from his curacy in Clunbury to the rectory at Hopesay in 1647, and then to the vicarage of St Alkmund's in Shrewsbury in 1651. In 1662, after the restoration of Charles II, he was ejected from his living. He moved to Wellington in Shropshire in March 1666 and died there in May.

Another clergyman with Bishop's Castle connexions appears on the national stage as one of Thomas Fuller's *Worthies of England*, in a book dedicated to Charles II as the 'revival of the memories of such persons which have in each county been eminent for parts or learning'. He was Jeremy Stephens (1591-1665), born in the town when his father was vicar *c*.1576-1629. Charles I presented him to the Northamptonshire rectories of Quinton and Wootton and he became the 'literary companion' of the great scholar Sir Henry Spelman, helping to bring out Part 1 of Spelman's *Concilia* in 1639. As a reward for his assistance he was given the prebend of Biggleswade in Lincoln cathedral in 1641 'by the interest of Archbishop Laud'. Unsurprisingly, he was deprived of all his preferment in 1644 and imprisoned. But he continued to work on further, posthumous, works of Spelman as well as his own 'small pieces on the controversies arising from the usurpation'. The Restoration made publication of this latter material unnecessary, and allowed him to recover his livings. He was also granted a prebend in Salisbury cathedral.

In 1645 the fortunes of the war in Shropshire turned definitively towards Parliament. In February Shrewsbury fell. Stokesay Castle followed at the beginning of June and Lea Castle in October. A Royalist attempt to regain Stokesay met with a crushing defeat. The Parliamentarians now felt secure enough to set up a local Committee for Sequestration. It was their task to seize the estates of those who were supporting the king. This confiscated wealth could, in principle, equip Parliamentary forces. However, in the uncertainty of war there were few buyers for property, so owners were given the option of compounding (buying back their estates) for the cost of one tenth of its value or two years' pre-war income from the estate. 'Delinquents' who thus compounded also had to swear the 'Negative Oath' – a promise not to take up arms against Parliament.

Richard Oakeley, who in 1644 was still signing warrants for the king, faced sequestration hearings in Bishop's Castle in August 1645. William Sayce, Richard Wooton, former high constable of Purslow hundred, and Esay Thomas, former mayor and town clerk of Bishop's Castle, gave evidence against him. Oakeley appears not to have entered any defence and officers of the Committee visited his house to make an inventory of his belongings. So that his children and servants might carry on living in reasonable comfort he compounded for part of his estates immediately and secured permission to petition the Committee for Compounding in London to settle a price for the rest. In September 1645, showing little gratitude for his three-years efforts for their cause, but resenting his 'co-operation' with Parliament, Royalists from Ludlow attacked and pillaged his home, leaving it devastated and bare. In November 1645 they imprisoned him in Ludlow but quickly released him, possibly for a ransom. In the same month he travelled to London to sort out his affairs. He paid a fine of £460 and took the Negative Oath early the following year. In January 1649, after the First Civil War was well over, the corporation of Bishop's Castle gave him the job of collecting levies for Parliamentary forces.

As for the burgesses of Bishop's Castle, the Royalists were now inclined to deem them Parliamentary supporters. The main garrisons at Ludlow and Bridgnorth, always hungry for supplies, planned to gather provisions by raiding a fair at Bishop's Castle on 25th August 1645. A troop of 400 horse and dragoons approached the town but local Parliamentarians had prior warning and sent 80 horse and 80 foot to meet them. The two forces met outside the town, probably near the foot of Stank Lane where the road was very narrow, and gave the Royalist cavalry no room to manoeuvre. Despite heavy odds against them the defenders won and Royalist losses were high.

A few days later in early September Sir William Vaughan returned to burn the town and destroy the church because it had been used by Parliamentary soldiers and had accommodated 'the preaching of sedition'. This deliberate gratuitous action reflected the erosion of morale and discipline in an army that was facing likely defeat. Ludlow, the last Royalist stronghold in Shropshire, fell in May 1646. Within six months King Charles had surrendered to a Scottish army at Newark, and people up and down the land faced the uncomfortable tasks of reconciliation within families and communities, and, nationally, of adapting to the constitutional experiments of the victorious Parliamentarians.

A contemporary letter gives a glimpse of the miseries faced by the ordinary people of Bishop's Castle in the four years of conflict: 'None of the inhabitants dare lye in their houses within 10 miles of the garrisons: some having been killed in their beds, and many having great sums assessed on them which not being able to pay are forced to fly to other places where they live in great want and misery.' Common folk were at risk whether they took sides or not. Unlike their commanding officers, they were not worth anything for ransom or exchange. Even if they escaped violence many went hungry as both armies lived off the land and plundered the area for provisions. As for the gentry, the holders of the same old family names continued to expect – and receive – the same old tugging of forelocks. Although its importance in the constitutional development of England cannot be doubted, the Great Rebellion had not produced a social or an economic revolution.

6   A ROTTEN BOROUGH POCKETED

Bishop's Castle borough was incorporated by charter dated 16th July 1573. Elizabeth I granted it probably at the request of Henry Herbert, Earl of Pembroke. The Herberts were pre-eminent in mid Wales and the earl had influence at Court, where his wife and his uncle, the Earl of Leicester (who was acquiring property in Bishop's Castle), were favourites. Thomas Jukes, in due course one of the borough's first two M.P.s, was a client of Pembroke's.[1] The charter conferred no right of representation in Parliament, but boroughs could be enfranchised or disfranchised, or have their chartered enfranchisement varied,[2] by other acts of Crown prerogative – the issue of letters patent or writs of summons.[3] So in 1584, for Elizabeth's fifth Parliament (the first since 1573), Bishop's Castle, with an electorate of *c.*40 burgesses and presumably answering a writ of summons, returned Thomas Jukes and John Cole as its first M.P.s.[4] (Most English boroughs sent two members to the old House of Commons.)

Only the burgesses could vote, but whether all burgesses could do so or only resident burgesses was from time to time a controverted issue when losing candidates petitioned the Commons, where decisions were very likely to be made in party interests. The size of the electorate grew over time as increasing numbers were admitted to the freedom of the borough, so becoming burgesses.

The local gentry, 1584-1690

Jukes and Cole had married nieces of Edmund Plowden, named first among the borough's original chief burgesses. Plowden and Charles Walcot (named second among the first chief burgesses), country gentlemen seated near the borough, may have been influential – through Sir Henry Sidney, their friend at Court – in securing the issue of a writ in 1584. Walcot sat for the borough in the next two parliaments (1586-7 and 1588-9). Not surprisingly the borough's M.P.s continued to be drawn from local gentry and office holders or their connexions: typical were Alexander King, an Exchequer official related to a burgess, who sat for the borough in three of Elizabeth I's last four parliaments, and Hayward Townshend, of a gentry family seated at Cound and son of Henry Townshend (kt.1604), an important official of the Ludlow-based Council in the Marches of Wales, who became recorder of Bishop's Castle. (A recorder was a barrister-at-law who, as judge in the civil and criminal cases tried at his borough quarter sessions, became a member of the corporation – often, because of his legal learning, a very influential member.) Hayward Townshend sat for the borough in Elizabeth I's last two parliaments (1597-8 and 1601), of whose proceedings he kept a full and vividly detailed journal – perhaps the best such record of the period.[5] He was a very active and influential member in 1601, and his parliamentary career would undoubtedly have been longer had he not died young.

The pattern continued under the Stuarts, though with some changes. Sir Henry Townshend's influence and that of Council in the Marches officials – often reinforced by connexions with the local gentry – had effect in the elections to James I's first three parliaments (1604, 1614 and 1621), but Sir Henry Howard, Earl of Northampton, who had acquired Bishop's Castle manor in 1609, also became influential in the borough's affairs[6] and secured the return of an M.P. at a 1610 by-election and at the 1614 general election. The most distinguished and effective parliamentarian of the seven men who represented the borough in the three parliaments was Samuel Lewkenor, who sat 1604-10.

In 1622 Bishop's Castle manor passed to Northampton's great-nephew Sir Robert Howard, and he was returned for the borough at the next four general elections (1624, 1625, 1626 and 1628). In 1624 he sat with Richard Oakeley, later a Royalist (until the 'Good Old Cause' was eclipsing the king's), and in 1625 and 1626 his colleague was William Blunden, of Blunden Hall, owner of much property in the town. Several dozen resident burgesses formed the electorate during these years.

When the Short Parliament was summoned in 1640, after Charles I's years of personal rule (1629-40), the borough again returned Sir Robert Howard; his colleague was Richard More, of Linley, an old burgess and the first of his family to sit for the borough. Both men were returned to the Long Parliament later in 1640.

The Long Parliament, sitting from 1640 to 1653[7] and more than halved in size – as the 'Rump' – after Pride's Purge in December 1648,[8] conducted the wars against Charles I and his son from 1644 to 1651. Howard, an active Royalist,[9] was 'disabled' from sitting in 1642 and died in 1653. More had died in 1643. 'Recruiter' by-elections saw Parliamentarian sympathizers replacing Royalists everywhere, and in February 1646 John Corbet of Halston (in Pontesbury) and Esay Thomas, the town clerk, were returned for the borough. Corbet, a successful lawyer and a minor country gentleman, became an active[10] 'out and out Rumper', one of only four Rump M.P.s from Shropshire – which had initially returned 12 to the Long Parliament.

Bishop's Castle was not represented in the next three assemblies – scarcely worthy of being called parliaments – summoned in the 1650s. All were elected under the influence of Oliver Cromwell, the Army and the Major-Generals. Cromwell, Lord Protector 1653-8, managed parliament incompetently and more ruthlessly than Charles I had ever dared to do.[11] Nevertheless the parliament summoned in December 1658, and in session January to April 1659 as the Protectorate regime crumbled, was elected in the old constituencies, and Bishop's Castle returned Col Samuel More, son of Richard, and William Oakeley. They differed in politics, each inheriting family views. More was an active army officer and a leading member of the county committee appointed by parliament in 1643;[12] he had sat in the 1656 parliament as a knight of the shire. At the Restoration Oakeley was named as a member of the intended Order of the Royal Oak.

The lord of the manor's interest was not exercised for some years after the Restoration, but four local gentry families, the Oakeleys of Oakeley, the Warings of Owlbury, the Mores of Linley and the Masons of Bishop's Castle on whom the manor was settled after 1671,[13] monopolized the office of borough bailiff – the returning officer at elections. Five of the seven men who represented the borough in the seven parliaments called between 1660 and the Glorious Revolution of 1689-90 were from those four families, and Francis Charlton, elected 1685, was a close connexion of the Warings besides having inherited the Blunden property in the town. The seventh man, Richard Scriven of Frodesley, elected in October 1679, was an 'old Cavalier' who had fought for the king in the Civil Wars. Indeed all but one of the borough's M.P.s during this period were Court supporters, and Sir Richard Mason, elected in 1681, was a courtier. The exception was Richard More: the third of his family to represent the borough, he sat in the third Exclusion parliament (1681) (see below) and the Convention (1689-90) summoned after James II's flight. In the strong traditions of his family[14] More had sided with Parliament in the Civil Wars and is presumed an Exclusionist and thus a proto-Whig – a political allegiance maintained by his Whig or Liberal successors at Linley until the late 19th century.[15]

The corporation interest had always been strong through its control of the electoral roll by the admission of burgesses and the bailiff's role as returning officer. A perennial anxiety was for cheap representation by avoiding M.P.s' expenses claims, which local gentlemen usually undertook not to claim[16] – Samuel Lewkenor's were still unpaid in 1612. Thus there is little in the first century of the parliamentary borough's existence to characterize it as 'rotten'. Representation of boroughs in parliament by local gentry – as at Bishop's Castle – was normal. It suited the times.

The 'rotten' borough, 1690-1763

The Exclusion crisis, dominating the three short parliaments between 1679 and 1681, had centred on legislative attempts to block the Roman Catholic James, Duke of York, from succeeding to his brother's throne. James's supporters, branded 'Tories' (Irish outlaws) by their opponents, in turn derided the Exclusionists as 'Whigs' (Scots cattle drivers). So began the national two-party system – producing in Bishop's Castle 70-odd years of election shenanigans inflamed by party acrimony and disfigured by corruption and bribery. These were the parliamentary borough's truly 'rotten' years, initially coinciding with the national 'Rage of Party' and constant election fever under triennial parliaments (from 1694) until the 1716 Septennial Act brought calmer times.

In 1690, at the first general election of William and Mary's reign, the votes of over 70 burgesses elected William Oakeley (returned at the four general elections between 1659 and 1679) and Richard Mason (d.1690). Their deaths during the 1690-5 parliament caused two contested by-elections which inaugurated the long period when cash came to determine everything, promises were broken and defeated candidates regularly petitioned the Commons to invalidate the elections[17] – as Richard More did after the 1695 by-election (caused by Oakeley's death), in which the borough bailiff, as returning officer, had been against him. More was returned at the 1695 general election with another Whig, Charles Mason, of Rockley. More, however, died in 1698, after which his family were not involved in local electioneering for a generation, and for over 30 years Bishop's Castle electioneering was dominated by the unprincipled Charles Mason (1661-1739).

Mason stood at Bishop's Castle in 11 of the 12 general elections from 1695 to 1727. In 1695 he was apparently allied to the Earl of Macclesfield, estranged husband of his cousin Anne, *née* Mason. Bishop's Castle manor had been settled on the couple at their marriage in 1683; Anne left her profligate husband two years later but they were not divorced until 1698,[18] and during the 1695 by-election the town had been observed to be the earl's. After the divorce Anne recovered most of her property, but Macclesfield continued to have influence even while his ex-wife's manorial interest was exerted for a decade from 1698, though not on Charles Mason's behalf. In the 1698 general election, when for the first time non-resident Bishop's Castle burgesses were excluded from voting, the manorial influence was put behind Anne's brother-in-law Sir William Brownlow, while her ex-husband supported his cousin Sir Gilbert Gerard, allied in the election with Charles Mason. Both sides bribed heavily, the price of a vote rising to £40 or £50 and one burgess holding out until the eve of poll when Brownlow and Gerard had 36 promises each and Gerard and Mason offered him any sum necessary to vote for Gerard. There was no petition against Mason – though he 'hardly escaped a censure, for being a tool under Lord Macclesfield' – but the Commons unseated Gerard and punished the borough for its flagrant corruption by leaving his seat vacant for the rest of the session. Mason was returned at the two 1701 general elections but unseated both times for notorious eve-of-poll bribery. Macclesfield died between the two elections, leaving £100 to the borough to be employed at the discretion of Charles Mason, who used it to promise bribes.

Macclesfield's death ended Gerard's prospects, and his ex-wife's new husband, Lt-Col Henry Brett, took Brownlow's place and was returned in November 1701, in 1702 and in 1705 – in alliance with Charles Mason. Thus were local political rivalries balanced in the first half of Queen Anne's reign. Mason was unopposed in 1702 and 1708; and having been returned for Montgomery Boroughs as well as Bishop's Castle in 1705, he chose the Welsh seat in 1706, probably to compromise with the defeated candidates, Richard Harnage and Charles Walcot, and thus obtain the withdrawal of their petition against his return for Bishop's Castle. At the by-election the Hon. Henry Newport, the lord lieutenant's son, was unopposed, perhaps another compromise. The Bretts, tired of Bishop's Castle, had put the manor up for sale in 1705,[19] and in 1708 Mason sweetened Harnage with overtures of marriage to his niece (his later dealings with her all of a piece with his shabby career) and they were unopposed.

Bribery was not the only disfigurement of Bishop's Castle elections. Treating, threats and promises of rent-free accommodation were used too. Moreover, as returning officer the borough bailiff was often far from impartial (as in the 1695 by-election), and – voting not being secret – rival poll books were kept: in the second 1701 election, when Mason's uncle was bailiff, Mason's book gave him 42 votes against George Walcot's 39, but Walcot's book, omitting the bailiff's vote, gave him 41 votes against Mason's 40. Both claimed the vote of a burgess who was reported to have said, as he went up to vote, that he was to have £5 whichever way he voted! The 1705 petition against Mason's election accused the bailiff, Maurice Pugh, of partisan refusal and acceptance of votes; scope for such behaviour arose, as in 1698, from uncertainties about whether or not non-resident burgesses could vote.

Mason's career as M.P. and placeman had prospered in the 1690s with the Whig magnate Macclesfield's support, and in the early 1700s local compromises reinforced his position in Bishop's Castle. He was made joint controller of the Mint in 1696 and, although quarrels with his colleague (which included mutual accusations of corruption) lost him that job in 1701, he went that year with Macclesfield's embassy to Hanover. The mission could hardly have been of greater significance for England's future: it was to present the Dowager Electress Sophia with a copy of the Act of Settlement making her Queen Anne's heir and to invest the future King George I with the Garter. Its composition – an atheist and two murderers[20] besides Mason, the fraudster – could not have been more unsavoury, and aroused much criticism.[21] But Mason continued in favour: voting in parliament with the Court Whigs made him receiver-general and paymaster for transports – entrusted (unwisely) with large amounts of public money! Outrageous mismanagement lost him the paymastership in 1708, just as he was returned, unopposed again, for Bishop's Castle. But thereafter his career went downhill, partly owing to the intrusion of greater powers on the local scene.

The Harleys of Brampton Bryan (Herefs.) had acquired Bishop's Castle property, and in 1710 a political revolution and general election allowed Robert Harley – in effect the new prime minister[22] – to get his new solicitor-general in at Bishop's Castle despite Mason's bribery. Mason did not challenge the new power at the 1713 general election, but in 1715, although heavily indebted, he engaged in colossal bribery and beat the Harleys' candidate. This, his last electoral victory, gave him parliamentary immunity from Crown process over his mismanaged paymaster's accounts and from private creditors.

So flagrant had Mason's bribery been that in 1718 the Harleys, castigating the 'villainous roguery' and 'perfidy' of the borough's 'profligate wretches' – between 70 and 100 voted in the earlier 18th century – sold Bishop's Castle manor to the rich Earl of Carnarvon (created Duke of Chandos in 1719), a recent paymaster-general. He got his man in unopposed, but not cheaply, at a 1719 by-election. But at the 1722 general election, when spending was 'prodigious', the Duke was allowed only one seat as Bowater Vernon, a 'South Sea man', determinedly outbid him for the other. Mason, 'not much prepared with *unum necessarium*' and beaten into third place, petitioned and was eventually awarded Vernon's seat for parliament's last three sessions (1726-7).

Standing for the last time in 1727 Mason got a derisory six votes; he died in miserable circumstances in 1739. By 1727 Chandos had sold Bishop's Castle manor to his nephew John Walcot, of Walcot. No Walcot sat for the borough again; but for over half a century – at six general elections, three of them not contested to a poll – Walcot's interest was exercised in favour of kinsmen and fellow Tories. One seat was secured for an old Tory friend of Chandos in 1727 and for another Tory in 1734; both times the other seat went to a strong hereditary Whig, Walcot's uncle, Robert More, standing on his own interest. There was no poll in 1734, but Walcot's servants paraded a drunken mob around the town crying 'Down with the roundheads, damn More, down with him'. (Shropshire memories were long.) Chandos's son, the Marquess of Carnarvon, and another Tory beat two ministerialists (government supporters) at vast expense in 1741. By then H.A. Herbert, chief of the Shropshire Whigs,[23] had been induced to nurse the borough secretly, and in 1744 an unopposed ministerialist secured Carnarvon's seat after his succession to his father's dukedom.

At three more general elections six Tories, none of them local, were returned on the Walcot interest, twice without a poll. Three were partners in Child & Co., the bank to which the Walcots were heavily indebted. A fourth was John Dashwood King, John Walcot's brother-in-law, initially returned at a 1753 by-election when 1,781 gallons of ale and other 'liquors', consumed over a few days, had to be paid for (Fig. 6.1). A fifth, Peregrine Cust, solemnly ascribed his unopposed return in 1761 'with the united hearts of the whole town' to his mother, the daughter and granddaughter of former M.P.s Sir William Brownlow and Sir Richard Mason. Only at the contested general election of 1754 did local men get involved. Corbyn Morris, a local associate of Herbert's 1744 ministerialist success, revived opposition to the Walcot interest, pledging that a Bishop's Castle seat was '£1,000 risk, £2,000 sure'. The eventual

Fig. 6.1 Some of the drink provided by John Walcot to help his brother-in-law to victory in the 1753 by-election. It seems that beer was then 2d a pint. (S.A. 151/4435/9)

candidate was Jeremiah Brown, a native of the town who had managed Vernon's bribery in 1722, but he and his colleague, a Herefordshire squire, were heavily beaten. One of the victors died next year and was replaced by Walter Waring, of Owlbury, a local Tory. Four years later, to raise money, Waring, who wielded an interest of his own in the town, resigned his seat and arranged for Henry Grenville, one of the ministerial clan, to succeed him.

All candidates had to spend heavily with doubtful guarantee of success; and the Walcots sank ever deeper into debt: by 1761 John Walcot owed over £48,000. In 1763 his son Charles sold the Walcot estate, with a promise of his interest in the borough, to Lord Clive for a greatly inflated price. So began the third period of Bishop's Castle's parliamentary history.

The 'Pocket' borough, 1763-1832

Clive of India, returning from the subcontinent with an enormous nabob fortune, was easily able to indulge the Bishop's Castle burgesses. (In the later 18th century *c*.150 were entitled to vote.) Secure of such great wealth he could be certain of getting his own way. Immediately determined to spend 'the utmost farthing', he got his cousin George Clive in at a 1763 by-election despite government backing for Walter Waring – Henry Grenville's brother George[24] having become prime minister. He soon rounded off his manorial estate by buying up other local properties, including Charles Mason's former estates and the mortgages on them and the estates of Walter Waring,[25] who had rashly opposed George Clive in 1763; negotiating the sale in 1767, Waring also promised Lord Clive his 'entire

Bishops Castle Market Hall —
July 24 - 1849.

Fig. 6.2 The Town Hall, built c.1765. Watercolour, 1849, belonging to Mr Nigel Gaspar; from a photograph in the Town Hall.

interest' in the borough. So Bishop's Castle passed from being 'rotten' to the slightly more respectable status of a Clive pocket borough – 'so safe and cheap', it has been said, 'that its representatives could be changed with ease and frequency'.[26] Safe it was; cheap, however, it was not.

At the first general election under Lord Clive's power, in 1768, two Clives – his younger brother William and his cousin George Clive – were unopposed. The pattern was set. After 1763 there was no poll for a Bishop's Castle seat until 1802, and the only other polls before 1832 were at the 1818 and 1820 general elections and an 1819 by-election. George Clive kept his seat until his death in 1779. William vacated his in 1770 to oblige his brother who wished to bring in Alexander Wedderburn, a Scots lawyer on the make; the Clives liked to oblige such rising men.

Until 1820 a Clive always occupied one seat. Clive's son brought his uncle William back in after George Clive's death, and William then kept the seat until 1820, eventually becoming Father of the Commons. In a kind of musical chairs the other seat was occupied by Wedderburn and Henry Strachey. In 1774 Clive found Wedderburn a seat at Okehampton (Devon), another borough he controlled, so as to make way at Bishop's Castle for Strachey, his highly valued private secretary. When Strachey was given a government job that made it necessary for him to seek re-election in 1778 he was found a seat for the Admiralty borough of Saltash (Cornwall) and Wedderburn returned to Bishop's Castle until he was created Lord Loughborough and promoted to high judicial office in 1780.[27] Strachey then came back again and held the second Bishop's Castle seat until 1802.

The 1768 election had cost Clive £1,200; a general election vote cost £20, a by-election vote less. In 1774 the Clives' estimate for Bishop's Castle was £3,028 – more than the combined estimates for Shrewsbury, Ludlow and Okehampton. By 1802–3, when the resident burgesses entitled to vote numbered *c*.170, electors expected 20 guineas, and at the time of the 1802 general election some local leaders were looking for 25 guineas a head. As the 2nd Lord Clive was away in India a contest was got up, the first for nearly 40 years,

Fig. 6.3 The Clive arms formerly on the 1781 Market Hall. The elephant supporter symbolizes the nabob wealth that enabled the Clives to control borough parliamentary elections from 1763. (Photo. Gavin Watson)

and after much confusion Strachey withdrew in order to preserve Clive's control of the borough, acknowledging that only a relative could hold the second seat. After an expensive contest Lord Clive's brother-in-law Col John Robinson joined old William Clive to beat J.C. Kinchant, who owned Blunden Hall and other property in the borough, and R.B. Robson, associated with opposition to Clive's Indian policy. But Robinson's victory was not overwhelming. Opposition survived to resurface in 1818-20, and during the years 1818-27 the Earl of Powis (as the 2nd Lord Clive had become in 1804) spent £24,129 to re-establish control. At the 1818 general election Lt-Gen. Robinson beat the radical banker, the Hon. Douglas Kinnaird. A few months later, however, Robinson was dead, and at the 1819 by-election Kinnaird narrowly beat Lady Powis's relation, Viscount Valentia. It was the only defeat of the Clive interest at Bishop's Castle. At next year's general election, when the Clive interest was perhaps feebly managed and no kinsman stood, 183 (out of an electorate of *c*.200) voted – more than ever before. But nine voters were rejected and the result was a dead heat: 87 votes for each of the four candidates. Kinnaird and a Warwickshire squire Robert Knight tied with the Clive candidates – the Tory chief whip William Holmes and the barrister Edward Rogers, of Stanage Park (Radnors.). Both sides petitioned. A Commons committee scrutiny gave Kinnaird and Knight a majority of one, but after a bribery investigation they were held to have been defeated by one vote.

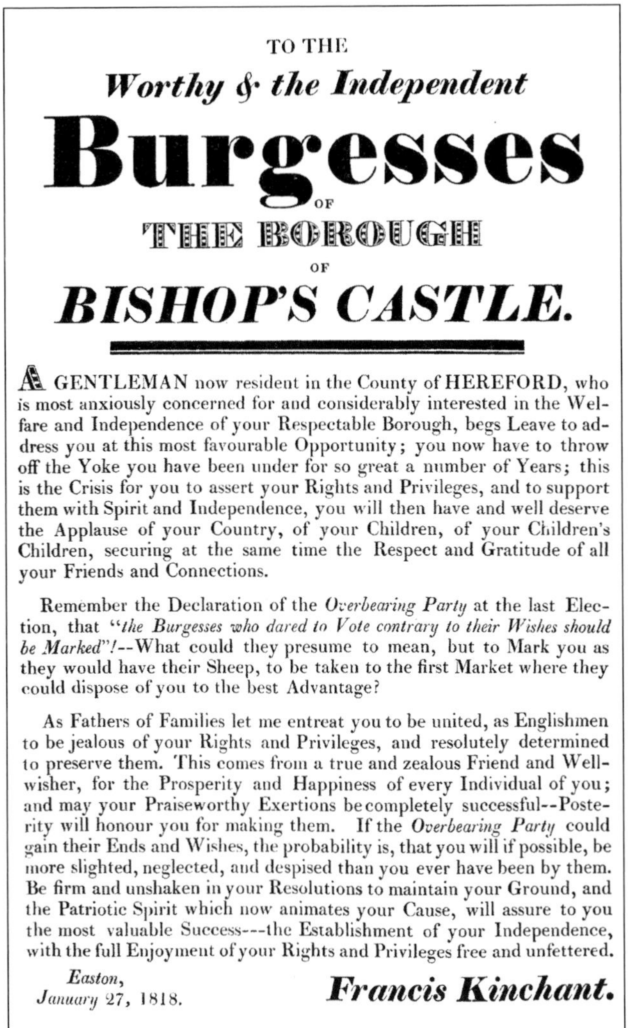

At the last three elections in Bishop's Castle, Powis's expenditure allowed him to resume

---

TO THE

Worthy & the Independent

Burgesses

OF

THE BOROUGH

OF

BISHOP'S CASTLE.

A GENTLEMAN now resident in the County of HEREFORD, who is most anxiously concerned for and considerably interested in the Welfare and Independence of your Respectable Borough, begs Leave to address you at this most favourable Opportunity; you now have to throw off the Yoke you have been under for so great a number of Years; this is the Crisis for you to assert your Rights and Privileges, and to support them with Spirit and Independence, you will then have and well deserve the Applause of your Country, of your Children, of your Children's Children, securing at the same time the Respect and Gratitude of all your Friends and Connections.

Remember the Declaration of the *Overbearing Party* at the last Election, that "*the Burgesses who dared to Vote contrary to their Wishes should be Marked*"!--What could they presume to mean, but to Mark you as they would have their Sheep, to be taken to the first Market where they could dispose of you to the best Advantage?

As Fathers of Families let me entreat you to be united, as Englishmen to be jealous of your Rights and Privileges, and resolutely determined to preserve them. This comes from a true and zealous Friend and Wellwisher, for the Prosperity and Happiness of every Individual of you; and may your Praiseworthy Exertions be completely successful--Posterity will honour you for making them. If the *Overbearing Party* could gain their Ends and Wishes, the probability is, that you will if possible, be more slighted, neglected, and despised than you ever have been by them. Be firm and unshaken in your Resolutions to maintain your Ground, and the Patriotic Spirit which now animates your Cause, will assure to you the most valuable Success---the Establishment of your Independence, with the full Enjoyment of your Rights and Privileges free and unfettered.

Easton,
January 27, 1818. **Francis Kinchant.**

Francis Went, Printer, Leominster.

Fig. 6.4 At the 1818 general election Francis Kinchant urges the electors to throw off the 'yoke' of the 'Overbearing Party' – the Clives, whom the Kinchants (of Blunden Hall) had long opposed. This time they failed, but at a by-election next year their man, Douglas Kinnaird, inflicted the only defeat the Clives suffered in the borough. (Bp.'s Castle Town Chest docs., BCB/H/2/9)

control without difficulty. Rogers sat until the end – in 1826 with Holmes as a colleague again; in 1830 with F.H. Cornewall, of Diddlebury, a kinsman of Lady Powis; and in 1831 with J.L. Knight, a rich and successful barrister.

In the Commons' committee debates on the second Reform Bill, Bishop's Castle found defenders. Knight claimed that the electors were quite free of 'improper bias'. Rogers rejected allegations of bribery. And the eccentric knight of the shire, John Cressett Pelham, strenuously opposed the borough's disfranchisement, dismissing Lord John Russell's charge that it was a corrupt nomination borough. None of that was taken seriously. The third Reform Bill received the Royal Assent on 7th June 1832,[28] and parliament's dissolution on 3rd December finished off the parliamentary borough of Bishop's Castle.

Further reading

H.T. Weyman, 'The Members of Parliament for Bishop's Castle', *T.S.A.S.* 2nd series, **10** (1898), pp.33-68.

J.R. Burton, 'Two Elections for Bishop's Castle in the eighteenth century', *T.S.A.S.* 3rd series, **9** (1909), pp.259-66.

J.F.A. Mason, 'Parliamentary Representation', *V.C.H. Salop.* **3**, pp.248-53, 297-308.

D. Preshous, 'Clive, Walcot & Bishop's Castle', *The Gale of Life: Two Thousand Years in South-West Shropshire*, ed. J. Leonard *et al.* (Logaston Press, 2000), pp.172-85.

The official *History of Parliament* volumes, published for all the time (except the years 1640–60) during which Bishop's Castle returned M.P.s, can be read online at http://www.historyofparliamentonline.org/ (accessed Dec. 2015).

The *Oxford Dictionary of National Biography* (2004).

A. and P. Theobald, 'Some Elections in Bishop's Castle', B.C.H.R.C., Heritage Pack nos. 15-26.

7 CHURCH AND CHAPEL IN GOOD TIMES AND IN BAD

A.G. Bradley, writing in 1911, described Bishop's Castle church as a 'church with an ancient tower and a more modern nave [which] occupies an unusually detached and lowly attitude towards the town it serves'.[1]

Bradley's comment neatly sums up two features of Bishop's Castle church, namely its location and the fact that the building has altered greatly over the centuries. There is a mystery about the site of the church: it is 'unusually detached' and does indeed occupy a 'lowly attitude towards the town it serves', which has suggested that the origin of the church might be earlier than the planted 'modern' Norman town seen today. Compared, say, to another border town like Monmouth (where Norman castle, priory and church are all adjacent to each other on high ground above the confluence of the Wye and Monnow), the church's site at the lower end of the planted Norman town is striking, though not without local parallels, as in Bridgnorth and Oswestry.

Bishop's Castle is a parish in the diocese of Hereford, which dates back to the 7th century. A legendary event was the gift of Lydbury North – the 'Lideberie' estate, perhaps 18,000 acres – to the bishop of Hereford c.780-792 by Egwin Shakehead, a Saxon thegn of King Offa, whose palsy had been cured by visiting St Æthelbert's shrine in Hereford cathedral.[2] This vast estate was to be a mainstay of the bishopric's finances for many centuries until Elizabeth I took over the estate in 1559, granting the town a charter in 1573. By 1167 the Lydbury North estate rent roll was yielding £124 per annum – 40% of the bishop of Hereford's income! After the Norman Conquest the bishop of Hereford was among the Marcher lords defending the borders against the unconquered Welsh. The building of the castle took place before 1127 and a new town was 'planted' with it. At first there was probably no church, perhaps only a castle chapel. By 1291, records were referring to a church dedicated to St John the Baptist and, although we have no documentary evidence of a precise date of its construction, the happy survival of the arcades of its fine south doorway, incorporated into the vicarage garden wall at the time of the church's wholesale re-building in 1860, can take us back to at least the first two decades of the 13th century. A neighbouring fragment of tracery from the old south transept shows us that a hundred or so years later the parish was thriving strongly enough to fund new building work in the latest fashions of the early 1300s, a period of which the tower bell openings can also give clear testimony. The presence of a 12th-century Norman 'tub' font is interesting, but not necessarily reliable evidence of an earlier building – fonts are portable items, and have quite commonly strayed from the place of their first installation.[3]

In 1281 Bishop Cantilupe carried out a major refurbishment and rebuilding of the castle, by which date the town had been known as Bishop's Castle for a generation or more. Bishop Swinfield visited the town four times during his episcopacy, which ran from 1282 till 1317.

Bishop Castle church was at first a chapelry of Lydbury North parish, with the advowson (the right to present to the living) of both, along with the great (rectorial) tithes, being given to Wigmore Abbey. But by the end of the 13th century, Bishop's Castle was detached from Lydbury North; the incumbent, however, continued to be presented by the abbey until the Reformation.

When Roger Mortimer (1287-1330) rebelled against Edward II, Bishop Orleton was accused of treachery and exiled, but by 1326 he was back and played a part in compelling Edward II to abdicate the following year.[4] In 1356 Bishop Trilleck and the dean and chapter of Hereford cathedral ordained that only the episcopal palace in Hereford, a town house in London and five manors, including Bishop's Castle, should be repaired and maintained in future. Buildings which ceased to be maintained included an 'old tower' in the manor of Bishop's Castle which was 'to be converted to the repair and maintenance of more useful buildings'.[5] This reduction in properties may have been due to the Black Death (1348-9), which ravaged the town and reduced the work force.

The parish church may have benefited from the importance of the castle and the Lydbury North estate. In 1336 the bishop ordained 27 acolytes, 34 deacons and 43 priests in the church. It also maintained worship and sustained pastoral ministry whatever storms raged along the border. A variety of devotions are recorded to the Blessed Virgin Mary, who had an altar dedicated to her, served by hired priests.[6] In the 1550s there were four bells in the church, of which one belonged to the corporation and was used to summon the burgesses to 'outcries', when they were required to assist the bailiff in suppressing affrays.[7]

Henry VIII's reign (1509-47) saw immense changes ushered in with the break from Rome. Cardinal Wolsey's failure to secure a divorce for Henry from his wife Catherine of Aragon led to the Reformation Parliament (1529-36) establishing the Church of England, with Henry as Supreme Head. The dissolution of the monasteries followed in 1536-40, overseen by Thomas Cromwell. By 1545 much monastic land, including Wigmore Abbey property, had been sold off, and the power of the medieval Church ended. The patronage of the living then passed to the Crown, but by 1661 it belonged to the Warings from whom it was bought (with the rest of their Owlbury estate) by Lord Clive, whose heirs, the earls of Powis (also, as lay impropriators, owners of the rectorial tithes), have enjoyed it ever since.[8]

In 1559 the first Protestant bishop of Hereford, John Scory, caused scandal by making his wife and sons prebendaries, so securing good incomes. Elizabeth I may have benefited from the uproar this caused for she required Bishop Scory to surrender four of his best manors, including Bishop's Castle, to the Crown in exchange for less profitable estates. Bishop's Castle town was compensated by the award of its charter of incorporation in 1573.

In 1592 the church was damaged by fire and was rebuilt. A year later, in 1593, plague hit Bishop's Castle and 174 people died. The parish register refers to the 'godlessness' of the bailiffs and leading citizens because they allowed a market to be held on 24th June, a Sunday. After a burial entry in the parish register of St John the Baptist, Bishop's Castle for 31st May 1593 and before others for 20th, 21st and 24th June, the vicar, Walter Stephens wrote the following (translated from the Latin):

At this time God began to punish us, with such severity that 174 adults and children died, snatched away by a most violent disease and contagious outbreak. God decided to afflict us thus because in many of our divine services and pronouncements of his Holy Word, we had not made known the just and holy rewards of the spirit, but, spurning the Word of God, had violated the Holy Sabbath, in that on 24 June which was the Lord's day, with the full consent of the elders and the majority of inhabitants of this Borough, a fair was held. On which account they were caught like thieves taken in the very act.[9]

This outbreak (which lasted from about 20th June to 21st October) of what is commonly known as plague was but one of many outbreaks in the 15th and 16th centuries known to have occurred in several local towns, including Shrewsbury, Ludlow and Presteigne, and which probably also occurred in Bishop's Castle at other times although there are no written accounts or early burial registers to confirm this. The only fact that the local population would have recognized was that episodes of plague were associated with crowds and the movement of people along the national and local trade roads. Concerning the outbreak in 1593, it is not recorded if the bodies were just put in communal plague pits inside or outside the churchyard or whether they were accorded normal burial rites.[10]

Walter Stephens 1576-1629 was a well-known Puritan; he had already quarrelled with his bishop for refusing to wear a clerical cap and surplice and over his views on baptism. He had also challenged the borough council over its laxity in alcohol licensing, describing drunkenness as 'the Friday Devil because of the Friday market in this Towne'. A picture of a 'Second Solomon' has survived in a monograph by a 17th-century rector of Brampton Bryan, Thomas Pierson, who saw Stephens as a 'faithful, diligent evangelical Puritan pastor, caring for his flock and leading his community by example. He catechized the young and was careful to instruct and advise the less learned and experienced clergy of the neighbourhood.'[11]

Nathaniel Eaton (*c*.1610-1674) – minister of Bishop's Castle

Nathaniel Eaton was born in Great Budworth (Ches.), where his father Richard Eaton, B.D., was vicar 1604-16. From Westminster School he went up to Trinity College, Cambridge, in 1630. Leaving without a degree, he went briefly to Franeker University in Friesland and returned to England to work as a schoolmaster in the 1630s. In 1637 he and his family emigrated to New England, and next year he became head of what was about to become Harvard College, in Cambridge, Massachusetts. His rule there – harsh, violent, and characterized by avaricious cheeseparing at the students' expense – was soon ended, and after his departure to Virginia he was found to have embezzled college funds. By 1646 his reputation for dissolute behaviour compelled him to leave America (where his Puritan brother Theophilus remained as governor and co-founder of New Haven, Connecticut), and in 1647 he obtained doctorates in philosophy and medicine from Padua University.

Minister at Bishop's Castle by 1651, he had left by 1661 but conformed to the re-established Church of England at the Restoration. He married a third wife, and in consequence of an arrest for debt in 1665 he resorted to perjury and bribery. In 1669 Sir John Granville, Earl of Bath, presented him to the rectory of Bideford (Devon), but in 1674 a final arrest brought him to the King's Bench Prison in Southwark, where he died.[12]

In the Civil Wars (1642-9) Bishop's Castle was caught in the cross-fire, with fighting in and around the town. In 1643 the Revd Gervase Needham was ejected from his living owing to his Royalist leanings, while in 1645 the church was set on fire by Royalist troops in retaliation for losses caused by Parliamentarians based in the town (see also Chapter 5). The church was substantially rebuilt in 1648.

Echoes of Walter Stephens's tirades against the borough council occurred in 1741, with the Revd Richard Mason's two sermons preached in May: an 'Exhortative to REPENTANCE' in the morning of Sunday the 10th and on the 'VANITY OF MAN' on the afternoon of Sunday the 24th. The sermons were printed and long remained in circulation. True repentance would lead 'to Peace of Mind while on earth and a Crown of Glory in the blessed Regions of eternal light, while overcoming the "Vanity of Man" would enable God to reunite our scattered "Atoms" in a new Body spiritualised, and together with the soul enjoy eternal and unspeakable bliss'.[13]

We know of church life in the late 18th century from Archdeacon Plymley's visitation records. He was highly concerned for church buildings and for the social and economic life of south Shropshire.[14] He visited Bishop's Castle in January and May 1793. Following initial information about the town (including its prospects for a canal) he lists the patron, Lord Clive, the vicar's tithe worth £160 a year, and his 7-acre glebe worth £20. The incumbent was Isaac Frowd, M.A., assisted by a curate, John Wingfield, on £50 a year, then a reasonable stipend.[15] A friend of Wingfield's, not finding him at home, wrote the following lines[16] and stuck them on the doorknocker:

Fig. 7.1 The parish church in the 1790s: the Revd. E. Williams's watercolour.
(S.A. 6001/372/2, no. 44)

The Bishop I find had a Castle behind
But the Bishop and Castle are flown
    For the Bishop God wot
    Could not dwell in a spot
Which Satan had marked for his own.

Then fly, Wingfield, fly
ere the wrath from on high
This damnable place has o'ertaken.
    What Curate of grace
    Would dwell in a place
By God and the Bishop forsaken.

Plymley described the church as 'in the form of a cross, with many irregular pews, and in general in good repair, though great awkwardnesses pervade the fabric both inside and out'. A new ceiling had been put in about 12 years before and 'some windows of modern shape'. He records 'the altar piece is Grecian'. He speaks of 'trifling repairs' needing to be done. The church was 'in general well filled with persons of all ranks'. The archdeacon's links with Bishop's Castle were strengthened in 1800 when he purchased an estate at Woodbatch, where there were possible deposits of lead ore.[17] The church then had five bells, four of them from 1718 and a treble (by Rudhall) added in 1767; a sixth bell (also by Rudhall) was added in 1820.[18]

From the turn of the 19th century, two headstones in the churchyard are reminders of contemporary conflicts. One commemorates John Davies, 'a native of Africa who died in this town September 9th 1801', with the text '[God] hath made of one blood all nations of men' (Acts 17:26).[19] Locally the Clives were opposed to the abolition of the slave trade while Plymley campaigned keenly for abolition. Another grave is that of a French officer, Louis Pagès, who died 1st May 1814, aged 40.[20] Over 50 French prisoners of war were quartered in the town in 1813 after the Peninsular War.

Since Reformation times Bishop's Castle, apart from masses in the recusant Plowdens' domestic chapel in Plowden Hall, had enjoyed an Anglican near-monopoly. There was little sign of dissent following the imposition of the Book of Common Prayer in 1662 – no Baptists, Quakers, Independents, or Unitarians. The first hint of future changes came with the arrival in 1769 of Richard Rodda, one of John Wesley's preachers. At that time John Wesley was still an ordained priest of the Church of England, and indeed remained so until his dying day. Rodda recorded 'In the strength of the Lord I went to Bishop's Castle, a town wicked to a proverb. I had nobody with me, but the Lord was with me to a truth. I put up my horse at an inn.' The town crier, having been given money, 'published me to preach under the Town Hall, the most public and convenient place in the town. At the time appointed, hundreds flocked to hear. I stood upon the steps and preached from Amos. v. 6. ['Seek the Lord, and ye shall live.']. Some threw their hats in my face but they did not hinder me from preaching. The tears trickled down many faces and after I had done, five or six came round me and begged I would come again. I believe the power of the highest reached many hearts and had my successors followed the blow the Kingdom of Satan might have been shaken in that wicked town.'[21] In spite of his enthusiasm, little seems to have come from Rodda's visit. Methodist influence really began in Shropshire with the Evangelical Revival associated with the Revd John Fletcher, vicar of Madeley 1760-85 and a close friend of John Wesley. Wesley said 'So unblameable a character in every respect I have not found, and I scarce expect to find another on this side of eternity.'

By 1807 Primitive Methodism had come into being – a fiery evangelistic mission born out of enthusiastic American-style camp meetings. The Primitive Methodists made a 'three-pronged advance into Shropshire', beginning with Wrockwardine Wood, the site of their first chapel, in 1822, Shrewsbury in 1824, and then Bishop's Castle in 1832, making the Bishop's Castle Primitive Methodist chapel one of the earliest in the county.[22] Again the early preachers were greeted with hostility, sometimes being pelted with missiles. By 1845 Bishop's Castle was the centre of a Primitive Methodist circuit of 20 churches, including chapels at Clun, Brockton, Lydbury, Kempton, Edgton, Clunton, Clungunford, Ratlinghope, Wentnor and Norbury. There were 23 local preachers on the plan (a list of chapels or meeting places with the ministers and lay preachers connected with them), and each preacher took an average of 8 services each quarter. Mr J. Prosser took most services – 16 on 11 separate Sundays – but eight others took between 10 and 14 services. This must represent a remarkable commitment for men who, we surmise, were mostly humble agricultural workers.

Nationally the Primitive Methodists were greatly outnumbered by the somewhat more conservative Wesleyan Methodists, but in south-west Shropshire the reverse was the case. The Wesleyans did, however, found a circuit based on Knighton which included a chapel in Church Street, Bishop's Castle, built around 1866; it closed in 1923, shortly afterwards becoming Bishop's Castle's first cinema and then a trouser factory.

The appeal of Methodism came at a time when an old rural world was giving way to a new urban one, and Primitive Methodism helped 'in making that transition possible by affirming individually one's soul in a divine order but also to a wider society'.[23] But life continued to be tough for early Methodists, as recalled in 1864 by Thomas Evans in a letter agreeing to the sale of the original chapel in Union Street. Referring to the early days, he said 'It rejoiced my soul when I read of your foundation stone laying, the prospect is brighter now than when I was stoned at the horseblock at The Old Fox and after when Mr Ward and me were stoned on the Green.'[24] In 1904 the chapel moved to its current site in Station Street, and in 1928 Bishop's Castle Primitive Methodism proudly celebrated the centenary of its arrival in the town with special services and a booklet recalling these struggles of earlier years.

An early Congregational Independent chapel was founded in 1810 (just off the High Street) and restored in 1883; but as it was reached through 'an unpleasant thoroughfare', it was replaced by a new building in Station Street in 1913. This chapel closed in 1975; the building has been used by the Army Cadet Force since 1976. Quakers in the area go back earlier to a meeting-house in Purslow in 1756, with a later one at Colebatch. In 1756 the Yearly Meeting for the whole of Wales was held in the town hall of Bishop's Castle.

The Church of England began to respond to the challenge of Methodism and revived Old Dissent rather late – not indeed until 1833 with the start of the Oxford Movement

Fig. 7.2   Opening of the Congregational chapel in 1913

following John Keble's assize sermon. It became clear that the Church of England had, in some ways, fallen behind the times. An example came in Bishop's Castle in 1835, when the Revd Isaac Frowd's long incumbency was remarked upon. It was revealed that because of infirmity he had done 'no duty for the last six or seven years', services being undertaken by his curate, the Revd John Daniel Lewis. (Such arrangements were not unusual before there were clergy retirement pension, and when resignation of a living meant the loss of one's income.) Local complaint was directed at the absence of a National or Sunday school, which was represented as 'a great abuse' by the Established Church. By contrast, the Primitive Methodists and the Independents had thriving Sunday schools.[25] Nevertheless parishioners were perhaps more appreciative of Mr Frowd's sermons: the memorial tablet put up in the church to commemorate his 60 years of ministry records him being endowed 'with a powerful understanding to which he added a rich store of theological and classical knowledge to his position'.

Nationally church building and improvement for the Church of England now became a high priority, with increased provision of pews for a growing population deemed necessary. Clearly there was a need to act. In 1852 Sir Stephen Glynne, Gladstone's brother-in-law, described Bishop's Castle as a 'poor church much altered and vilely arranged'. The church was then cruciform without aisles, and the western tower and the chancel were not in line with the nave. Glynne saw the chancel as 'low and mean, with many bad windows'. Worse still, the whole church was 'miserably dark and encumbered with pues and galleries'. And, Glynne added, 'there is a bad barrel organ'.[26]

Clearly there was much to be done. By 1851 the Religious Census showed that the Anglican monopoly had long since gone. Bishop's Castle parish church had a congregation of 250 in the morning and 200 in the evening, while the Primitive Methodist chapel had 115 in the afternoon, including Sunday school children, and 99 in the evening. The Congregational chapel had 70 in the morning, including children, and 80 in the evening. Thus the number of nonconformists was nearly as high as the Anglicans.[27] The physical state of the parish church and the numbers supporting the chapels prompted the need to rebuild the church. As a result Bishop's Castle church was entirely rebuilt in 1859-60, apart from the tower.

The appointed architect, Thomas Nicholson of Hereford, chose an Early English style for the arches of the chancel, nave and transepts. The nave roof was raised to take clerestory windows, and a new north porch added. The stone used in the rebuilding, as might be expected six years before the coming of the railway, was mostly locally sourced shelly limestone. But the stone for quoins, buttresses, windows and a string course may well be Permian limestone from south Yorkshire, also used in the rebuilding of Parliament in the 1830s.[28]

Returning to Bishop's Castle in 1867, Glynne spoke of the church as a rebuilding rather than a restoration.[29] And in 1939 Arthur Mee was impressed, stating that the 'colour scheme of the interior is effective with cream walls and black roof timbers thrown into relief by blue ceilings'. Further, he speaks of 'graceful arcades on clustered pillars' and says that 'a lofty and beautiful arch frames the chancel and apse'.[30] Excellent stained glass by Powells, O'Connor and Holiday was installed in the windows. The tower of the old church, containing the six bells of 1718, 1767 and 1820, remained. Ringing customs recorded or recollected *c.*1900 included a half-hour ring before the Sunday morning service and the tenor rung for 'celebrations' at 8am; the tenor was also tolled for vestry meetings.[31]

Fig. 7.3 The church today, seen through the lych gate

Peals were rung on New Year's Eve, and there was occasional ringing for weddings; before funerals the tenor was tolled for an hour, and when the cortège came in sight three bells were chimed to alert the vicar to get to church – a practice said to have been introduced by 'the late vicar' (the Revd W.M. Rowlands).[32] The six bells were restored in 2007-9, while the one-handed church clock, dating from 1720, was restored in 2000.

So Bishop's Castle was bequeathed the Victorian church we know today, with 'the arcade of the nave being the best feature' according to one assessment. Little has survived from the older church apart from the tower, a plain Norman font, the demi-figure of an Elizabethan divine (perhaps the Revd Gervase Needham, vicar, d.1649) in the south-west corner of the south transept, and the Early English doorway in the garden wall of the former vicarage.[33]

Late Victorian incumbents could be quite well remunerated. In 1909 the living was worth £290 a year with ten acres of glebe.[34] Perhaps that is why there were two long-serving vicars at this time. The Revd W.M. Rowlands enjoyed a ministry of 50 years and his successor, the Revd C.M. Warner, one of over 20 years. Victorian and Edwardian churches and chapels were immensely active in the community, and Bishop's Castle was no exception. There were Mission plays, choirs and amateur dramatics, a Girls' Friendly Society, a Band of Hope, Scout troop, Mothers' Union and Church Lads Brigade.[35] There was a Church Room next to the Six Bells public house. Methodists were equally active with societies, tea meetings, Sunday Schools, Club outings, 'treats' and trips to the Long Mynd, processions, and chapel anniversaries.

In 1921 an obelisk of white Hollington stone was dedicated as a memorial to the 33 men who died in the Great War of 1914-18 and unveiled by the Countess of Powis. The names of 11 killed in the Second World War 1939-45 have been added since.

Thankfully, post-war ecumenism has drawn church and chapel together. Anglicans and Methodists at times shared services and evolved a very effective Christian Aid week. Methodists saw their ministers stretched further with circuits growing in size. Bishop's Castle chapel is now in a circuit extending from Oswestry to Builth Wells. Many small rural chapels have closed, though the chapel in Station Street survives, helped by the addition of a modern hall in the 1990s. In the Church of England, reduction in the Church Commissioners' funding for stipends and pensions in the 1980s and 1990s led to reduced numbers of stipendiary clergy and growing numbers of multi-benefices. Mainstone was added to Bishop's Castle as early as 1935, thus ending the unusual practice whereby the vicar of Mainstone, who lived opposite Bishop's Castle church, hired a car on Sundays to take him to Mainstone for services there. Canon Harold Smith, vicar of Bishop's Castle 1929-45, then took over Mainstone; by 2000 Lydbury North and Edgton had been added to the benefice, and in 2004 Sarn was added to make up the present 'Ridgeway' benefice.

It was in Canon Smith's time that a Young Anglican People's Association, following on from the Church Lads Brigade, did much to foster faith among the younger generation. Roy Davies, curate at Clun and vicar of Bishop's Castle in the 1970s, revived Midsummer Rejoicings at the time of the Patronal Festival – St John the Baptist's day, June 24th – which has become a popular annual event. In the present century, the church has also become active in promoting art and music. The congregation has organized three major art exhibitions on religious themes. In 2000 it presented 'Windows on Christendom', a celebration of two millennia of Christianity. This was followed in 2006 by 'World Religions' and in

2010 by 'Faces of Faith' – two thousand years of Christian art. In 2000 a Millennium choir was formed to sing Handel's *Messiah* as part of a Georgian Festival and continues as the Marches Community Choir, regularly giving concerts in the church. Improvements in the church have continued; a long kneeler taking in the full width of the altar rail was dedicated in 1995 by the bishop of Ludlow, the Rt Revd John Saxbee. The kneeler was given and made by Katherine Bossom in memory of her husband; it is decorated with local scenes and comprises 1.3 million stitches. The refurbishment of the Church Barn in 2004, in origin a tithe barn though smaller than the huge one once located in Station Street, was successfully achieved with the aid of local and lottery fund-raising.

Recent events have included a strange echo from the past. In 2010 the chancel floor of the church gave way to reveal a vault containing 17 wood and lead coffins, some with inscriptions. The first to be identified was that of Byne Oakeley, who died on December 9th, 1825, aged 81. She was the widow of John Oakeley (1744-1811), known as The Old Retriever for his retrieval of the family fortunes;[36] his memorial plaque is in the north transept. The family originally lived at Lower Oakeley under Oakeley Mynd, then built Oakeley Manor (now Lydham Manor) in the 18th century. Although there were clues, no-one had realized that the Victorian church of 1860 had been built over the crypt containing so many Oakeley coffins. Dr Henry Oakeley, of Beckenham, Kent (author of a book on Richard Oakeley, 1590-1653, M.P. for Bishop's Castle before the Civil War), inspected the coffins and later dedicated a plaque marking the sealed-off crypt. The later members of the Oakeley family of Oakeley are buried in Lydham, and after that branch of the family died out, Lydham Manor was bought by the Sykes family in 1900.[37]

An impressive lych gate, which had been erected in 1894 in memory of the Griffithes family, was well refurbished by Castlewoods in 2010. A new heating system was installed in the 2000s and re-ordering of the west end of the church to include a kitchen and toilet is planned. At the Community College, a recent initiative by the curate, Sarah Hare, called 'Sanctuary', has encouraged young people to discover faith and explore prayer. So for over 700 years, and probably with some kind of existence for many years before, the church, from 'its unusually detached and lowly attitude', along with the chapels, in good times and in bad, has sought to witness to God's presence in the town and to care for its people.

8 COMMUNICATION BY ROAD, TRACK AND TURNPIKE

For a town whose history can boast some strategic and economic importance, it is perhaps surprising that Bishop's Castle does not stand on any modern main road. The A488 Shrewsbury to Knighton road now passes to the east of the town, the A489 Craven Arms to Welshpool and Newtown to the north – and it is possible to pass by, unaware of the town's existence. This was not always so, and in earlier centuries the town was firmly situated on commercial routes.

The earliest of these routes were the prehistoric trackways, one of which, the Kerry Ridgeway, originating in Mid-Wales, followed the high ground above the Vale of Kerry to Pant Glas and Bishop's Moat, descended to the town along what is now Kerry Lane, and proceeded east to Crowgate, Stank Lane, Edgton and the junction now called Craven Arms. This route later became an important drovers' road, allowing sheep, cattle and other livestock to be moved from Wales to the markets of central and southern England. The Kerry Ridgeway linked up at Plowden with another ancient route, the Portway, which passes along the high ridge of the Long Mynd before descending to Leebotwood, where the Pound Inn marks one of the stopping-points for the drovers. A few miles to the south of Bishop's Castle was another ancient east-west track, the Clun-Clee Ridgeway.

The nearest Roman roads are those from the city of *Viroconium* (Wroxeter) near Shrewsbury. One of these (Watling Street South) followed the route taken by the modern A49 through the Church Stretton Gap to Leintwardine (*Bravonium*), Kenchester (*Magnis*) near Hereford, and finally Caerleon (*Isca Augusta*). The other passed to the west over Long Mountain to the military base at Forden near Welshpool (*Lavobrinta*), and on to Caersws (*Mediomanum*).

It is easy to assume that the network of roads we use today has always been there. But around Bishop's Castle, as everywhere in our countryside, there are a number of tracks and 'green lanes', now overgrown, which were once the main links between communities. An Ordnance Survey map of 1832 clearly shows a changing scene from lanes and tracks to surfaced roads.

By Acts of Parliament in 1555 and 1563, highway maintenance became the responsibility of parishes, a responsibility initially discharged by churchwardens who could require parishioners to work four days a year on the roads, under the supervision of unpaid surveyors. In the 17th century legislation provided for parishes to levy rates for road repairs, but little use was made of these powers. Wheeled traffic was very limited. Rich people rode their horses; ponies and mules carried the loads that could not be borne on the backs of the poor, who walked. In winter, many roads were virtually impassable. As the economy developed, the inadequacies of these arrangements (which could not be described as a 'system') were increasingly seen as an obstacle to trade, and remedies were sought through Turnpike Acts, which permitted private organizations to improve or build roads and charge tolls to cover the costs of their construction and maintenance. The first such turnpike authority was established in 1663 on the New Great North Road through Hertfordshire and Huntingdonshire. South-west Shropshire had to wait another hundred years before the Bishop's Castle Turnpike Trust was formed in 1768.

What became a national network of turnpikes (but was never planned as such) significantly reduced the isolation of this area. Relatively fast coach services, run to regular timetables, put Bishop's Castle in communication with London and other major cities. Glamorous in retrospect, such services were uncomfortable, tedious and very expensive. *Bailey's British Directory* of 1791 records the London mail coach leaving Bishop's Castle at 9am on Monday, Thursday and Saturday and taking the best part of two days to reach its destination. Return services struggled into Bishop's Castle at 5pm. There was also a horseback mail service from Ludlow, and from Shrewsbury via Welshpool on Monday, Thursday and Saturday. By 1822 there were coaches twice a week (tellingly, only available between May and September) linking Bishop's Castle with Shrewsbury, Ludlow, London, Montgomery and Aberystwyth. *Pigot's Directory* of 1828 tells us that the mail coach to Ludlow left the Castle Hotel daily at 8am, arriving back at 6.30pm. There was also a daily 8am horse post to Welshpool. Named coaches appear in 1830 – the *Royal William* linking Bishop's Castle with Ludlow, with connexions to Leominster, Hereford, Cheltenham, Worcester, Bewdley, Kidderminster, Birmingham, Oxford and London, as well as to Newtown, Llandrindod Wells and Aberystwyth. In 1836 *The Dart* was plying between Aberystwyth and Kidderminster twice a week, and in 1856 and 1861 *The Telegraph* served Craven Arms station on Mondays, Wednesdays and Saturdays.

There are many reminders of this system still apparent to the observant traveller. The most obvious is the fine coaching inn which has given its name to Craven Arms, built

Figs 8.1 and 8.2 Milestones in Stank Lane, east of Bishop's Castle, and on the former Shrewsbury road.

c.1830 at the junction of the Hereford to Shrewsbury turnpike and the road to central Wales and Holyhead and, across the road, the handsome 20ft-high obelisk indicating distances to destinations (36 of them) at every corner of the kingdom. More modestly, former toll houses can still be seen at Crowgate at the foot of Stank Lane and at Pultheley near Hyssington. Milestones showing distances from Shrewsbury and Bishop's Castle are still in place along the original main roads, at the Lea, along the Pulverbatch road and up Stank Lane (Figs 8.1 & 8.2).

Between 1833 and 1841, thanks to a generous contribution from the More family of Linley, a road was driven from Minsterley up the Hope Valley to Pultheley, Hyssington and Churchstoke, with a further branch to Bromley's Mill, Lydham and Bishop's Castle. This also served the growing lead mining industry, and is today's A488.

The coming of the railways in the 1840s signalled the beginning of the end for long-distance coach travel, but in the 1850s the turnpike trust was still active, with major improvements to the road from Bishop's Castle to Shrewsbury via Norbury, Wentnor, Ratlinghope and Pulverbatch – for centuries the main road to Shrewsbury. In 1869 the trust recorded an annual expenditure of £1,318 on its 92¾ miles of main road, 25 main gates and one side gate. By then, however, the consolidation of the national railway network had left the turnpikes with little more than local traffic. Toll income was no longer adequate, and the trust was wound up in 1879. In 1889 the care of roads passed to county councils, and was devolved further to rural district councils in 1894, returning to the counties in 1974. Street names in Bishop's Castle still reflect the network of roads leading out of the town: Welsh Street, Salop Street (of old 'Salop' meant Shrewsbury), Montgomery Road, Kerry Lane, Brampton Road.

The 'turnpike age' had enabled the growth of a network of carriers which extended to all but the most isolated country towns and provided an essential service, not only for goods, but also for local passengers. Trade directories show that Bishop's Castle was served by a number of carriers. In 1785 a weekly service to and from Smithfield, London, was in operation. In 1828 Thomas Groom operated a service to Chester, via Oswestry, Shrewsbury and Wrexham, on Mondays and Wednesdays; John Jones went to Newtown and Ludlow on Mondays; Charles Morris to Shrewsbury on Wednesday mornings; and J. Davies to Shrewsbury on Wednesdays and Saturdays and to Welshpool, Wales and the North of England on Mondays and Wednesdays. Services left from various hostelries – most often from the Castle Hotel, the Three Tuns or the Boar's Head.

Even after the arrival of canals and railways, carriers remained busy with traffic to and from stations and wharves. Indeed, the coming of the railway produced additional services to Craven Arms station (recorded in directories of 1836 and 1861) and from Clun to Broome station and Bucknell. Minsterley and Montgomery are also specified as destinations. It is recorded that in 1844, 87 carriers from 62 different villages made 181 calls in Shrewsbury each week. In 1899 this carrier traffic had increased to 91 carts from 79 villages, though the number of Shrewsbury calls had fallen to 135 a week.[1]

Local postal services were erratic, often depending on private arrangements. An exchange of letters between the Earl of Powis, of Walcot Hall, and the Postmaster General (Lord Clanricarde) resulted in the establishment of a foot messenger 'to serve Lydbury and Walcot with their letters', commencing on 1st May 1850.

*Fig. 8.3 The Post Office: mail-cart and staff, c.1903.
Postmaster Alfred Bore stands on the right in the doorway.*

A fine photograph taken outside the Post Office in High Street, Bishop's Castle, about 1903 shows the postmaster, Alfred Bore, with the mail cart and no fewer than 11 employees (Fig. 8.3). Miss Molly Puckle, remembering the town before 1919, spoke of the mail man driving to Craven Arms every night and returning with the letters in the early morning ready for an 8am delivery. Some mail was carried on the afternoon service of the Bishop's Castle Railway.

Later the mail was taken to Craven Arms by a Mr George Chappell. Mr Reg Corfield (b.1902) remembered teaching him to drive a van. Mr Chappell was grateful not to be out in all weathers, but he missed the companionship of the horse. 'Mr Alfred Bore was at the Post Office when I used to get called upon, at the end of the First World War, to go and deliver a telegram, on an old fixed-wheel bicycle ... and I've gone out to Wentnor for fourpence or fivepence to take a telegram – biked to Wentnor and back.'

The motor car arrived in the area around 1903. One of the first, a Daimler Wagonette registered AW 98, owned by Jack Roberts of Clun, was photographed outside the Six Bells, Clun (Fig. 8.4), and later outside the Six Bells, Bishop's Castle. In the latter picture it has an elaborate roof, possibly built by the Six Bells coachbuilder, Charles Jones. It was referred to locally as 'the Black Maria'. The pioneering Greenhous family set up a garage in the town and ran the first local buses in 1912.[2]

In 1920 D. Lowther started to operate a service, two years later handing his business over to Jim Rose. In 1928 Bishop's Castle Railway started its own Bishop's Castle Transport Company, a subsidiary of the railway company, registered on 6th January 1928, with an authorized capital of £1,000, of which £900 was issued. The registered office was 2 Argyle

Fig. 8.4 The first motor car in Bishop's Castle – AW 98 – photographed in Clun.

Street, Wrexham, where Mr H. Roberts, the railway's manager since 1922, added to his portfolio the posts of secretary and manager of the new company. The first vehicles were a 14-seater Chevrolet 'Salon' bus and two goods lorries. The route mileage was 32 miles, with a twice-daily service to Craven Arms, and on Saturdays to Ludlow. Services began in February 1928. For a while, the railway used its bus to replace the last train of the day. The railway also owned a Shrewsbury-built Sentinel steam waggon to haul stone from More (Squilver) quarry to Lydham Heath station.

When the railway closed in 1935, S.W. Brisbane and T.A. Owen of Knighton took over the road services, still trading as the Bishop's Castle Transport Company. A slight variation in the route took the service through Colebatch, Brockton, Lydbury North, Red House, Kempton, Little Brampton and Aston-on-Clun to Craven Arms. In 1936 some journeys ran to Craven Arms through Lydbury North, Plowden and Horderley. Two buses were needed to operate the service on Mondays, Fridays and Saturdays (auction and market days in Craven Arms and Ludlow).

In 1939 W.A. Thomas, a driver for the company, bought the business from his employers. He agreed to pay £350 for the assets, £50 as a deposit, and the remainder when the licensing authority formally consented to the transfer. Mr Thomas took over officially in July 1939 and continued to trade as the Bishop's Castle Transport Company. By 1945 he had replaced the old buses and changed the name of the company to the Plowden Valley Motor Service. He put his business up for sale in 1946, finding a willing purchaser in Yeomans Motors of Canon Pyon (Herefs.).

In 1948 the Yeomans' services in the Bishop's Castle area passed to the Radnorshire Motor Services, a concern operated by Mr H.J. Yeoman of the original family. Yeomans sold out in 1951 to R.W. Carpenter, the best-known Bishop's Castle operator before, during and after the Second World War. Robert Carpenter had bought the railway's goods shed after the line's closure in 1935 to 'supplement' his own garage, and for many years his buses provided an excellent and friendly service through the surrounding countryside – winter and summer, market days and ordinary days.[3] Bill Hailstone was an equally well known operator.

A variety of vehicles was used – Bedford, Leland, Chevrolet, Daimler, Commer and Tilley Stevens. The network of routes became very extensive, as efforts were made to ensure that even the remotest settlements were served by at least a weekly bus. The list of stopping points 'off the beaten track', en route to towns like Ludlow, Welshpool, Newtown and Shrewsbury, is impressive – including Asterton, Prolley Moor, Mainstone, Cefn Einion, More, Norbury, Wentnor, Criftin, Colebatch, Church Stoke, Priest Weston, Middleton, Rorrington, Meadowtown, the Lyde, Stiperstones, Ratlinghope and the then daunting Cothercott Hill. A number of the routes climbed to over 1,000 feet above sea level, and would be affected by severe snowfalls in winter. To ensure that he could serve the narrowest lanes Bill Hailstone took a basic Bedford chassis to a firm in Lowestoft to have a slimmer body fitted. This bus, UJ 9058, was a successful venture, but eventually the council removed some of the sharper corners, enabling a standard 20-seater to cover the routes.

The services were intimate and delightfully friendly. Drivers would carry baskets for elderly passengers to their front doors, and deliver messages, letters, orders and unofficial goods. The fittings in some of the vehicles were basic. Driver Norman Gwilliam wrote 'we had slatted wooden seats. You can imagine how cold they were, and the passengers had some very numb bums by the time they reached their destination!'

Fig. 8.5 Bill Hailstone's bus picking up in Claremont Street, Shrewsbury, some time during the Second World War. The headlights have cowls to maintain the blackout. (© Omnibus Society)

Luggage was often stored on the roof, with the driver climbing a ladder on the side of the bus to place a basket of eggs on the roof rack. On one occasion a lady loaded her precious new bicycle onto the rack. Reaching her destination, she discovered that the bicycle was missing. On the return journey, the driver found it safely suspended from the branches of an overhanging tree! One unusual cargo was baskets of yeast from Trouncer's Brewery in Shrewsbury, to go to the Three Tuns.

Drivers had to be patient and understanding. In some remote farms a shopping basket hung on a roadside gate indicated that someone wished to catch the bus and needed to be alerted to its arrival by a toot on the horn!

Buses were popular and often overcrowded. The late Gwen Roberts, daughter of Bob Carpenter, and herself a bus conductress, recalled 'One Sunday we had a bus that left Bishop's Castle at a quarter to one – it was a hospital bus, plus soldiers going back off leave. We had a 32-seater Leyland. We got as far as the Port Hill island, and there was no way we could take all these people into Shrewsbury, because we always had the police on our track for overloading. We counted the people getting off and there were 96!'

Bishop's Castle High School (later the Community College) has always had a complex network of buses and minibuses to convey pupils to and from school over an area of some 200 square miles, including many isolated hamlets and farms. In days gone by some of the buses were retired and antiquated vehicles ... one, on the Clun route, was irreverently referred to by its passengers as 'Conky's Henhouse!' One morning a school bus, travelling down the straight section of road from Little Brampton to Purslow, was overtaken by one of its rear wheels. The bus stopped safely and pupils were delighted to scramble into a neighbouring field to retrieve the wheel!

In recent years, with the increase in private car ownership, bus services have been reduced. Nevertheless Bishop's Castle is still linked with Shrewsbury, Ludlow and Newtown by regular services, and once a week there is a bus to and from the Princess Royal Hospital in Telford. The main operators have been Valley Motors and its successors, Minsterley Motors, M. and J. Travel, and Long Mynd Travel. The town also has Dial-a-Ride minibus and voluntary car services.

Rural bus companies have always had to respond to particular local needs, such as operating services not on a simple day-to-day basis but according to specific events, such as the different market days in Ludlow, Welshpool or Newtown. Quite recently a special service has been operating to take ardent Shrewsbury Town football supporters from Bishop's Castle to the Greenhous Meadow stadium in Shrewsbury, for all 'home' fixtures. This affords the fans opportunities to share pre-match expectations and sometimes, sadly, post-mortems!

In the late 19th and 20th centuries cycling became popular and the town had accommodation for the Cyclists Touring Club (CTC) at the Old Brick Guesthouse. The Castle Hotel visitors' book records that the Anfield Bicycle Club, formed in 1879, visited the hotel, as did a famous record-breaking individual cyclist, George Pilkington Mills. His main claim to fame was winning the 1891 Bordeaux to Paris Race, a precursor of the Tour de France. Since 1985 the town has organized an annual Tandem Triathlon (involving swimming, running and cycling). Bishop's Castle is also on a new National Cycle route.

For travellers on foot the network of public rights of way has been carefully mapped and preserved, and some paths furnished with modern gates replacing old stiles. Open Access

Land and Permissive Paths have greatly increased walkers' options. Long-distance footpaths such as the Offa's Dyke Path (opened in 1971) and the Shropshire Way pass close to the town. There are good leaflets describing the routes available, including *Walking with Offa* (a series of pub walks and days out in the Shropshire Hills Area of Outstanding Natural Beauty), and *The Bishop's Castle Ring*, a set of walks which encircle the town, taking in the best of its scenic attractions. The Town Hall Information Centre offers advice and a wide range of leaflets and maps.

Bishop's Castle is some distance from any navigable water (the Montgomeryshire Canal at Welshpool being the nearest), but there existed in 1793 a dream to create a waterway across south-west Shropshire between two canals then under construction, from the Leominster Canal south of Ludlow, passing through Lydbury North, Brockton, Bishop's Castle and Lydham, to enter the Montgomeryshire Canal at Garthmyl, just a couple of miles north-west of Montgomery.

Planning for a canal to reach Leominster had begun in 1777, at the height of 'canal fever'. This was to link Kington with Stourport on Severn, with a short branch to Leominster. By 1796 a stretch would be open from Leominster through Woofferton (for Ludlow) and Tenbury Wells, as far as Marlbrook (Mamble), where coal could be loaded from the nearby mines. At this point, however, as with many other such ambitious ventures, the project ran out of funds and was discontinued, reaching neither Kington nor Stourport. However, the canal engineer Thomas Dadford Jr. was already assisting his younger brother, John (then aged just 24), to draw up plans for a link from Woofferton to the Montgomeryshire Canal across south-west Shropshire. John Dadford's plan, dated 11th November 1793,[4] includes a section of canal from Lydbury North to Lydham, passing through Brockton, and then east of Bishop's Castle past the houses of Snakescroft and Oakeley, to Lydham. In July 1794 John Dadford was appointed engineer for the Montgomeryshire Canal and commenced work, but problems with water leakage from the (very heavy) aqueducts on weak ground led to his resignation in 1796.

On 18th December 1793 a meeting was held in Bishop's Castle to invite subscriptions to fund the link project, chaired by Lord Clive of Walcot Hall. The project was considered to be too expensive, but it was thought that a canal from the Leominster Canal to Lydham Heath 'may be of advantage'. Proceedings were adjourned. Subsequent meetings in Ludlow in 1794 referring to 'The Ludlow and Bishop's Castle Navigation' were also adjourned, and nothing came of this intriguing concept.

The 20th and 21st centuries have brought a huge transformation in travel and communication. Today the Digital Revolution has taken its place alongside the Agricultural Revolution and the Industrial Revolution in its capacity for changing lives. We now have an Information Age with its computers, laptops, cell phones, Sat-Navs, databases, the Internet and the world-wide-web. Personal and commercial transactions can be carried out from the comfort of one's home. Bishop's Castle has responded with its own Information Technology Centre at Enterprise House, where, despite some serious variations of reception among the hills, people can benefit from most of the new technological connexions. Perhaps this will afford us the leisure time to enjoy the beauty and solitude of the ancient trackways and drovers' roads!

9 THE BISHOP'S CASTLE RAILWAY

The Bishop's Castle Railway (B.C.R.) was conceived in 1859, a decade after the Shrewsbury to Hereford line had reached south-west Shropshire. To the west the Oswestry to Newtown Railway struggled through many difficulties to open on 1st May 1860. Others were to follow – a line from Craven Arms to Knighton opened in 1861, eventually becoming part of the Central Wales Line, and in the same year a branch of the Shrewsbury and Welshpool Railway opened to Minsterley.

Bishop's Castle found itself with railways to the east, to the west, to the south and to the north, but there were at least a dozen miles of inadequate turnpike roads to negotiate to reach any of them. The town's dignity, as well as its prosperity and convenience, demanded a railway to secure a modern connexion with the outside world. Enter Thomas Savin, an Oswestry draper who had branched out into the railway-contracting business and done well in the third railway boom by building the first lines in mid Wales in the 1850s. He had a grand vision for a network of tracks running from Wolverhampton through Bridgnorth to Craven Arms, up the Onny Valley to link with his expanding Welsh system at Montgomery. There were to be connexions to Bishop's Castle and from Chirbury to Minsterley and thus to Shrewsbury.

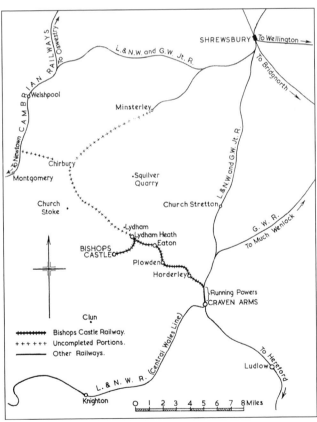

Fig. 9.1 Map of the Bishop's Castle Railway in relation to other systems in the Pre-Grouping era. (Drawn by D.E.H. Box, via Gavin Watson)

In 1860 the route was surveyed, and plans and sections prepared, to put a Bishop's Castle Railway Bill before Parliament. It proposed a total line of 19¼ miles running from the Shrewsbury and Hereford line at Wistanstow to Montgomery, with a branch from Lydham Heath to Bishop's Castle. Public meetings were held in 1861 to explain the plans and to encourage investors to buy shares in the new venture. There were rival schemes, including one for a direct line from Minsterley to Bishop's Castle, which was favoured by a significant section of the local community. To assuage these concerns the Bill's promoters inserted a provision requiring that the branch from Lydham Heath to Bishop's Castle was to be opened at the same time as the main line, and in the end, on 28th June 1861, the Bishop's Castle Railway Bill alone received royal assent. The new company's capital was fixed at £180,000 in £10 shares, with powers to borrow £60,000 when half the capital was subscribed. The amount raised locally was disappointing, and the company directors also struggled with opposition from local landowners and the established railway companies at each end of the proposed new line, who feared it would siphon off their existing traffic.

Thomas Savin was confirmed as contractor and R. & B. Piercy were the engineers. By 1862 working plans and drawings were complete and negotiations for the land were under way. The company was originally unsure whether its trains would be allowed on to the main Shrewsbury and Hereford tracks at Wistanstow so the plans provided for a new railway to run parallel with the line to Craven Arms. In the end permission was secured, thus saving the B.C.R. the expense of building half a mile of line, but burdening the company with continuing costs for 'running powers' into Craven Arms station. The planned junction with the Shrewsbury and Hereford line was then moved south from Wistanstow to Stretford Bridge. By early 1863 enough land was available for the contractor to start. But all was not well. The directors admitted at a board meeting in August 1864 that they had been forced to file a bill in Chancery against Savin to recover £20,500 advanced to him. By that time he had lost interest in the B.C.R. and was building the coast railway in Wales. In the end he overstretched himself and was declared bankrupt in 1866; it is doubtful if the B.C.R. directors ever got the money back.

A new contractor was appointed – G.M. Morris, of Plowden, who undertook the work – and on 24th October 1864, when many had already lost hope, a start was made on construction between Lydham Heath and Bishop's Castle. Progress was quick, marred only by an accidental fall of earth which broke a workman's legs. Stations were planned for Horderley, Plowden, Eaton, Lydham Heath and Bishop's Castle. By October 1865 the line from Stretford Bridge to Lydham Heath and the branch to Bishop's Castle had been laid, and the directors decided to open that portion of the railway from 24th October 1865.

The opening ceremony was a typically Victorian affair. The locomotive hauling the first train carried banners declaring 'Better Late Than Never' and 'Long Looked For – Come at Last'. The town was decorated with flags, greenery and triumphal arches; bells were rung, guns fired and speeches endured. Three hundred sat down to a banquet in a marquee on the bowling green at the Castle Hotel, and the navvies who had worked on the construction were entertained to roast beef, plum pudding and ale. In the evening there were fireworks and the following night a public ball was held at the Castle Hotel. Unfortunately the directors had overlooked the need for Board of Trade inspection and approval, and when the inspectors did arrive they refused to sanction the opening, citing the line's unfinished condition. Hurriedly the company completed the outstanding work, and three months later, after re-inspection, the line opened to traffic on 1st February 1866.

Commander Henry Oakeley, R.N. (Retd), kept a meticulous diary. He lived at the Roveries, More, followed the Railway's progress, and made sure that he and his family obtained the first seats when it finally opened: '1.2.1866: Walked to Lydham Heath Station with Sophy. Bishop's Castle Railway opened for passenger traffic. Took the two first class tickets for Craven Arms from this station numbered respectively 00 and 01. At Craven Arms met Mrs and Katarina [his wife and daughter] who took the two first from there to Lydham's Heath, numbered as above.' Henry Oakeley succeeded his brother as squire of Lydham – his 'awfully sudden death' was reported in *Eddowes's Journal* on 14th March 1877. The town clerk had been reading a letter to him concerning the Bishop's Castle Railway when 'he fell back and shortly afterwards breathed his last'.

The rest of the line, from Lydham Heath to Montgomery, and the branch from Chirbury to Minsterley, were to be started as soon as possible, an ambition that was destined never to be fulfilled. In those early days the B.C.R. tried to behave like a thoroughly respectable railway. It dressed its station staff in smart blue uniforms with silver braid and caps embroidered with its initials, and it provided decent housing for its employees – a row of pretty little cottages, complete with fancy bargeboards and dormer windows, which survive to this day in Welsh Street.

Fig. 9.2 Railway Cottages, Welsh Street. Built by the Bishop's Castle Railway Co. for their employees, the row was taken over by E. Beddoes & Sons in payment for repairs to buildings, rolling stock, etc., that they had not been paid for. (Postcard in S.W.S.H.A.S. Collection)

Later in 1866 the Overend & Gurney bank collapsed spectacularly, bringing other banks down with it. Interest rates surged and the subsequent financial waves swept through the country. Businesses struggled, many went bankrupt. The Bishop's Castle Railway was forced to abandon its extension plans, but worse followed when the company experienced severe cash-flow problems and was unable to pay its creditors. Bailiffs were called in, and eventually the assets were sold off at auction at the George Hotel in Shrewsbury on 23rd January 1867. Most of the carriages and wagons were bought by the Midland Wagon Company on behalf of debenture holders who, believing that the company was capable of generating a satisfactory profit, installed a receiver to manage the accounts, and the railway continued as before with the same staff. All profits then went to pay interest on the debentures, and this prioritizing of dividends over investment had serious effects on the railway over the years.

Operations settled into a routine for the next ten years, but in February 1877 the death of Dr Beddoes, one of the original company directors, threatened the railway's very existence. He had been a keen supporter and had sold land to the railway for which he had not been paid. His widow, with a son still in his minority, was keen to protect his inheritance and pressed for payment. The sum of about £1,300 of capital and accrued interest was not forthcoming, so Mrs Beddoes obtained a court judgement. The railway could make no settlement; so on 27th February bailiffs took possession of the land which, in default of payment, was still her property. They erected fences at the boundaries, removed a rail and awaited the next move.

Fig. 9.3 The Red Lion, Horderley. (Photograph from Basil Wood)

The railway attempted to maintain a service of sorts between Bishop's Castle and Horderley, but with no income from traffic and demurrage charges mounting up on a large number of London & North Western Railway (L.N.W.R.) wagons trapped at Bishop's Castle, an enduring solution seemed to be beyond the company's means. In desperation, a plan was hatched in the back room of the Craven Arms Hotel. The February nights were no doubt cold, so when approached by a couple of locals suggesting a few drinks by a warm fire, the bailiffs were more than happy to accompany their new friends to the Red Lion at Horderley.

As soon as they were out of sight and sound, B.C.R. gangers replaced the rails and removed the fences. A train with the empty wagons crept silently from Bishop's Castle down the gradient to Stretford Bridge and Craven Arms, where the locomotive picked up a loaded train and, with a good shove from the L.N.W.R. shunter, made for the town as fast as possible. The bums – a perfectly respectable 19th-century term for bailiffs – now couldn't fail to hear what was going on, but it was too late as they staggered out of the inn. The manager of the railway was threatened with prosecution, but was able to provide the alibi that he was not in the Bishop's Castle area that evening and had no knowledge of his staff's extra-curricular activities. The night's excitements did little to solve the long term problem and the railway remained closed. A single decade of existence, and already two openings and two closures. Eventually, a local committee of wealthy supporters organized subscriptions to pay off the debt, but it was not until 24th July 1877 that the railway re-opened.

Closures of the B.C.R. were not uncommon over the years. They could be precipitated by problems with the courts due to non-payment of debts or as a result of brushes with the railway inspection authorities. Notable episodes occurred in 1878 and 1889. In the first case the railway was closed for many months by the Board of Trade after a very unsatisfactory inspection which brought forth stinging comments from the inspecting officer, who summed up his concerns: 'I consider the travelling public are exposed to constant danger in travelling on this line.' Re-inspection in June 1879 following overdue repairs allowed goods traffic to resume, but it was several more months before the inspectorate were satisfied that passenger trains could run again.

Ten years later the Board of Trade was looking to implement the new Regulation of Railways Act, 1889, which included important new provisions for railway safety, incorporating lessons learned from bitter experience of accidents throughout the country. The new requirements for 'block signalling and interlocking' would mean new equipment and expense. The B.C.R. looked at the regulations and did nothing, the company solicitors fending off the authorities.

From 1893 the position of receiver and manager were combined, with the incumbent drawn from the staff of the Wrexham, Mold & Connah's Quay Railway based in offices in Wrexham, an arrangement which continued even after that company had been absorbed into the Great Central Railway in 1905. This absentee management was sometimes resented in Bishop's Castle, and may go some way to explaining the feebleness of 'grip' on local operating practices.

An inspection in 1895 was highly critical of both procedures and equipment. As in 1878, urgent work was demanded. The arrangements for safe operation of the level crossing

Fig. 9.4 Bishop's Castle Railway Station and staff in the early 20th century.
The late Ken Lucas identified most of those in the picture: left to right, they are Jessie Jackson
(in the doorway), unknown, Mr Harris (station master and manager), Tommy Hurdley,
Arthur Meredith, Jack Cadwallader and (by the open carriage door) Will Lucas, guard.
(Photograph from Ken Lucas, Bishop's Castle Railway Society)

gates at Horderley and Eaton stations aroused particular concerns in the mind of Col Yorke, the inspecting officer. Interlocking machinery was in place to ensure that the crossing gates could not be opened to road traffic unless the signals controlling trains were at danger. But the signals in each direction were 200 yards away from the gates, thus requiring a tedious walk to set or unset them every time a flock of sheep or a cart presented itself at the crossing. The B.C.R. had worked out a delightfully simple solution to this problem: set the signals permanently at danger, but allow engine drivers to ignore them! Col Yorke, through gritted teeth, ordered that 'the signals for the protection of the level crossings must be brought into regular use and the most dangerous and improper practice of running past signals at danger must be stopped'. After re-inspection in 1896 he gave grudging acceptance that things were as good as they were ever going to be. The signal posts remained in position until the railway closed, but in the final years they had lost their warning arms and were serving merely as aerials for the stationmasters' new wireless sets.

By 1901 the B.C.R. was well known for court cases over unpaid debts, and in that year a milestone case brought the railway into the High Court again. William Plowden, like Dr Beddoes, had sold land to the railway, but had never been paid. He had, in 1880, secured a judgement which entitled him to reclaim his land and required the B.C.R. to pay compensation of £1,345 16s. That would have forced the railway to close. Plowden, however, was keen to keep the railway going as a public amenity, and he had used this judgement as a lever to negotiate an agreement that the company would pay an annual rent of £224 6s. No payment had ever been made, but Plowden had not pressed the matter. At the same time he was considerably irritated by the behaviour of a Mr Fraser, a London accountant acting for the debenture holders, who was insisting that any trading surplus should be paid to them. This 1901 case was an attempt to secure what he thought would be a more equitable sharing of the slender earnings of the railway service. The case was heard by Mr Justice Kekewich, who observed that 'Bishop's Castle Railway cases always were complicated'. In the end judgement went to the debenture holders, but once again local notables came to the aid of the railway. They formed the Bishop's Castle Railway Defence Scheme ('Trust' after 1903), raising £9,000 to pay off debts and to provide a financial cushion. They were to watch over the receiver and to suggest improvements.

In 1903 the death of Robert Jasper More, the local M.P., removed an important friend of the railway. A tireless and vocal supporter of the railway over the years, he used his position to promote the area, bombarding ministers with suggestions for strengthening the economic basis of his constituency by completing the railway's extension to Montgomery and building golf links, a hydro and an army training ground to generate more traffic.

The 1914-18 war demanded large quantities of timber both for pit props at home and for trench shuttering in France. The B.C.R. took advantage of this and thus paid its first and last dividend.

After the war more and more freight went by road; army lorries had been sold off cheaply and many transport companies sprang up to undercut the railways by picking the

The Football Special, 1924

In 1924 a memorable cup-final football match between Bishop's Castle and Craven Arms took place at Bishop's Castle. The railway company laid on a special train from Craven Arms. After the match and a certain amount of good-natured horseplay, the passengers assembled on the platform for the return journey. Craven Arms was a railway town, so the throng of supporters included several experienced railwaymen from bigger (and, they thought, better) lines. They decided to test the professionalism of the B.C.R. and managed, without being noticed, to uncouple the locomotive from the coaches. The Craven Arms supporters climbed aboard. Cadwallader, the B.C.R. guard, waved his green flag and blew his whistle in the approved manner. Hotchkiss, the driver, opened the regulator and the engine pulled away smartly ... The train remained where it was, alongside the platform. The engine was nearly at Love Lane bridge before Driver Hotchkiss or anyone else on the footplate noticed that something was wrong. So much for the rule book, which required the footplate crew to watch carefully that the train and all the coaches were following correctly. One wonders how smoothly Hotchkiss performed the humiliating duty of returning to collect the trainful of 'superior' colleagues.

Fig. 9.5 Carlisle *on stocks, 1929.*
Improvisation kept the railway running. Hand-operated screw jacks (one is visible under the front buffer beam) have been used to hoist almost 40 tons of locomotive 6ft on to timber piles. The six wheels, along with the engine's valve gear, braking equipment, buffers and couplings, have been removed – and all in the open air. The railway's small staff needed resourcefulness and muscle power to deal with the complexity of jobs to be done.
The huge pieces of felled timber and the cattle van indicate the railway's staple freight. The dire state of the carriage shed behind the engine is evident, and the railway's lorry in the background is far from pristine. Also visible are the railway bus and an old L.N.W.R. carriage fitted with the palaeotechnic 'chain brake' long condemned by the Railway Inspectorate.
(Photo. Alan Keef Collection)

best loads. As 'common carriers' the railways were legally bound to carry any load offered, at a fixed price, whether the transaction was profitable or not. The railway became seriously run down, and when the line was left out of the compulsory 'grouping' of the country's main-line railways into four very large companies in 1922-3, the B.C.R. lost its last real chance of renewal and repair. (There is a suspicion that, expecting to be taken over, the B.C.R. management had neglected repairs and had thus given the debenture holders a final chance to cream off any operating surplus.)

Hope still flickered for a few years and several attempts were made in the 1920s and 1930s to get the neighbouring Great Western Railway (G.W.R.) to take over the line. All failed. The final throw was an appeal to Col Holman Stephens to take over the railway. He had a history of rescuing decrepit rural and run-down railways that others had given up as hopeless and operated a dozen or so disgraced lines up and down the country. His assistant, Mr W. Austen, came to view the line; he considered that the costs involved could never be justified and recommended that Stephens should refuse. With real concern now in the area about the fate of the railway, a Railway Users Committee came into being on 1st July 1931 to look after passengers' interests; but it had no legal powers and the receiver was not bound to give answers or divulge information, so it faded away fairly quickly. In 1934 the borough council discovered a plan, possibly inspired by the debenture holders, to close the line, and at a special session passed a resolution in support of the railway, highlighting the loss to the area if it were closed. It is not known when the courts became involved, but they deferred closure. However, by spring 1935 the Defence Trust reported that their funds were exhausted, and there were rumours about the safety of some of the bridges. As an example of the poor state of maintenance of the railway it was said that it was possible to tell the direction of the last train by the direction in which the grass and weeds between the rails were bent over. The debenture holders withdrew the receiver and the courts decreed that the railway should close on 20th April 1935.

Trains ran for a short time clearing outstanding goods, and the railway then sank into a temporary slumber until December 1935 when demolition started. A few of the former employees found work with Alan Morris of Chester, who had won the contract. Demolition started at the Bishop's Castle end and was complete by 21st February 1937. The track was found to be unsafe in several areas; alder logs being used to replace sleepers were found sprouting leaves and small branches. The junction at Stretford Bridge was taken out on 27th May 1937, and *Carlisle*, the last locomotive on the line, was cut up in the yard at Craven Arms by a Mr J. Brocklebank shortly afterwards.[1]

The weight of scrap from the demolition was estimated at 2,500 tons, but after the costs of demolition and all the legal bills were taken into account, the debenture holders received only a few pounds as a final payment. Shareholders and outstanding creditors got nothing.

Throughout its existence the Bishop's Castle Railway relied upon second-hand equipment; very little was ever bought new. The only locomotives in later years were *Carlisle* and *No. 1*. All the routine maintenance was carried out at Bishop's Castle, the company being unusual in that it combined the duties of fitter and driver. Extensive repairs to the locomotives were carried out as a matter of course, although both locomotives would be

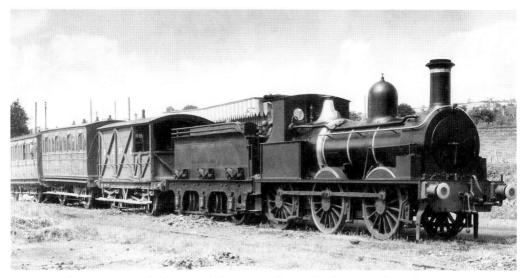

Fig. 9.6 An impressively clean Carlisle *awaits the 12.45 departure from the town in 1935 (the photographer's notes are on the back of the original print). The train includes brake van No. 2 followed by a 4-wheeler coach (ex-Brecon & Merthyr Railway), with 2nd- and 3rd-class compartments, and a 6-wheeler brake (ex-London & South-Western Railway), 3rd-class. Freight was the railway's priority, and the absence of goods vehicles is surprising.*
In the line's latter days, when there was no freight for the last train of the day, passengers would be consigned to a bus.
(Photograph from K. Woodward, Peter Broxholme)

sent to the Wolverhampton works of the G.W.R. for major refurbishment as required. Over the years *Carlisle* thus acquired some characteristics of the 'house style' of that company's locomotives.

Carlisle was an 0-6-0 tender engine built by Kitsons of Leeds in 1868, supplied new to Thomas Nelson, railway contractor (and sometime mayor of Carlisle), who used the locomotive on construction projects throughout the country. It arrived at Bishop's Castle in 1895 and was in service until the end, finishing by hauling all the demolition trains.

No. 1 was an 0-4-2 tank engine built by the G.W.R. as No. 567 of their '517' class at Wolverhampton in 1869. Bought by the B.C.R. in 1905 for £700, it had an extended smoke box with wings which gave it an old-fashioned appearance. The G.W.R., well aware of the reputation of the B.C.R., cashed the cheque before releasing the locomotive. It was never named officially and continued to the end known simply as *No. 1*, but was affectionately named *Tankie* by the crews. *No. 1* played no part in the demolition, being stored at Plowden awaiting a potential buyer. A colliery company considered purchasing the locomotive but after inspection decided that the driving wheels were too large for shunting heavy coal trains. (In steam engines small wheels are preferred for heavy haulage and large wheels for speed – not that velocity was ever a quality much in demand on the B.C.R.) *No. 1* was scrapped where it stood in 1936.

From February 1928, the railway operated motor bus services through a subsidiary Bishop's Castle Transport Co. Its registered office was in Wrexham, with Mr H. Roberts,

90

Other locomotives and rolling stock

Bee, an 0-4-0 saddle tank built by Brotherhoods of Chippenham, was used in the construction of the line. It was acquired from the contractors who built the line but was found to be underpowered and was disposed of in 1870.

Plowden, an 0-6-0 tender engine, was acquired for the opening; it came from the St Helens Railway and was disposed of in 1874.

Perseverance, an 0-4-2 tank engine built in 1854 by Dodds & Co of Rotherham, ran on the Newport, Hereford and Abergavenny Railway as *No. 22*. In 1861 it became *No. 92* on the West Midland Railway and *No. 227* when that railway was absorbed by the G.W.R. Purchased by the B.C.R. in 1870, it was used to thwart the bailiffs as described above. In 1887 it was sold to the Wrexham, Mold & Connah's Quay Railway, which scrapped it in 1890 as *No. 14*.

Progress, an 0-6-0 tender engine, was built by George England & Son in 1861 for the Somerset and Dorset Railway, where it was *No. 1*. It was purchased by the B.C.R. in 1875 and scrapped in 1904.

Bishop's Castle was a similar 0-6-0 tender engine, *No. 5* on the Somerset and Dorset Railway. The B.C.R. acquired it in 1877 and scrapped it in 1905.

The coaching stock was equally miscellaneous. The carriages ordered new for the opening (and sold and leased back after the B.C.R.'s collapse into the arms of the receiver) eventually went to the Golden Valley Railway and were replaced by six anti-quated L.N.W.R. coaches, used until 1924 when the Board of Trade banned vehicles equipped with the Clark & Webb chain brake. The B.C.R. then purchased three ancient vacuum-braked vehicles from the G.W.R., where they were already second-hand. One was a six-wheeler of London & South Western Railway (L.S.W.R.) origins, and two four-wheelers, one from the Brecon & Merthyr and the other from the Hull & Barnsley. They were all painted a smart red before delivery, but became much run-down at the end; it was said that in heavy rain an umbrella was required inside.

The goods stock was the Railway's life blood, and the B.C.R. was well equipped to handle large quantities of timber, some of which were of very large section. There were several modern cattle trucks and steel vans in addition to the usual wooden goods wagons.

the railway's manager since 1922, adding to his portfolio the posts of secretary and manager of the new company. A brief account of its doings has been given in Chapter 8.

So why did the railway struggle to survive? First, the hopelessly ambitious plan to build a main line to Montgomery to capture trunk traffic between the Midlands and north Wales was never realized, but distorted priorities at the expense of a direct route to Shrewsbury which was what many local people actually wanted. Secondly, the Overend & Gurney Bank failed creating enormous financial and economic difficulties. Thirdly, the debenture holders' were unwilling to invest in the business or accept a reasonable offer when the opportunity for a sale or takeover appeared. For many years the railway actually covered its operating costs, but with all the surplus regularly creamed off by the debenture holders the Bishop's Castle Railway was condemned to a life of make-do-and-mend.

Nevertheless, over the years the railway was held in great affection not only by the townspeople but also many railway enthusiasts and photographers who came to witness a railway whose employees were almost like a family.

The memory of the Bishop's Castle Railway is still cherished. Following a 'Living History' exhibition at the Community College in 1986, Ken Lucas and a team of enthusiasts formed the Bishop's Castle Railway Society and established the Railway and Transport Museum in School Lane.

In 2015 a plaque was installed in Station Street to commemorate 150 years since the railway's opening. Karen Bavastock, who as mayor unveiled the plaque, recalls that her grandfather, George Morris, had kindled her interest in the town's history with his account of seeing the last train leave Lydham Heath station. He had started working for his living at the age of 12 (he looked older than his years) and in 1935 was employed as a waggoner at Newton Farm. He painted a vivid picture of looking up from his work and raising his hand to wave to Dick Matthews, standing on the footplate of the engine as the Bishop's Castle Railway passed into history.

10 A MARKET TOWN – SHOPS, TRADE AND BEER

It has been said of the town, 'It is a natural market centre, and it must have been selected particularly with a view to trade. And though it has had its periods of depression, Bishop's Castle has always had trade.'[1]

The foundation of the castle and the planted town was described in Chapter 4. In the 13th and 14th centuries the bishops were granted charters allowing them to hold weekly markets and annual fairs. The markets were probably held just outside the castle walls around the present Market Square and were the starting point for the town's subsequent commercial life.

There would have been skilled workmen as well as labourers involved in the building of the first wooden motte and bailey and later the stone castle that replaced it. Some may have settled into the new burgage plots, contributing their skills to the town's emerging role as a service centre for the surrounding area. As trade developed, houses in High Street and around the market square became shops and workshops. Once the border with Wales became more settled in the late 15th century the town could focus on its commercial development.

Elizabeth I's charter of 1573 brought further confidence to the town, and the markets flourished. Around that time some of the town's more substantial houses were built, and a number of houses of distinction have been identified. The Porch House (dated to 1564 with alterations made early in the 17th century), is an L-shaped two-storey hall with some elaborate carving. The House on Crutches (1610-30) has a large jetty overhanging the Cobbles Passage, described as 'an imaginative extension to a box-framed mediaeval house'. At the southern end of the town Blunden Hall, birthplace of the lawyer Edmund Plowden (see Chapter 4), is a substantial 16th-century house, with an intriguing figure of a bearded man in Jacobean dress carved under one of its jetties. Among other interesting buildings are nos. 8-10 Church Street, 25, 27 and 39 High Street and 26 Church Street (Harp House), a timber-framed building which has herringbone work in its upper storey.[2]

Interior decorations would have graced many of these houses. Wall-painting was a development from painted cloth hangings or more expensive tapestries. The paintings could be simple geometric patterns or friezes, but were sometimes more elaborate, with heraldic devices, texts or figures intended to impress guests or reflect the tastes of the owners. In the ground-floor parlour of Harp House, there is a painting of a female figure in Elizabethan dress, in part over-painted with a floral design. This is dated from between 1500 and 1575. The ground-floor parlour of the Three Tuns has floral-scroll decoration, now in a poor condition. In the ground-floor hall of the Porch House, High Street, there is geometric wall painting of black and white squares and lozenges,[3] and in an 18th-century rear extension there is a wall painting of a castle, possibly Bishop's Castle as it then was, but it is obscured by whitewash.[4]

Archaeological evidence has established the existence of a Jacobean Market Hall near the top of High Street. On 16th November 2000 a serious fire spread into Bishop's Castle Railway Museum from an adjoining builder's store. It revealed previously unknown architectural features, which were investigated by a team of archaeologists and historians led by Madge Moran

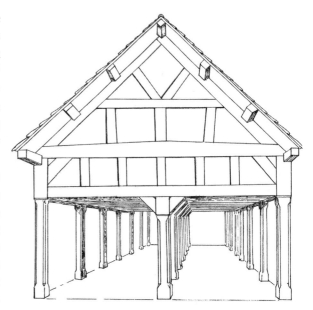

Fig. 10.1 The Market Hall of 1618, end-on from the west (High Street). (Drawn by Henry Hand)

and Henry Hand. There emerged an open-sided building, 82 x 22ft, set end-on to High Street. It was supported by 21 wooden pillars, in three lines of seven, providing a two-aisle space (Fig. 10.1). This was identified as a market hall, which must have been an imposing feature of the upper end of High Street. The timbers were felled in 1618.[5]

At that time there were potential rivalries and opportunities for co-operation between local market centres. In 1609, with the Earl of Northampton's aid, Bishop's Castle succeeded in thwarting the grant of a market in Church Stretton. In 1611 the borough moved to take advantage of an arrangement (brokered by Richard More) whereby its burgesses and those of Shrewsbury could enter each town toll-free. Then in 1616, despite continued opposition from Bishop's Castle, a market in Church Stretton was granted and a market house was built. That must have been the stimulus for the building of Bishop's Castle's market house in 1618.[6] It probably did duty until superseded in 1781 by a new market house provided by Lord Clive on the corner of Salop Street and Bull Street. Clive sold the 1618 building in 1804 and it virtually disappeared as it was adapted to more mundane uses.

In due course the successor building, proudly bearing the Clive coat of arms on its gable end, became known in the town as the 'Old Market Hall' Fig. 10.2). It became the Powis Institute and Men's Reading Room but fell into disrepair and was demolished in 1951. It is remembered today by the stone coat of arms which was carefully removed and stands in Market Square.

Market and fair days would see a great flurry of farmers and farmers' wives coming into town on foot or by horse and cart. Some of the farmers would be driving their sheep, cattle, pigs and goats, to sell in the street, while their wives unloaded their produce – chickens, ducks, geese, rabbits, butter and cheeses. The horses would be stabled safely and young lads from the town given a penny each to brush them down and water them. Particular care was

Fig. 10.2 The 'Old' Market Hall of 1781. At the top of the street (on the right) is Bradley's clothier's shop. It is recorded that a workman, who fell from a roof but was saved when his shirt-tail caught in the scaffolding, reassured his wife:

Fear not, fear not, my darling wife,
For Bradley's shirt has saved my life:
It did not tear and let me down,
Although it cost but half a crown.

taken of horses as they were the only means of transport. The occasions of such scenes were frequent: *c.*1840, as well as the Friday market 'well supplied with grain', there was a fair in February for cattle and sheep, a very large one on the Friday before Good Friday for horned cattle, a pleasure and 'statute' fair on the Friday after May Day, and fairs for horned cattle, sheep and horses in September and November; a July wool fair was described as 'formerly ... great'.[7]

Farmers would not be the only traders. Sellers of charms to ward off the murrain (a disease of cattle and sheep) would be there, and so would fortune tellers, chair caners, bodgers (chair makers), a music man, perhaps a poacher or two and chapmen selling songs and carols. As in centuries past, an official from the borough council checked weights and measures. To deal with miscreants the town had stocks and a whipping post. In the 19th century, before an official lock-up was installed under the Town Hall, a constable called Bogey Weaver is said to have shackled anyone arrested to the bars of his fire grate in New Street. By 1840, however, there was a gaol in the Town Hall basement with a debtors' gaol above.[8] The formation of the Shropshire Constabulary that year[9] was followed by the establishment of a proper police station at 1 High Street in 1842.

Fig. 10.3 Fletchers, Grocer and General Merchant, on the corner of Market Square below the Castle Hotel and Bull Street, 1888-1913.

Fig. 10.4 Mrs Edith Pickford outside her daughter Grace Bowen's shop, 13 Market Square, one October day in the early 1930s. The House on Crutches can be seen in the background.

About 1790 there was a wide range of trades and services being carried on in the town. There are ten victuallers recorded with the names of their public houses, as well as three maltsters and an innholder. The trades include butchers, grocers and chandlers, glaziers, shoemakers, joiners, haberdashers, a hat maker, clock and watchmaker, tanner, blacksmith, mercer, milliner, apothecary, gardener, bookseller-stationer-printer, peruke maker, currier, saddler, stay maker, glover, mason, cooper, ironmonger, painter and heel maker.[10] By 1793 the range of occupations included weavers, carpenters, turnpike operators, a sawyer, crockery man, baker, barber, thatcher, ballad singer, carrier, pattern maker, cricker (an itinerant dealer in coarse earthenware) and sportsman; 12 public houses were named.[11]

Most of those trades (except for peruke and stay making and turnpike operating) survived into the 20th century,[12] demonstrating the town's continuing importance for the surrounding rural population and their needs. There were two wheelwrights in Church Street, two smithies in Union Street and another in Station Street, while at Castle Green Mrs Emma Gough had a threshing machine for hire. We can guess that she was probably a widow, carrying on her husband's business, as many women had done centuries earlier after the Black Death. The town had a haulier and a tinplate worker, and close by at Colebatch was a brick maker.

To provide a more modern comparison, by 1937 there was a very similar range of basic entries with the addition of a substantial number of new (or more specialized) trades: solicitors, bus proprietors, motor garages, an electrical and wireless engineer, chimney sweep, surveyor and sanitary inspector, china warehouse, ladies' outfitter, coal merchant, fishmonger, auctioneer, hosier, confectioner, fruiterer, plumber, cycle agent, firewood merchant, fried fish dealer, draper, wheelwright, bill poster, beekeeper, corn and flour deliverer, and refreshment room proprietor. From c.1700 until the mid 19th century the town boasted a remarkable number of skilled clock and watchmakers.[13]

Over 150 probate inventories for Bishop's Castle parish for the period 1661-1756[14] record the possessions of deceased persons and their value and confirm the wide range of trades and professions followed by citizens of the parish. Twenty-two different occupations are recorded. They range from wealthy farmers and yeomen to poor tradesmen who left little more than their clothing. The wealthiest recorded was John Bason, a farmer who died in 1739 leaving among his possessions 700 sheep, 12 oxen for ploughing, 12 cows and a bull, and whose inventory was valued at £724 5s. At the other end of the scale were Richard Evans, tanner, who died in 1679 leaving chattels valued at £4 2s, including his wearing apparel and 'one oulde booke cauled the practise of piety';[15] Edward Bright, tanner, who died in 1697 leaving wearing apparel worth only 10s; and Francis Colebatch, a glover who died in 1702 leaving chattels worth just £4 16s 8d.

The most remarkable inventory found was that of William Mall, a mercer who died in 1668. His possessions were valued at £48 5s, and the inventory has 65 entries, 58 of which detail precisely the amounts of materials, trimmings and fittings he supplied for tailoring and dressmaking. It is a document of substantial historical importance.

In the mid 17th century, when there was a shortage of government-minted coinage, private tradesmen began to coin small tokens, usually in copper or brass, to be used in exchange for goods. They were mostly to the value of a penny, a ha'penny, or a farthing. A few of these trade tokens exist from Bishop's Castle, notably coined by well known trading families: Jeremy and Richard Ambler, apothecaries, 1670; William Mall, mercer (mentioned above); Thomas Mason 1670; and Edward Wollaston, 1670. The tokens are of various shapes – circular, squared and heart-shaped – and carry the value and the emblem of the family issuing them (see Chapter 11, Fig. 11.1).

Fifty apprenticeships were taken up in Bishop's Castle parish between 1812 and 1828. The recipients were aged between 9 and 15 years. Boys were expected to serve for at least 10 years, and girls until they were 21 or got married. Fourteen were apprenticed to domestic housework, eight to farm work, three to butchers, two to innkeepers, two to carpenters, and two to masons. There were single apprenticeships to a tanner, grocer, surgeon, solicitor, saddler, skinner, joiner, plasterer, chair maker, brazier, maltster, mercer, glover, baker, draper and shopkeeper.[16]

The presence of several large estates in the proximity of the town had a big impact on employment. Within six miles of the town were Walcot Hall, Oakeley (later Lydham) Manor, Linley Hall, Owlbury Hall, the Hut (Colebatch), and Plowden Hall. All employed numbers of male and female domestic servants, gamekeepers, huntsmen, stable boys, coachmen, craftsmen, foresters and large numbers of farm labourers. The landed gentry also owned tenanted farms.

Houses in the town c.1840 were 'in general meanly built of unhewn stones, with thatched roofs'. In 'detached situations', however, there were 'several handsome edifices of modern erection'.[17] In fact, the handsome edifices apart, Bishop's Castle acquired some of the characteristics of an 'open village': demolition of substandard cottages in neighbouring villages forced local farm labourers to rent houses of the worst kind in slummy parts of the town and to traipse to and from their ill-paid work in the countryside.[18]

The locations of many of the original shops and workplaces cannot now be traced. At the bottom of Church Street, however, the last building on the east side displays clear

Fig. 10.5 Robert Weaver, wheelwright, and his family outside his workshop in Church Street, 1890s. (Photograph from M. Jukes, Lydbury North)

Fig. 10.6 The Six Bells, Church Street, with the coach-building workshop behind, to the left.

evidence – three full-height pilasters framing the façade – that it started life as a bark barn for a tannery. It provided the raw material for craftsmen and women to fashion leather goods – boots, saddles, harnesses, leg gaiters and travelling cases. Close by were the premises of Mr Weaver, the wheelwright (Fig. 10.5), and, just across the road, at the back of the Six Bells inn, was a coach-building business; the rather makeshift building, remarkably, still stands (Fig. 10.6). It appears to have been spatchcocked together from re-used materials and comprises a long two-storey wooden shed, open on the courtyard side at ground level. At the rear, a small forge projects backwards (just far enough to reduce the risk of sending the whole workshop up in flames). Here metal components were worked. The upper storey, generously glazed, is supported on spindly cast-iron columns, and contained the upholstery department. The open ground floor sheltered the assembly of the various components to produce the finished vehicles. Opened in 1904-5, it cannot have prospered for long after the coming of the mass-produced motor car. Its survival is almost unique in England.

The railway line built from Craven Arms to Bishop's Castle in 1865[19] was a boon to the town. It very substantially reduced the price of fuel for households and workshops and carried a heavy two-way timber traffic. It enabled the creation of a gasworks beside the station, at the bottom of Station Street. The essential coal could be brought in easily and cheaply to run the processes, and the valuable by-products, especially coke, could be dispatched to customers anywhere. Small plaques (marked 'Junction Indicator'), showing that a house had gas supplied to it, can still be found low down on the walls of houses in the town: 2 Tan House, Church Street; 18 and 27 Church Street; the Boar's Head, Church Street; 8 High Street; Jane's Petals, High Street; and 1 Bull Street. Gaslight was a great improvement for businesses and households previously lit only by oil lamps and candles. It was a mark of considerable status to afford a gas supply. The advent of electricity in 1914 brought the telephone, and businesses' bill heads indicate the adoption of this new means of communication. Electricity, the railway's closure in 1935, and nationalization of the gas industry in 1948 contributed to the demise of the gasworks, which was demolished in 1988.

Ale production and consumption in the town was always important. Ale was brewed using malts and flavourings such as wormwood, henbane, wild rosemary, heather, ginger, spruce etc., and would last only a few days before becoming noxious. Much ale was brewed domestically, and an alewife would sometimes hang a sheaf over her door to advertise that ale could be bought there.

With the introduction of hops, used primarily as a preservative, the Three Tuns at the top of the town built its own brewery producing hopped beer (Fig. 10.7). The brewery, said to be the oldest in continuous use in Britain, commenced operation in 1642. It is still visited today by real-ale pilgrims from across the globe. Today the Six Bells at the bottom of the town also supports its own brewery, producing award-winning brews.

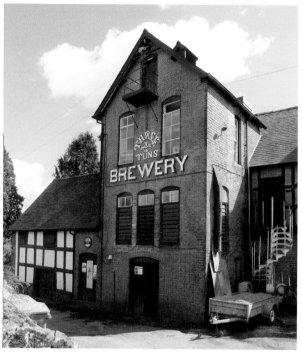

Fig. 10.7 The Three Tuns Brewery 2016. (Photo. Gavin Watson)

Bishop's Castle has always been noted for the number of its pubs and alehouses. The accumulated list of those that have come and gone (see Table opposite),[20] or indeed have survived till today, is impressive. Local research has produced the names of 35 inns or hotels, as well as one Temperance Hotel.

At present there are six public houses in Bishop's Castle, generous provision for a small population. Earliest known are the Three Tuns and the Boar's Head (both licensed in 1642); then come the Castle Hotel (1719), the Six Bells (1750), and the King's Head and the Crown and Anchor Vaults (both 1832). An annual beer festival helps to celebrate their diversity. The Castle Hotel, built in 1719, was important as a coaching inn with accommodation, a staging post on routes between London and towns in mid Wales.

There was a branch of the North Wales Bank in the town as early as 1790. Today there is a single bank, although in the recent past there were two. One of the earlier establishments, the Ludlow & Bishop's Castle Bank, was producing its own banknotes in 1820 but failed in 1826. The first issue of a town newspaper, *The Bishop's Castle Advertiser and Clun News*, appeared on 5th October 1900; it was incorporated with the *Ludlow Advertiser* in November 1966.

The post office was at first housed at the junction of High Street and New Street, where the shadow of its built-in post box can still be seen in the wall at the corner of New Street. Later it moved a short distance down the street, and most recently to premises behind the Boar's Head.

Former Inns and Pubs, Bishop's Castle

The Harp	Church St, opp. garage	1642
Old Talbot	High St (Jane's Petals)	1755
The Butchers' Arms	location unknown	1791
The Owl	Welsh St	1791
Black Lion	Welsh St	1792
The Bull	The Square	1792
Red Lion	Church St	1792
Crown & Star	High St	1793
The Plough	The Square (Wellfield House)	1793
Unicorn	Church St (below 'Stars')	1793
Old Nag's Head / Broughton Arms	High St	1807
Bricklayers' Arms	Bull Lane	1809
White Horse	corner of the Square/Salop St	1809
Hit or Miss	Union St	1832
Old Crown	corner of Castle St/Welsh St	1841
Stone House	Old Primary School (Chemists)	1841
Old Black Lion	above Burd's	1848
Cross Keys	Castle Green	1851
Railway Tavern	Burd's, corner of Church St	1865
The Oak or Royal Oak?		1870
Toddy Hall	Castle St	1936

Dates unknown:

The Angel	Church St
The Fox/Foxholes	top of Station St
The George	Welsh St?
London House	location unknown
The Old Club	Union St
Old Swan	Church St (Lymes)
White Swan	Welsh St, opp. Black Lion

and the Temperance Hotel!

For such a small town Bishop's Castle has kept a surprising range of shops and services. This is at least partly due to its remoteness at the heart of a sparsely populated rural area. Although travel and communication are now much easier and quicker, there is still a vital need for local sources of basic commodities and services.

A reliable water supply has been a problem for the town in the past.[21] About 1840 inhabitants without 'pumps attached to their houses' were 'indifferently supplied ... from a reservoir under the town hall' fed by pipes from 'neighbouring hills'.[22] Local springs were inadequate, and in 1893 an impounding reservoir of 1½ million gallons was constructed for the corporation on the river Unk, some five miles away at Maes Gwyn in Mainstone parish. Eventually the fissured rock of the reservoir bed caused leaks, and in droughts supplementary water from the stream below Maes Gwyn had to be pumped in. By 1946, when further improvements were being considered to the supply (of 30,000 gallons every 24 hours, from the service reservoir at Cabin on the Kerry Ridgeway road), 376 of the estimated 400 premises in the town were supplied indoors, 4 premises relied on standpipes, and 20 had no mains supply.[23]

A small stream, the Pennal, flows along the southern edge of the town, eventually joining the Kemp near Brockton. It provided water for the tannery's operations. The absence of any larger watercourses near the town must have presented a problem, since water mills were vital facilities in early economies. Near Bishop's Castle, however, are several rivers with flows regular enough to sustain small scale mills, not all of them flour mills. The East and West Onny had mills at Ratlinghope, Upper Mill, Walkmill, Whitcot, Myndmill and Plowden; and a watercourse (now unusable) left the West Onny near Newton Farm and powered the mill at Lydham. The Camlad had mills at Bromleys Mill, Pell Mell, White Mill, Snead and Broadway Mill, all within a few miles of Bishop's Castle. A mill has recently been uncovered at Walcot by the Lydbury North Field Group. Among the mills on the rivers Kemp, Unk and Clun were those at Brockton, Purslow, Oaker, Aston-on-Clun, Newcastle, Birches, Bicton, Clun, Hurst and Clunton.[24]

The absence of any major water supply and the distance from large centres, motorways and railheads has to some extent curtailed the establishment of larger industrial concerns. Farm Gas, a major enterprise producing bio-digesters, which began life near Bishop's Castle, eventually moved its operations to more commercially accessible centres. The former Wesleyan Chapel in High Street, after serving as the town's cinema, housed a branch of Walters clothing factory, employing many local people.

The town has nurtured successful entrepreneurs such as John Wright, the London merchant whose relict generously endowed the free school in 1785.[25] J.P. Wood & Sons started as game and poultry dealers, building up a major firm (Chukie Chickens) at the Grove, near Craven Arms, with a shop in Bishop's Castle. Members of the family founded Woods Brewery in Wistanstow and for a time owned the Three Tuns in the town. In 1912 Vincent Greenhous, from a family of Bishop's Castle ironmongers, founded a business which grew to become Greenhous Group Holdings, one of the country's largest car dealers. Several bus companies were also started in the town (see Chapter 8).

Today the town maintains a long-established and flourishing timber business (reflecting the numerous forestry plantations on neighbouring hills), an egg-packing plant, and a number of smaller but thriving industrial units mainly serving local needs: woodwork and joinery, agricultural machinery, etc.

Enterprise South-West, housed in a former factory building in Station Street, provides an extensive and well-used range of IT, computer and reprographic services and advice, as well as an equipment hire service (Village Outreach). The Library now has a home there – an important factor in its survival at a time of severe financial pressure.

The wide range of skills, trades and enterprises which Bishop's Castle has continued to support over several centuries is a manifestation of a community with considerable creative energy and determination, as well as a well-judged appraisal of the particular needs of a sparsely populated rural area.

11 Caring for the People: Health and Welfare

Two factors have characterized Bishop's Castle throughout its history: relative geographical isolation and modest size. The town lies a good 20 miles from other established urban centres (an insignificant distance for motorized transport but important when travel depended entirely on human or animal muscle), and its population has remained remarkably stable at *c*.1,500. The 2011 Census counted 1,893 inhabitants in the town, not very different from the 1,369 noted in 1793[1] or the 1,592 at the 1901 Census.

Isolation has enforced a long tradition of self-sufficiency in goods and services, but a restricted market means that their provision has often been economically marginal. This chapter examines how those contrary forces have been balanced in the important matters of medicine and 'welfare'.

Fig. 11.1 Trade token of Richard Ambler, Apothecary, trading in Bishop's Castle. (© British Museum)

Medicine

Regulation of medical practitioners in England began in 1422,[2] and the College of Physicians was founded in 1518,[3] when distinct classes of medical practitioners were emerging: physicians, apothecaries and druggists or herbalists. Physicians were university men (women were explicitly excluded). Between 1779 and 1783 there were five in Shrewsbury and two in Ludlow,[4] but there is no record of any practising in Bishop's Castle before the 19th century. Their fees were high. Apothecaries, trained through a seven-year apprenticeship, were more affordable, deriving their living from selling drugs and medicines in their shops. Nevertheless, their services would have been beyond the means of many ordinary townspeople. Richard Ambler, in 1661, was the first recorded in the town; he was a burgess, and bailiff in 1670.[5] He issued trade tokens, a device used by many traders in times of coin shortage (Fig. 11.1).[6] Four apothecaries are noted in Bishop's Castle burial registers between 1684 and 1715, the last of whom was Mr Ralph Waring.[7] Other documents[8] add a couple more.

In 1793 the town had a surgeon and two apothecaries.[9] Druggists provided cheaper services, and among early ones was Edward Griffiths, who in 1828 combined the trades of printer, bookseller, stationer, druggist and patent medicine dealer.[10]

For self-medication wealthier gentry and yeoman households often had their own family recipe books, perhaps based on Culpeper[11] or other herbals, but poorer people had to rely on traditional wisdom and experience, and on informal treatment by local tooth pullers, bone setters and 'wise women' – who continued to provide invaluable help for women in childbed, as they had throughout ancient and medieval times.

By the early 1800s apothecaries were styling themselves surgeons, a word then used to describe those who today would be termed general practitioners, suggesting a shift from a trading to a consulting profession. In Bishop's Castle two of the earliest surgeon-apothecaries were John Wollaston, senior and junior,[12] scions of a family established in the town since at least 1613; both were elected head burgess and bailiff in the early 19th century.

In the 1860s Bishop's Castle boasted two well established pharmacies. One was the business of Martha Cam Bills, one of only 400 female pharmacists registered in England. She started in Market Square and Salop Street but moved to 26 High Street where the pharmacy remained until the end of the 20th century. The second was Edward Davies, also in Market Square. In 1868 he was charged by an over-zealous police sergeant with selling an arsenical poison and convicted by ignorant magistrates, even though the law prohibiting the sale of such substances had not yet come into effect. George Strawson, at Yarborough House, took over the business. He was a prominent man in the town, alderman and chief of the fire brigade. These pharmacies continued as separate establishments under different owners[13] but amalgamated in the 1950s as Compston & Gourdie at 26 High Street.

Medicines

Most 18th- and 19th-century medicines were based on plant materials such as dandelion, willow bark, cascara, foxglove (digitalis) and poppy juice (opium). Some metallic materials were employed: mercury in the form of calomel and ointments for syphilis; iron pills for anaemia. Most were ineffectual and many were downright dangerous. In mid-Victorian times surviving prescription books for Bishop's Castle show that medicines were dispensed as oral mixtures or hand-made pills, with a few ointments and lotions, the most common ingredients being potassium bromide and Ipecacuanha wine – sedation and cough suppression were obviously necessary in this community. Synthetic medicines began to appear in the late 19th century with salicylic acid, aspirin, etc., used to combat pain and fever. Although the causes of infection were known by the late 19th century, treatment of bacterial infections was not effective until sulphonamides and penicillins appeared later in the 20th century.

Pharmacies also supplied animal medicines, always important in an agricultural area even though many farmers had their own remedies, including 'magic spells'.[14] The pharmacists' prescription books include many recipes and formulae for animal treatment. The 1841 Census records a specialist veterinary surgeon for the first time. Samuel Dayus was followed by Henry Danks in 1861 and five others were noted into the 1920s; they included Frederick Whisken of Castle Green (1900) and Roy Bickerton at 33 High Street (1909), followed there by Ernest Beaumont.[15] They would sometimes examine and treat larger animals in the street outside their premises.

'General practice' as we know it today took shape in the 19th and early 20th centuries. Gradually a distinction arose between physicians and surgeons, who together specialized to hold hospital appointments, and doctors, who chose to provide what we now call 'primary care'. The National Insurance Act of 1911 formalized this split, requiring all eligible working males to register on the 'panel' of a named general practitioner, who received an annual capitation fee to provide for their general medical care. General practitioners thus became responsible for the provision of primary health care within a national system funded by the state. In 1948 the introduction of the National Health Service extended the 'panel' to everyone.

In 1861 the town's medical men began to note their qualifications in trade directories.[16] They took surgeries at their residences and visited outlying patients in all weathers. Some employed dispensers, taking in apprentices from the parish. Many held public office: Dr Selwyn Hale Puckle, B.A., M.B.C.M., was mayor in 1889 and from 1910 to 1914. Patients not on the 'panel' would pay the doctor, some at the consultation; others, more credit-worthy, were billed quarterly 'for professional services'. There was no hospital in Bishop's Castle until the workhouse in Union Street was demolished in 1962 and a small hospital built on the site. It has so far (2016) survived recurrent threats of closure.

England's first organized district nursing service was pioneered in Liverpool in 1859, with Florence Nightingale's active support. The idea spread, and subscription schemes – essentially a form of insurance – were used to meet the cost. It was reckoned that, with

Fig. 11.2 Local general practitioner Dr Bremner c.1900, brother-in-law to Dr Puckle.

Fig. 11.3 The Former Nurses' Home, Castle Green, on the right.

subscriptions at a shilling (5p) a year for an individual or half a crown (12½p) for a family, a nurse could be supported by a population of *c*.4,000, but that was more than twice the size of Bishop's Castle's. Nevertheless, with the help of a charitable trust endowed by Arthur Sykes, of Lydham Manor, a Bishop's Castle District Nursing Association was established in 1912 and a Nurses' Home built at Castle Green (Fig. 11.3). The Association worked until taken over by the N.H.S. in 1948.

The first dentist, Emmanuel Lovekin, set up in the town in 1917. His name still appeared in trade directories in 1941.

Public Health

The idea of organized protection of 'public health' is relatively new. Medieval and early modern societies had little grasp of the causes of infectious diseases or their effective prevention. Plagues were sometimes ascribed to acts of God in punishment for sin. In a long Latin note in the parish register Walter Stephens, vicar of Bishop's Castle, attributed the plague of 1593 to the unholy custom of holding markets on Sundays (see Chapter 7).[17]

Lay people identified other suspects: foreigners, or 'people from off'. In 1636, having news of plague in London and, ominously close to home, in Radnorshire, the corporation ordered that the town be quarantined:

> upon Consideracion had to the great daunger of Sicknesses & the infection that is at this Instant time both in London & divers other partes of this kingdome & in the Towne of Presteigne within this our neighbourhood, ffor prevention of daunger It is at a Comon Hall concluded upon, that noe manner of person or persons whatsoever Inhabitinge within this Towne shall offer to Receave & entertaine within his or their howsse or howses or any part or parcel therof any straunger or person unknowen either to drincke or Lodge therin without notice therof ffirst geaven to mr Baylif ffor the time beinge.[18]

The relative remoteness of the town and its airy hillside position probably spared Bishop's Castle many of the outbreaks of disease which afflicted larger busier places in valley bottoms, and perhaps the singularity of not having a river reduced the risk of water-borne disease. Drinking water came largely from springs and wells. There was also a public supply with a spring-fed cistern under the town hall. The first borough minute book has several entries about the condition of the 'pompe' and 'conditt',[19] and in the early 18th century the chamberlain made many payments for their repair.[20] Increasing consumption during the 19th century outran supply (see the extract from Dr Puckle's letter, below) and the borough took a £4,000 loan under the 1875 Public Works Act, together with further loans from local friendly societies, to construct a reservoir in the upper Unk valley above Mainstone and a water works at the Cabin, about 1 mile to the west of the town. Unfortunately the fall between the reservoir and the Cabin was only 40ft, so that at the opening of the works it took two weeks for the water to reach the town. Those arrangements served into the 20th century, but there were still episodes of shortage when the town crier came round warning that the supply was to be cut off.[21] One resident recalls that into the 1950s an essential requirement for home confinement was to fill the bath with water in case of a stoppage.[22] A borehole sunk in 1956 near Snakescroft, east of the town, improved matters.

During the 19th century public authorities began to concern themselves with prevention of disease as well as its cure. The Vaccination Act, 1853, required every healthy child to be vaccinated within three months of birth by the public vaccinator or some other medical practitioner. Doctors in Bishop's Castle acted as public vaccinators for the three local vaccination districts and as medical officers of health for the borough.

Extract from a letter of Dr Puckle to his fiancée, 23 July 1887[23]

I hear to-night that our water supply such as it is, has failed. That is a pretty state of things. The town is supplied, or rather, not supplied now, by a large spring, there being no regular water supply, and all water has to be carried from the town pump or tap in buckets. It is a great shame that a town like this, on the side of a hill with hills all round should have no water supply. But they are that pig-headed that they won't do it. It was proposed a while ago to celebrate the Jubilee either by having a regular water supply or patching up the rotten old Town Hall. Of course they chose the latter, as a town council naturally would. If they get an epidemic here, it will serve them right and will decimate the population. The smells in some parts of the town are awful just now. The Health Officer is always trying to get them to do something. They will, when anything breaks out, go about the place saying 'the visitation is from God' and the Dissenters will rant and rave .... I can only say, as Amyas Leigh said when fever broke out on his ship, that it is the 'devil's visitation', coming from the devil who has so prompted them to be so wilfully neglectful. If I live, and have luck, I shall leave no stone unturned until something is done. It is only the pure bracing air of the place that saves it. If cholera came to England, and got up here, we medical men would have our hands full. There was a meeting to-night of the Sanitary Board to consider the case, and much good will they do. I had a long talk with the Mayor about it the other day; he seems keen on a water supply, but he is all jaw and talk, like an old woman.

Throughout the century the town still had neither mains sewerage nor, as far as it is known, night soil men (to remove the human waste). At Shropshire quarter sessions grand juries dealt with many complaints of nuisance from privies and dung heaps, and in Bishop's Castle the corporation served many notices under the 1875 Public Health Act requiring abatement of nuisance from privies and cesspits.[24] For example, in 1891 a house owner was given notice to clean, disinfect and lime wash all rooms of his property in Church Street on account of his tenants' contracting typhoid.[25] In 1910 the borough took action, borrowing £4,500 to fund the construction of a sewage system and works off Stank Lane, and inviting householders to apply for connexions to the system.[26]

Welfare

It is widely believed that medieval monasteries provided some relief for the poor and that their dissolution in the 1530s removed a principal source of such assistance. Even if that were true, the closures cannot have had much effect on Bishop's Castle, since there had never been a religious house nearby. In any event, there was no general policy to promote new lay institutions to replace monastic provision. Helping the poor, the sick and the old had always been the private Christian duty of those with money, and the establishment at Clun in 1617 of the almshouses known as the Hospital of the Holy and Undivided Trinity is a good example of continuity. Alone among Shropshire municipal boroughs, however, Bishop's Castle never had an almshouse.[27] Nevertheless, charities founded from the mid-17th century on did aim to relieve poverty outside the poor law. By 1830, although some charities had been lost owing to trustees' negligence, 12 poor people of the town, carefully selected and regular at church, were given a 1d loaf every week after Sunday morning service (and the parish clerk received the same for checking the bread quality and distributing the loaves). Besides that, twice a year on 1 January and 2 June, 1s doles were distributed to poor townspeople: the endowments would have benefited some three dozen recipients, but added sacrament money and a donation from the vicar probably increased their number on those occasions.[28]

Charitable endowments, however, could not do all that was necessary, and as the 16th century wore on there was increasing concern about bands of 'sturdy beggars' tramping the country threatening public order. Acts of 1597 and 1601 established the essentials of the poor-law system – the 'Old Poor Law' as it became known after the 1834 Act super-seded it – which endured for over two centuries throughout England and Wales. The churchwardens and the vestry became responsible for relieving poor native parishioners and raising a poor rate to cover the cost of doing so, the work being devolved to the parish officers known as the 'overseers' of the poor.[29] Each parish could choose its own ways of implementing the Act, either setting the able-bodied to work in a House of Industry, apprenticing pauper children, sending the idle to a House of Correction or prison, or – as most parishes did at first – by providing 'outdoor' relief in the form of money, food or clothing. Strangers were, in principle, returned to the parish of their birth, but the 'settle-ment' process was often difficult to implement. Bishop's Castle records show that between 1709 and 1826 the overseers held 106 settlement examinations (to determine whether people were entitled to the parish's assistance) and issued 50 settlement certificates and

161 removal orders. Around 230 children were indentured as apprentices: over a century, not big numbers.

In 1793 there were 44 'poor' parishioners – 11 men and 21 women, besides 12 in the parish workhouse; that was *c.*3% of the parish's population (1,369).[30] Children of the poor were 'bound apprentice at nine years of age for 12 years, but few insist upon the contract being performed. There are frequent instances of the master putting them in sufficient cloathing and giving them their liberty when capable of earning wages. Some are taken upon honour from the parish.'[31] The parish rented its workhouse, as is shown by a 1794 receipt for £2 5s – a year's rent 'for Mount Pleasant for the youse of the poore of the parish', paid by William Hoskin.[32]

Three years later a thorough survey of the national operation of the poor law provides a comprehensive account of the social state of Bishop's Castle parish:[33]

> The Poor of the borough have generally been, and are now, farmed in a work-house; the present contractor has £105 a year; for which he agrees to feed and cloath them; and to defray all other expences; except what may arise from appeals; in consideration of the high price of provisions, the parish gave him an additional gratuity of £5 the last half-year. 14 Paupers, (consisting chiefly of old, infirm, or insane,) are at present in the house. Those, who can work, are employed in spinning lint, or in other common work, according to their ages and abilities ... The house is kept pretty clean; of the 10 beds six are stuffed with feathers, and four with chaff; both beds and bed-cloaths are very old. A committee of 12 gentlemen visit the work-house very regularly. The contractor has now, upon his list, 11 or 12 out-pensioners, who receive from 6d. to 1s. a week, each; and a bastard, who costs 1s. 6d. a week: he also pays several house-rents. His rule is, not to allow more than 1s. a week to each family of out-pensioners; and if that sum does not satisfy them, he requires them to come into the house; but a reluctance to enter it, often induces a poor family to acquiesce in a very small out-allowance. It is generally believed, that if the Poor were not farmed, the Rates would be much higher than they at present are.

The workhouse diet was described. Breakfast and supper were broth or milk-and-water gruel; dinner was hot meat and vegetables on Sundays and Wednesdays; cold meat and vegetables for the rest of the week. 'No bread is allowed at dinner; sometimes potatoes and milk are served for supper: the matron always gives each person a little bread and cheese after breakfast.'

A corporation register of apprentices for 1812-28[34] lists 25 poor boys and 22 girls bound until 21 years of age (or until a girl's marriage). Boys learned a trade while girls performed household duties.

The first known workhouse was Stone House in Stonehouse Shut (later New Street), housing paupers of the parish and liberties in separate quarters. An inventory of 1821 gives an insight into conditions in the house, listing furniture and basic tools including a spinning wheel.[35] In 1830 Mrs Mary Chester covenanted with the churchwardens to keep the parish poor house,[36] and appeared as its keeper in the next year's census. Then in 1832 the churchwardens and overseers contracted with John Bright for the maintenance of paupers in the borough in a hired house, probably Norton House in Church Street. He was to

Fig. 11.4 This aerial photograph appeared in The Shropshire Star *on June 12th 1965, on the occasion of the opening of 'the new Stone House'. It captures a significant moment in the history of Bishop's Castle's health care. In the foreground on the left are the rather gaunt buildings of the former workhouse (about to be demolished); on the right, standing back from the road, are the new buildings, a unique combination of old peoples' home and hospital, now Coverage Care Residential Home and Bishop's Castle Community Hospital.*

employ an able and skilful Apothecary and Surgeon (to be approved of by the said church-warden and overseers) who shall attend the said poor persons and administer all necessary and proper medicines to all and perform all necessary and proper operations on them, and also shall and will in like manner provide proper nurses to take care of the said poor persons during the continuance of their respective illnesses or ailment, and also shall and will in like manner decently inter such paupers who happen to die.[37]

By the 1830s the growing burden of poor rates and the difficulties of operating a system based on birth parishes, when thousands were quitting the countryside for rapidly growing manufacturing towns, led to the 1834 Poor Law Amendment Act; it replaced the old parish system with newly formed poor-law unions (of parishes) run by guardians under the supervision of a Poor Law Commission in London – the 'three Bashaws [Pashas] of Somerset House'.[38] Clun union, which included Bishop's Castle and 18 other parishes, was formed in 1836, and at first it used the Bishop's Castle workhouse for pauper children. The guardians – 'farmers and shopkeepers of a very inferior grade', described as ignorant and timid rather than ill-willed – were dogged from the start by disagreements among themselves and the inadequacy of Whitling, their architect. Eventually Edward Haycock, the county surveyor, replaced Whitling, and a new union workhouse built in Bishop's Castle opened in 1844. The originally planned 'Elizabethan' almshouse-style façade was made much plainer. Designed for 150 inmates,[39] it never held more than the 86 recorded in the 1861 Census. An isolation hospital built in 1872 was apparently never used.

A late Victorian prescription book has a separate formulary for the workhouse medicines. It naturally specifies the cheapest ingredients, which were dispensed in bulk as workhouse dispensary stock.[40] The inmates' diet was plain and monotonous but improved considerably after an outbreak of cholera in 1849.

In 1930 Stone House became a county-council public assistance institution, and the severities of the workhouse may have begun to be softened. There are local memories of the staff's kindness towards the inmates. In the 1930s they collaborated in making a wedding dress for one inmate,[41] and children living nearby recall people from the workhouse 'coming for hot water to make tea, sometimes whole families, and their own mothers being kind to them'.[42] After the abolition of the poor law in 1948 some modernization of the institution was achieved in 1951-2.[43] Stone House became a home for the old and sick. In 1964 the old building was demolished and replaced by a residential home and a small hospital. It is still known as Stone House. The ghost of the old union workhouse still haunts the site in its 'Union Street' address. The Coverage Care Home and Community Hospital are still under the same roof.

Outside the workhouse, friendly societies offered some security to people below the richest levels of society. For modest regular subscriptions members could be assured of payment for medical expenses and funeral costs. A 1793 Act facilitated their establishment, and by 1797 the town had three with a total membership of 220. The movement continued to grow throughout the 19th century, spawning the Bishop's Castle Union Friendly Society in 1828[44] and the Bishop's Castle Mutual Improvement and Provident Society in 1882.[45] Better known national societies, like the Manchester Unity of Oddfellows, had branches here, still flourishing into the 1920s. Women were not left out: the Bishop's Castle and Lydbury North Female Friendly Association was also active from 1840 to 1900, with typical payments in 1889 of £16 7s in sick pay, three funerals for £6, and £43 3s paid to 13 pensioners.[46] The establishment of the welfare state in the 1940s and '50s effectively rendered them unnecessary.

This chapter has described some of the developments in health and welfare over the centuries in Bishop's Castle. Something of the advance of medical knowledge is reflected in the arrangements discussed above, but until the advent of the N.H.S. the greatest benefit to the health of the town's inhabitants at large came from improved sanitation and water supplies. Welfare of the poor and needy has similarly developed from a patchwork of local charities to the provision of services under the aegis of national and local government. Bishop's Castle, like other small English towns, has seen and experienced all these changes, some welcomed and others fiercely resisted or resented. But always there has been the kindness and consideration of ordinary people. The town has looked after its own and continues to do so.

Bibliography

Census (1851): *Education. Eng. and Wales: Report and Tables.*

N. Culpeper, *The English Physician* (1652); idem, *The Complete Herbal* (1653).

A. Goff, 'The Clun Poor Law Union Part 1: From Poorhouse to Workhouse 1636-1845', *S.W.S.H.A.S. Jnl.* **15**, pp.25-35; 'The Clun Poor Law Union Part 2: The Victorian Workhouse', ibid. **16**, pp.6-15; 'The Clun Poor Law Union Part 3: The Workhouse 1900–1948', ibid. **18**, pp.7-17.

R. Logan, *An Introduction to Friendly Society Records* (Bury Federation of Fam. Hist. Socs. 2000).

L.G. Matthews, *Antiques of Pharmacy* (Bell, London, 1971).

R. Moore, *Shropshire Doctors & Quacks* (Amberley, 2011).

R. Porter, *The Greatest Benefit to Mankind* (HarperCollins, London, 1997).

J. Preshous, *Bishop's Castle Well-Remembered* (privately published, 1990).

L. Smith, *Refuges of Last Resort: Shropshire Workhouses and the People who Built and Ran them* (*T.S.A.S.* **82**, 2010), pp.94-99.

12   CARING FOR THE PEOPLE: EDUCATION

Education was once the privilege of the upper or middle classes who had the option of sending their sons to public schools like Shrewsbury or grammar schools such as Ludlow. Daughters could be educated at home or at private academies for young ladies. The poorer classes either remained uneducated or were served by small charity or private schools. In Bishop's Castle schools have been located in various places round the town: Church Street, Union Street, Welsh Street, Market Square, Castle Green, Bull Street, School Lane and Station Street. But the story of education in the town is a complicated one, influenced by charity, local opinion, county and national education policies, and in later years by the need to serve a widely scattered population.

Charity and private schools

Charity schools were the first institutions to provide elementary education on a large scale for girls as well as boys.[1] The first record of a school in Bishop's Castle comes from 1646, during the Civil War. The vicar, Gervase Needham, had been ejected from his living for loyalty to the king; his house and goods were burnt, 'and he was prevented from keeping a private school for the subsistence of his family any longer'.[2]

The Society for the Promotion of Christian Knowledge, founded in 1698, promoted numerous schools during the 18th century which were maintained by the local inhabitants, but south-west Shropshire was long a neglected area,[3] and many charity schools catered for few pupils, their influence declining by the 1780s. This made way for the Sunday School movement, which blazed a trail towards popular education for all. Evidence for any Sunday school in Bishop's Castle came late, with a mention of Abraham Thomas as master of the Primitive Methodist school in 1870.[4] There would surely have been others. The need for universal education was being promoted by the non-denominational British and Foreign School Society from 1808 and the National Society for Promoting the Education of the Poor in the Principles of the Established Church from 1811; both societies built schools throughout England.

Generous endowment of a free school in the town was made under the will (1785) of Mrs Mary Morris, a native of the town and relict of a successful London merchant. It was recalled in 1793 by Archdeacon Joseph Plymley[5] that

> A poor girl went from this town a servant to London, she afterwards married a merchant there and in the event of his death became entitled to £20,000. She has

established a school at Bishops Castle and endowed it with money ... charging there-from the payment of £30 a year to a master and £20 a year to a mistress. She left also £200 to build a schoolhouse, and a good one has been recently built.

Moreover

There is another school in the town endowed with £3 a year, and a third school kept over the market house in a room given by the late Lord Clive for that purpose, but to which there is not any salary.[6]

There is no information on the second school mentioned.

Fig. 12.1 Wright's Charity Old School House

Wright's Charity School, named in memory of Mrs Morris's first husband, was endowed with £1,000 for the instruction of 25 boys and 25 girls in reading, writing and arithmetic. Built on land given by Lord Clive, it stood at the top of the town – perhaps in Old School House (Fig. 12.1) – with William Wild as schoolteacher during the early period and the Bishop of Hereford as the school's trustee. In the 1830s the boys were taught in the room (mentioned in 1793) over what is now remembered as the Old Market Hall, girls and infants in the original school house. The bishop was still the sole trustee; he appointed the master and visited regularly. The master had a house and garden and £40 a year with 'allowances' of £7; he nominated the 'free scholars'.[6]

Later in the 19th and 20th centuries Wright's endowment provided scholarships to the board and county schools.[7] Another educational charity was endowed by Richard Wollaston in 1844.[8]

A sampler worked in 1804 by Sarah Morris, overseen by her governess, provides evidence of private education in the area,[9] and in the later 19th century three local families – Pardoe (solicitor), Puckle (medical practitioner) and Roberts (Three Tuns, brewer and publican) – employed governesses for their children. Several academies and schools for young ladies or gentlemen are also known in the town during the mid 19th century.[10]

Workhouse teachers

Under the old (Elizabethan) poor law, scant provision had been made to educate the poor. As a result of the new poor law introduced in 1834, a union workhouse was built in Back Lane (now Union Street) and opened in 1844.[11] The governors were directed to employ an apothecary to care for the inmates' health and a schoolmaster to teach the pauper children. The workhouse schoolmaster in 1851 was Joseph Dorricot, salaried at £25 a year; Henry Trubshaw, there in 1861, taught *c*.30 children. By 1891 the children were being taught by Elizabeth Waine, the workhouse master's daughter.

After a report from the Inspector of workhouse schools, it was decided that the boys had to get up at 5.45am (in summer), make their beds, put the rooms in order, and wash the younger boys. Prayers were to be read at 6.30 and breakfast taken at 7. The younger children were to be under the charge of the matron and one of the older girls, and instructed in reading until noon. The older boys were to work in the garden and building and the girls to do household work until dinner and recreation between noon and 1.30. The afternoons were to be spent in school until 5 o'clock, receiving instruction in reading, writing and arithmetic. After that, more duties were specified for the children until their bedtime at 8.[12]

National schools

By 1840 the need for universal education was recognized and the 1841 School Sites Act facilitated the purchase of land for school buildings. In Bishop's Castle a National school was built in Back Lane (now Station Street) during 1839-40 to mark Viscount Clive's coming of age. It was erected, through subscription, on land later conveyed by the Earl of Powis to trustees;[13] at least 70 subscribers subscribed a total of £319 13s.[14] Earlier, in 1809, the land had been described as 'a house, building and garden' tenanted by John Marston, weaver.[15] Some 40 years later a map shows a school on the site, and this small school served the town's educational needs for over 30 years.[16]

Fig. 12.2 Station Street showing the The National School on the right

115

An education census was carried out in 1851 alongside the decennial population and religious worship census. For Clun union, which included Bishop's Castle where the union's workhouse was built, 12 publicly maintained schools, 8 private day schools, and 7 Sunday schools were noted, with 729 children in day schools and 428 in Sunday schools,[17] but the schools' locations were not specified. In 1863, however, the Inspector's report lists 63 boys and 52 girls attending the National school in Bishop's Castle. Elementary education was not free until 1891:[18] families had to pay 'school pence' for each child at school, nominally 3d a child each week.

School board

With the 1870 Education Act came school boards to provide elementary schools 'on the rates' wherever voluntary school provision was inadequate, for children aged between 5 and 12 years, with optional religious instruction. There were few boards in Shropshire,[19] but in Bishop's Castle the National schools in the area were transferred to a school board elected on the 26th November 1873. Next year the borough borrowed £1,600 from the Public Works Loan Board to build the Bishop's Castle Board School[20] for 120 girls and 120 infants on land at the corner of Church Street and the present New Street; it was the site of the old Stone House, which during the 18th century the parish had let variously as a school, two workhouses, and then a dwelling – before demolition. The school board agreed with four local residents to build the school for £1,456,[21] and it opened in 1875. Meanwhile, with the introduction in 1880 of compulsory school attendance until the age of 10, the school needed enlargement. In 1881 an

A Bishop's Castle School Board Candidate
(adapted from Gilbert and Sullivan's *Patience*)

Conceive me, if you can –
A hard-headed shrewd old man,
Vicar and veteran, get not a better 'un,
Grey-in-the service old man.

Conceive me, if you can –
An honest Dissenting young man,
A popular minister, truthful minister,
Do-what-is-right young man.

Conceive me, if you can –
A middle-aged festive young man,
Folks say salacious, a little too gracious,
All-things-to-all young man.

Conceive me, if you can –
A red hot Irishman,
Famed for sagacity, choked with veracity,
Speak-the-truth-always young man.

Conceive me, if you can –
A thoroughly decent young man,
Bucolical steadily, come to Board readily,
Ratepaying - largely young man.

Conceive me, if you can –
A squabby old henpecked man,
In his own estimation, a wondrous creation
Skin-a-flint-quick old man.

Conceive me, if you can –
A purse proud, mean old man,
A filius rutius trying to bully us,
Ne'er-had-a father old man.

Conceive me, if you can –
A rather stout young man,
Quiet respectable, highly delectable,
Ought to get in young man.

H.M. Inspector observed that 'the want of a classroom must often be severely felt and I am glad to understand that one will probably be built before long'. The board received a loan from the Education Department to build the classroom, and by 1884 a cloakroom and covered shed had been added.

The school-leaving age was raised twice before the end of the 19th century: to 11 in 1893 and 12 in 1899.

The Board of the United District of Bishop's Castle was run or managed by a committee drawn from the local clergy and influential residents. Elections to the board were triennial with a consequent abundance of paperwork acquired from London and the local stationer Annie Hughes. The town then had two board schools: the Boys school in Station Street and the new Girls and Infants school, designed by J.L. Randal, at the junction of New Street and Church Street. Managing schools on two sites would have been an onerous task. The infants were taught in a smaller room adjoining the Girls school, the boys moving to the Station Street school, and the girls changing classrooms.

Board-school teachers

Board-school teachers and pupil teachers were generally drawn from the same ranks in society as the pupils themselves. Fortunately it has been possible to compile a partial list for Bishop's Castle.[22] A few teachers had grown up in the town, and pupil teachers were drawn from aspiring nearby families. There were fewer boys interested in teaching, but some of the girls returned as qualified teachers to work in the town. School records tell us little about them, but other sources are more revealing. Isabel McMinn's father was a tea merchant. Henry Coward taught variously at a boarding school and at the board school, played bowls, and became a member of the Corporation.[23] Louis Copson taught at the board school alongside Miss McMinn and Miss Baldwin, previously the teacher at Mainstone. In his free time Copson joined the crown-green Bowling Society, where on occasion he exercised his considerable talent as a caricaturist. In 1893, however, he received notice of dismissal from the Board in the following terms: 'that as Mr Copson was informed by the Board that there was no cause for the action "Copson v. Biggs" and that the Board meant to support their vice-chairman in said action, but as Mr Copson took no notice of our communication, we now give him 3 months' notice to leave our employment.' In July 1893 H.M. Inspector requested 'that you will state in detail in what way the Board was dissatisfied with Mr Copson's conduct',[24] but the board's response has not survived, and no further information on the case has come to light.

Copson left on 28th September 1893 and was replaced on 2nd October by Richard Ridge. On 13th September 1895 J.J. Lane became the board-school master, retaining the post for around 30 years. He

> **A heartfelt observation from the Boys' School log book for 17th Oct. 1893**
>
> A considerable number of boys leave this School immediately they pass the Standard for Exemption, and can be seen idling away their time loafing about the town, learning bad habits very probably and certainly acquiring a taste for idleness and unlearning all they have learnt, which is the pity of it, considering the labour Schoolmasters &c. go to over them.

also became the secretary of the Bowling Society for at least 27 years. In the early 20th century Jane Spink, an infant teacher, experienced the system's harshness when she was required to find, and pay, a temporary replacement teacher while one of her own children was ill. School attendance was dogged by the prevalence of familiar children's diseases: diphtheria, whooping cough, ringworm, chicken pox etc., some of which have become rare in our century.

Schools in rural areas were always kept sharply aware of the turning seasons and the demands of agriculture. Attendances were affected by parents keeping children at home for lambing, haymaking, harvesting, potato picking and sorties into the hills to pick wimberries.

School boards apart, there was no universal system of local education authorities before the creation of school attendance committees when elementary education became compulsory in 1880. In 1903, under Balfour's 1902 Education Act, elementary schools – board and voluntary (the latter in due course 'aided' or 'controlled') – passed to county and county-borough councils or to 'Part III' authorities.[25] In 1918, at the end of the First World War, the school-leaving age was raised again, to 14.[26]

The National Union of Elementary School Teachers (now the National Union of Teachers) was founded in 1870, and it conducted quarterly pupil-teacher and scholarship student examinations. In 1904 Emily Bowen and Lily Lockley sat the examination for scholarship students and Henrietta Bosey sat the second year pupil-teacher examination. The examination sessions were spread over two days and included a choice in one paper between French, Latin and Welsh. Frances Sinclair, another pupil-teacher of that generation, was absent from school for three days in 1917 to sit Part I of her examination in Shrewsbury. Her father, an engine driver on the Bishop's Castle Railway, could not afford to send her to college, so she taught half-time and studied half-time. Later she taught at the Bog school and at Shelve school. She became Mrs Cooper, and was visited by grateful former pupils until her death in 2003 aged 104.[27]

Log books and minutes

School log books were introduced in 1862-3 as part of a general move by the government to promote efficiency, economy and accountability in elementary education. These documents have variously survived from 1863 to 1993, after which date they were no longer a statutory requirement. The Bishop's Castle Council Schools managers' minutes (1915-29)[28] reveal some of the problems faced. During this time the managers, always the 'great and good' of the district, included the Revd C.E. Warner, vicar of Bishop's Castle, the Revd W.H. Thornley, Congregational minister, A. Scott, Mrs W.A. Pugh and R.W. Francis, with P.H. Newill as correspondent. The managers met monthly, in the boys and girls school alternately, to deal with repairs, lettings, notifiable diseases, medical inspections, accounts, staffing and salaries, reports from teachers, and returns to higher education authorities. They also fixed the length of school holidays, curiously in half-day units (the summer holiday, for example, was fixed at 52 half days). A manager was deputed to inspect the schools each month and sign the log books. A number of initiatives, including a savings bank, were started. In 1916 the managers authorized the loan of the school carbines (used for drill and shooting practice) to the Volunteer Training Corps 'provided they were returned periodically'. A reminder of the war came with an entry recording the death in action in France of an assistant teacher, James Keenan, while serving with the King's Shropshire Light Infantry.

In 1916 the girls' head teacher informed the managers that it was 'not possible to carry on the school efficiently with two teachers and a pupil teacher' – so an assistant mistress was sought. Several female teachers declared their intention to marry and offered their resignations (invariably declined), and then continued teaching. On one occasion of staff illness a teacher from the Infants class was transferred to the Girls school and subsequently appointed as an uncertificated teaching assistant at £70 a year.

In 1919 the schools needed much repair and painting after the stringencies of the war years. There was a general shortage of teachers in the country, but the managers advertised for a male teacher in *The Teacher* and managed to recruit one. In 1924 nine applications were received for a teaching post in the Boys school. Discipline at that time in the Girls department was reported to be poor; the school was not opened on time and the head teacher was not there by 9 o'clock. In 1926 the local organizer for physical training wished to have the playground concreted – the boys' yard was in a dangerous condition and the low wall around the Girls and Infants school caused problems with neighbours when ball games

Fig. 12.3 The old Girls School, Church Street

were played: 'Please may we have our ball back'! In 1928 Dr Adams, a school manager, presented the school with a primus stove for warming dinners. That same year Major H.R. Sykes, of Lydham Manor, joined the management team and immediately proposed 'that the local education authority be invited to hold an inquiry as to whether the dual system of education [essentially grammar and secondary modern streams] could be profitably introduced at the Bishop's Castle Council Schools'. At that time the long-serving head teacher, J.J. Lane, resigned owing to ill health and was succeeded by Mr Green; the two streams were not introduced till the 1940s.

From a surviving Infants department log book[29] we learn something about the calendar of activities and visits over the 30 years from 1914: a Peace Holiday in 1919, regular inspections, prize giving, visits by teachers from other local schools, sports days, music festivals and seasonal treats. In 1929 the Inspector's report was encouraging: 'This Infants School is a place of happy, busy, cheerful children, where neatness, orderliness, cleanliness and habits of attention and obedience, consideration for others, kindness to younger children, truthfulness and love of work are fostered.' There were similar reports from the religious inspections.

In the 1940s this little school welcomed evacuees, four from St Michael's Roman Catholic School and ten from St Athanasius's, both in Liverpool. Space was at a premium and extra accommodation was secured in the Women's Institute Hut. When the head teacher of the infants stepped down in 1944, according to the log book there were 66 pupils on the roll (though only 54 local and 8 evacuees are mentioned).

The Girls' Council School, as it was known by 1922,[30] had three staff and 99 pupils, but owing either to defective heating apparatus or lack of fuel, the school was often too cold to follow the timetable or teach properly. Although the town had its own electricity supply in 1913, the Boys school was not connected until 1930, while the Girls school was still waiting in 1933. The school attendance officer, the dentist and the nurse visited regularly. There were also periodic changes of teaching staff before Margaret Metcalf took charge of the school in 1930. In 1933 the inspection report stated that 'the school was maintaining its good reputation ... admirable tone in school ... creditable to all concerned'. Next year most of the girls attended a Ludlow performance of the Shropshire Historical Pageant with tickets and a bus funded by Major Sykes. At that time the local education authority requested a reorganization of the school buildings and provision of a field for recreation, to relieve pressure on facilities during the statutory dinner hour.[31]

During the late 1930s a new headmaster of the Boys school, Mr Finlayson, was appointed, but his period of tenure was impaired by his preference for living at some distance from the town, which rendered winter attendance difficult. Also, relations between the head teachers of the Girls and Infants departments were strained, a situation brought to the attention of the National Union of Teachers. The school managers instructed staff to resolve the problem or resign. The year 1939 marked the centenary of the opening of the school in Station Street.

Miss Metcalf continued as head of the Girls school until war broke out in 1939, when she joined the Voluntary Aid Detachment, leaving Miss Mary Hayward to 'hold the fort'. In 1940 and 1941 the school welcomed evacuees accompanied by several of their teachers. That put a strain on the building, especially on the water supply, which needed to be turned off at night and during school holidays by order of the borough surveyor. During the war years finding a suitable garden plot for the schools became an important project, and a woodworking centre in the old chapel in Chapel Yard was also suggested.

The 1944 Education Act[32] brought far-reaching changes. The Girls and Infants departments were combined to become the school which in 1950 was described as a junior mixed and infants school. It had four classrooms, a staff room and a small store; one head teacher with three assistants taught at least 92 pupils. Inspectors described 'a happy family with much co-operation between teachers and parents'. Sadly, there was no school hall and the playground fell below local-authority standards. School canteen meals were excellent in quantity and quality at 5d a meal, gardening plots were re-introduced, and pressure was applied for the 11+ children to be transferred to the High School. When Miss Metcalf returned to her post after the war – with a certificate for distinguished war service presented by Queen Elizabeth, wife of George VI – times were already changing, especially in the local managers' attitudes towards male or female head teachers. While warm tribute was paid to Margaret's excellence as a teacher, the managers felt it would be 'in the best interests of all if she did not return to her duties after sick leave'. They referred to a lack of space and a shortage of male teachers – 'the bigger boys are a challenge' – and in 1952 a headmaster, Mr P. Robinson, was appointed.

In the 1950s the pupil numbers ranged from 131 to 141; the number of classes containing over 30 pupils rose, and the timetable was hampered by conditions in the buildings. To commemorate the coronation of Queen Elizabeth II the school managers presented the pupils with 140 Testaments and three Roman Catholic prayer books. Loudspeakers were wired up around the school for radio reception, the school library flourished and school dinners were now served in the Church Barn. The children adopted the Motor Vessel *Lucien*, continued with National Savings, and supported Dr Barnardo's charity. During this period the Boys school building in Station Street was taken into use for a time by the High School, which itself was being adapted to suit county secondary school requirements.

The late 1960s brought a new headmaster, Leslie Cunnick, the introduction of the Initial Teaching Alphabet system, a school television set and further alterations to the old Boys school building – this time given new life as the Annexe for the Primary School. A Parent Teacher Association was formed and 75 members attended a dinner in February 1967. There were also swimming lessons at Ludlow baths, football and netball matches, attendance at concerts and shows in

Fig. 12.4 Certificate presented to Bishop's Castle Primary School celebrating 50 years' participation in the National Savings Scheme

local towns, and performances of nativity plays for the Stone House Hospital patients. By 1969 the staff consisted of four full-time teachers, two part-time teachers and a headmaster.

At the beginning of the 1970s plans were drawn up for the proposed site of the new primary school. A new head teacher, Mr M.E. Thorne, was appointed in 1971, but it was not until 1973 that the first drawings of the new school were produced. That was also the year when there were celebrations to mark the 400th anniversary of the town's 1573 royal charter, and the school closed for a day to take part in an Elizabethan street market. Next year the two buildings in the centre of the town were finally replaced by a new school in Oak Meadow.

Secondary Education

With the 1902 Education Act came new powers for the county council to provide secondary education, and, as noted above, by 1918 the school-leaving age was raised to 14 years. There followed a long contested local debate about the location of the new High School which was to serve a large area of south-west Shropshire, from which Bishop's Castle emerged as the most appropriate place. The school, called the County High School, was built around a central quadrangle and constructed of asbestos panels. It was officially opened by the Earl of Powis on 25th October 1922.

The school prospectus stated that courses were designed to give a thorough preparation in the usual subjects for the school certificate, matriculation, university and professional examinations; the science course was arranged to provide thorough instruction in the principles on which a later specialized study of agricultural science might be based.[33] Scholarships and free places were available. The first headmaster was C.W. Dodson, a strict but fair disciplinarian, and the senior mistress Miss Thomas, 'a wonderful teacher who never had any trouble with discipline'.[34] From its inception, the school and its successor

Fig. 12.5 The masthead from a 1930s News Sheet

college has always aimed to instil pride in learning, good manners and self-discipline. The Old Pupils' Association issued an annual news sheet, and one has survived from 1937 with the motto *Non Sibi Sed Scholae* (Not for Self but for the School) and an elaborate masthead (Fig. 12.5).[35]

By 1938 there were seven teachers for 35 boys and 48 girls; five pupils passed the School Certificate in the following year when a small sixth form was established.[36] Fees had to be paid, but assistance was available for the purchase of uniforms. Most pupils cycled to school before the provision of school buses. During the 1930s the vision of a university place after secondary education became a reality for some pupils. The Sykes Foundation Trust, set up in 1929, provided grants for further and higher education.[37] Initially one or two awards of £20 per annum for three years were given after receipt of satisfactory reports. The final grants were made in 1995, when 23 pupils gaining higher education places were awarded grants of £10 each.

During the war pupil numbers expanded and included 16 evacuees, rising to 23 during 1941; more staff were urgently required. The school was now overcrowded and classrooms designed for 25 were housing up to 36 pupils.[38] School meals for all children in the town were provided in the Women's Institute Hut off Union Street. In 1947 the school leaving age was raised to 15, fees were abolished in maintained schools, and secondary education graded into grammar, modern and technical schools. At that time 12 pupils passed the school certificate and four gained the higher school certificate. Miss Thomas, the long-serving senior mistress, retired, only to be called back later to teach Latin to the sixth form. The headmaster retired in 1945, and R.A. Bowman was appointed. During his tenure he extended the scope of the establishment to a bilateral grammar and modern school.

The High School was extended in 1947 with three new prefabricated HORSA (Hutting Operation for the Raising of the School-leaving Age) huts to accommodate the increased

Fig. 12.6 Aerial view of the High School showing the three HORSA huts added in 1947

intake. A new head, R.H. Hawking, was appointed in 1949 by which time 145 names were on the register. Next year the numbers on the roll doubled: 151 in the grammar stream and 158 in the modern stream. Unfortunately the HORSA buildings were causing problems with porous walls and water ingress, cured two years later by spraying with bitumen and repainting. The High School admissions register listed 158 pupils leaving between 1945 and 1953: 39 of them went on to further education, 27 undertook vocational training, 13 had apprenticeships and 14 enlisted in the armed forces.[39]

The school saw a number of important changes in 1951: ballroom dancing classes, a school choir, and an enlarged sixth form; an Evening Institute commenced with 120 members attending 11 classes. The 'school cert.' examination was replaced by a new General Certificate of Education (G.C.E.). But after about 30 years the buildings were no longer fit for use and a new secondary school was erected on the existing playing fields. Work began in 1955 and the building was completed in time for a visit by Princess Margaret in 1958. A new headmaster, J.D.M. Preshous, was appointed in 1973, and after much local campaigning and fund-raising the long awaited swimming pool was opened by the chairman of governors, Lt-Col A.P. Sykes, on 16th October 1974.

The school was especially fortunate to have been designated to offer post-16 courses for the G.C.E. 'A' level. Although sixth-form classes were small, the older pupils contributed a mature element to the school's life.

As well as maintaining a full range of team sports and musical and dramatic opportunities, the High School held an annual camp in Wales and organized a regular London trip aimed at pupils who had never had the chance to visit the capital. Overseas visits were arranged to European countries and pupil exchanges with French schools.

The Community College
By the 1980s the antiquated buildings from earlier periods had been demolished to make room for modern extensions. Following a campaign to retain the sixth form and extend the public use of the school, the county council agreed to a two-year pilot scheme with teaching-staff co-ordinators to link with the local community.[40] This was highly successful, and the school, Shropshire's first co-educational comprehensive school, now became the county's first rural Community College, serving a catchment area of over 200 square miles – almost the whole of south-west Shropshire, from Ratlinghope to Knighton and from Marton to Aston-on-Clun. It had a roll of some 500 pupils.

The College opened its community operation on 18th September 1987, with conducted tours, displays and opportunities to enrol in adult education classes. It became possible for members of the

> A community school is a unified, self-governing institution in which the educational function is inseparable from the function of assisting the individuals and the communities, which generate and support it, to grow in accordance with their own perceptions. It is open and responsive to the whole community, sharing its resources and encouraging a deeper understanding of the value of education as a life-long process. (Dominic Swainson, headteacher of Ansford School, Somerset, writing in *The Management of a Rural Community School*[41])

Fig. 12.7 Aerial view of the Community College

community to participate in daytime classes and buy lunch in the canteen. Additionally, for the period 1987-99, a much appreciated Community College newsletter called *The Rabbit* was published.

David Preshous retired in 1997. In 2006, during Terry Hunt's headship and after a long and determined campaign for improved leisure facilities (typical of local tenacity), the SpArC (Sports & Arts in the Community) building was opened. It comprises the original swimming pool, a theatre, squash courts, fitness centre, sports hall and a floodlit all-weather playing area – a great asset to both school and local amenities.

In 2016 the South West Shropshire Learning Trust was formed, under the College's headmaster, Alan Doust, and head teachers of local primary schools. The Trust will bring together all the schools in the College's catchment area. The aim is to support each other and enhance the educational experience of young people in the area. Membership is open to anyone interested in the future of education. All of this serves to demonstrate that the College was, and indeed remains, at the heart of the communities of south-west Shropshire.

Conclusion

Over the centuries Bishop's Castle, in its sparsely populated location in the hill-country of the Welsh border, has moved to improve its education services, always dependent upon the resources available. Even when funds were forthcoming from central government, the town frequently relied on the private initiatives of its people to get things done. Although its education story is not unique, Bishop's Castle has always worked to serve the needs of its young people – and continues to do so – in its own inimitable way.

Bibliography

Census (1851): *Education. England and Wales, Report and Tables.*

S. Curtis and M. Boultwood, *An Introductory History of English Education Since 1800* (University Tutorial Press, 1966).

M. Daniel, 'The Old Boys School, Bishop's Castle', *Jnl. of S.W.S.H.A.S.* **4,** pp.21-4.

E. Humphries and K. Baker, 'Hockey Sticks and Bicycles', *The Gale of Life*, ed. J. Leonard *et al.* (Logaston Press, 2000).

J. Preshous, *Bishop's Castle Well-Remembered* (privately published, 1990).

P. Theobald, *The Bowling Club, Bishop's Castle* (2009; copy in B.C.H.R.C.).

13   LIVING HISTORY

Introduction: local history research in Bishop's Castle

In 1973 Bishop's Castle celebrated 400 years since the charter was granted by Queen Elizabeth I. There was an upsurge of interest in local history and Keith Ritherdon initiated a Local History Research Group, which after his death was continued by Dr Barrie Trinder and James Lawson. In 1988, with the development of the High School into the Community College, the South-West Shropshire Historical and Archaeological Society was founded. The Research Group went on working on the parish registers under the late Marion Roberts and continues with George Baugh.

A reminiscence (RECALL) project was launched in 1984 at the Stone House Residential Home and Hospital, and *Bishop's Castle Well-Remembered – Memories and Photographs of a small Shropshire Market Town* was published in 1990. The House on Crutches Museum was opened in 1993, and the Bishop's Castle Heritage Resource Centre (B.C.H.R.C.) came into existence in 2004. Latterly the refurbishment of the Town Hall in 2014 and the staging of varied talks and exhibitions have stimulated renewed interest in the town's history.

In small close-knit communities such as Bishop's Castle one can tap into a vein of continuous memory. In such a settled rural area, largely cut off from major towns, there is a tradition of handed-down memory through several generations. It has been possible to record and transcribe first-hand oral memories and copy a huge number of photographs. These, with access also to family memoirs, letters, diaries, local news reports, school log books, tickets, posters and bills, have built up a picture of everyday experiences, underpinning the documentary or 'historical' reporting of events, both locally and nationally. In the more distant past it was rare to hear the personal views of 'the man – still less the woman – in the street'. Just occasionally a phrase from a court case or a note in the parish register comes to life.

Photographs and objects are very important in triggering memories, or confirming the accuracy of recollections and anecdotal material. Recording actual voices carries immediacy and authenticity even further. Locally this has had the added value of catching Shropshire rhythms of speech and word order as well as dialect words, phrases and sayings, which can be related to the 19th-century collections of Georgina Jackson and Charlotte Burne. From these tape-recorded memories (now digitized by B.C.H.R.C.), it has been possible to build up a composite picture of life in Bishop's Castle from the 1890s.[1] The similarities as well as the differences of communal memories, collected from a wide selection of local people from different backgrounds can conjure up the actual moment, or a lifetime's experience.

In 1979 Miss Molly Puckle gave a talk to Bishop's Castle W.I. about her life in the town up to 1919, as daughter of the mayor, Dr Selwyn Hale Puckle; this was later recorded. She also produced photographs (taken by her aunt Miss Isabella Bremner) of 'Bishop's Castle Celebrities 1902', which included the Engine Driver, the Town Crier, the Church Cleaner and even the Grave Digger. Those memories by a privileged member of Bishop's Castle society, educated at home by a governess, were complemented by recorded conversations with Mr Alfred Shakespeare, who had left the Boys' School in Station Street at 14, and had been 'minding cattle in the street' even in his schooldays. These two recordings, with relevant photographs, were used as the framework for triggering memories in all subsequent interviews.

The material was also used in the RECALL project at Stone House Home and Hospital partly as a stimulus to reminiscence, but also for the residents to help to identify personalities and events from the past. Artefacts from Acton Scott Farm Museum have triggered accounts of farming methods, and household skills such as butter- and cheese-making. Memories, anecdotes, songs, recitations and jokes were also recorded. Mr Tom Pryce (1914-2007) of Linley gave a vivid account of the 'Black Winter' of 1947 as the frozen gorse bushes thawed out: 'The rabbits was thin, thin, terrible thin – like rakes they was'. He also described how the dealers came to collect holly at Christmas: 'They'd rather have the slike holly – that other holly's got all pricks all the way round it'. ['Slike' – smooth, sleek: Georgina Jackson, *Shropshire Word Book*.]

In August 2015 the Friends of Bishop's Castle Community, Residential Home and Community Hospital celebrated the 50th anniversary of the demolition of the old Clun Union Workhouse (built in 1844), and the launch of the new Stone House, a residential home and hospital under one roof. One former resident, Mary Louise ('Lou') Davies (1911-99), lived at Stone House for 46 years, having been born in 'the Union' at Knighton. The hardship of her life was exemplified by her memory of a night when it was 'raining heavens hard' and the master kindly allowed her to reach her bedroom for once by the inside stairs instead of having to go outside to get there. She ended her days in the comfort of the modernized Coverage Care Home, having contributed many valuable memories to the RECALL group, and taken part in a video on farm-life made with Acton Scott.

Transport: road and rail

Some of the earliest memories concern methods of getting about: walking to school or to work, and vivid recollections of the role of horse transport – with carts and traps in the town, and wagons and drays carrying produce and timber. Cattle and sheep would be driven in from the outlying farms and there are many childhood memories of cattle in the street, straying animals and horses impounded. Boys would be helping to drive cattle; little girls would be warned to keep to the doorstep as the horses and men of the Yeomanry passed by: 'I can see them now – we were all excited' (Miss Eva Hinksman 1903-91).

Before the Second World War all the heavy work on the farms was done with horses. Horse sales were held in 'Horse Fair', at the bottom end of Station Street, opposite 'Pig Fair' in Union Street. All the inns had stabling for the horses and carts: the local farmers would come in to the auctions, and their wives would come to buy necessities at the market. Most of the local shopkeepers had a field where they kept a horse for deliveries

– milk was delivered by pony and trap: 'Milk was tuppence ha'penny a pint, fivepence a quart. I used to be proud of Kitty the pony.' (Mrs Doris Bourne, *née* Evans (1916-2001), one of the first women in Bishop's Castle to drive a car – a 'Clyno'.)

Mr Roly Marston (1904-86) started work for Morrays the bakers in 1917 at the age of 13 and delivered quartern loaves with a pony and trap, 'I was like a tom-tit on a round of beef!' Other bakers would take round the loaves in a 'whisket', a basket on three wheels.

Alf Shakespeare (1904-92) used to deliver the orders for Gaius Smith, grocers, and Bowens the butchers, round the Stiperstones area with a

Fig. 13.1 Delivering the milk: Doris Evans (Mrs Bourne) with her brother Eddie and 'Kitty', the pony. (Photograph from S.W.S.H.A.S. Collection)

horse and cart: 'The Bog Mines was running at the time, and we used to carry a great big box full of medical goods, Beechams Pills and the lot, apart from the orders ... They used to run all round Newcastle, up by Clun – terrific area, all out to Plowden and Lydbury North and The Down ...' People in the surrounding countryside depended on these deliveries, or used the carrier's cart for their shopping if it was too far to walk.

Mr Jack Davies (1896-2000) cycled from Edgton to Bishop's Castle to learn the shoe-maker's trade at Ross's shop: 'and I was paid the lordly sum of a shilling a week for three years!' Mrs Annie Burd (1901-88) used to cycle in with a friend from Prolley Moor to work at Scotts in Market Square: 'all the ladies in the town had their dresses made up by Miss Bason, very smart she was'. Burd's grocery shop has been in Church Street for three generations.

Dr Puckle did his rounds in a dog cart or on horseback, and a groom would meet him with a second horse in the afternoon. His daughter Miss Molly Puckle (1896-1987) would wake at night (before the advent of the telephone of course) 'and hear, a long way off, the sound of fast trotting hooves, ... and the bell pealing through the house ... and hearing him riding off into the darkness'.

The vicissitudes of the Bishop's Castle Railway (1865-1935: see Chapter 9) led to many anecdotes about the slowness of the train – that boys could overtake it on their bikes and that passengers had time to get out and pick mushrooms. 'The first Guard was a fellow of the name of Broome, and he was dressed up there in his uniform, that proud of the train, and up come one of these travellers, a cocky sort of feller: "Oh, this is the train they get out to pick mushrooms from, don't they?" And when they got to Bishop's Castle, coming along on the train, like, he was sticking his head out, and he lost his hat. And he could see Broome, and he kept shouting to Broome to stop; anyhow, Broome never stopped. When he got out he said to Broome "Why didn't you stop to pick my hat up? I shouted at you!" "No", Broome says, "We only stop to pick mushrooms!"' (Alf Shakespeare, recorded 1987).

129

The railway was nevertheless vital to the town's prosperity before the roads were opened up, and the advent of cars and lorries. As well as ordinary passengers, there were regular visits from the travellers, dealers, the dentist, the music teacher and 'the skin man' (the dealer in rabbit skins). The railway carried coal and timber, stone, milk, cattle, sheep, horses, fish and rabbits. The stone for the roads came from Squilver Quarry at More, and hauliers and roadmen were employed – the roadmen also took pride in the maintenance of their allotted 'length', and there are vivid memories of the steamrollers and the smell of tar being laid. Some of the stone for the roads was broken up by 'roadsters', tramps who travelled from one workhouse to another, perhaps from Forden to Bishop's Castle, where they got a night's lodging in exchange for their stone breaking, and on to the workhouse at Knighton. Many people remember their mothers boiling a kettle to fill a roadster's tin can with a few tea-leaves.

The railway also carried the steam engines to the annual May Fair, which seems to have continued as a hiring fair up to the time of the 1939-45 War. Mrs Lucy Hemmings (1906-98) remembered that 'They used to stand under the Town Hall, the maidservants

Fig. 13.2 A 'Roadster': one of the itinerants who lodged overnight in the workhouse casual ward in return for stone breaking. (Photograph from Emmanuel Beddoes)

and the farm-workers ... They had their wages from the last place, and they had this roundabouts business, the May Fair that goes round, and all the amusements, they would go and spend their money on this (after they'd been hired for next year) ... and there was a lot of drunkenness about, and they used to have these stalls, selling sweets and fruit and that, and they had these flarey lamps, paraffin or something – I always remember them.' Mr Shakespeare vividly remembered men and boys being hired: 'They used to grade them ... they used to feel their muscles in the street!' Mrs Hemmings also remembered the visits in her youth of the man with the dancing bear, the umbrella man, the knife-and-scissor grinder, the coconut-mat mender; as well as the sales of cork-lino, and that fish was sold door-to-door. Mr Harry Fletcher (1898-1989), a veteran of the Great War, remembered meeting his future wife at the May Fair when they watched a Charlie Chaplin film together. They were married for 60 years.

Bishop's Castle – market centre

Bishop's Castle was very important as a market centre. Farmers came in from the surrounding districts to sell their sheep and cattle, pigs and horses, often driving them in from considerable distances. They would stable their horses and traps at the local hostelries, while their wives would take their eggs and butter and poultry to sell at stalls in the Town Hall or the old Market Hall in Market Square. Even now the oldest residents remember coming with their grandparents to sell their wares, especially at Christmas, to the Dead Market with dressed turkeys and chickens. Two postcard images survive of iron-mongers' shops (Davies and Greenhous) both obviously flourishing two doors away from each other, showing the hardware needed locally – buckets, butter-making equipment, tools, bicycles etc. There were dressmakers and milliners, and it was possible to buy hand-made boots and shoes at Cookes in Market Square.

Many people had memories of the town crier going round the town on foot: 'a vener-able old man with a white beard and a bowler hat; with his bell and his "Oyez, Oyez" he announced sales, entertainments and lost property' (Miss Molly Puckle). Mrs Lucy Hemmings and Mrs Ivy Evans (1920-2015) remembered later town criers letting everyone know when the water or electricity would be turned off.

Printers and Photographers

The role of the printers had always been very important from the time of the notorious parliamentary elections, producing printed announcements, bills and lampoons by the contesting parties. Christopher Hughes was a printer at 18 Market Square in 1881 and produced the short-lived news-sheet, *The Pepperbox*. After his death in 1895 his widow Annie kept the business of 'printer and stationer' going until 1911. Between 1910 and 1915 several editions of *Picturesque Views of Bishop's Castle* were issued, many of which appeared also as postcards. Later, a succession of other printers – Moretons, Oldburys and Spracklens – occupied the same premises. Mr Marston remembered that Oldburys 'printed all the ballot papers, all the rate papers, all the auction things ... they printed the parish magazine, electioneering papers, all the tickets – everything'.

The development of photography, and eventually access to affordable camera equipment, enabled ordinary people to be shown taking part in historical events and the depiction of

Fig. 13.3 Mr W.T. Spracklen, printer and stationer, Market Square, with his son Lewin, c.1925.

Fig. 13.4 Shropshire Imperial Yeomanry in Walcot Park, 1912. (Photo. Madge Strawson)

Fig. 13.5 Memorial Service Procession, 20 May 1910, on the death of King Edward VII.
(Photo. Madge Strawson)

everyday life. Postcards and the penny post allowed everyone to keep in touch with friends and family, and to express their impressions of a visit or an event. Sir Benjamin Stone was one of the first to take pictures of Bishop's Castle as part of his scheme to record all the towns of Britain at the time of Queen Victoria's Diamond Jubilee. At least four of the images he took of Bishop's Castle in 1897 are held at Birmingham Public Library.

Several Bishop's Castle photographers have been identified: W.L. Foster, 'Artist & Photographer' (1891 Census), S.C. de Medewe (1871-1902) and Tom Jones. Some had studios and took portraits of the mayors and other notables of the time. Mr George Strawson and his daughter Madge had the advantage of his chemist's shop and facilities for developing photographs. Even before the First World War, they were taking pictures of the Shropshire Yeomanry camped at Walcot Park near Lydbury North, and Madge Strawson went on to photograph regiments in training on the Long Mynd and as far away as Rhyl. She took a huge series of pictures of the 1911 coronation of George V, and printed many postcards of Bishop's Castle streets and shops and local scenes.

In the early 1900s Emmanuel Beddoes (1882-1961), a local undertaker and carpenter, captured on glass plates the likeness of many of his neighbours, as well as pictures of local workmen. He is recalled as 'having his head under a black thing ... a bit frightening to a child'. Miss Isabella Bremner's selection of 'Bishop's Castle Celebrities 1902' has already been mentioned.

Childhood memories of the early 20th century include Sunday School outings, and the 'wimberry picking' (gathering bilberries on local moorland). As well as the chance of a day out with their mothers, families depended on the sale of the wimberries to local dealers (sent to Lancashire for dye in the cotton industry) to be able to afford boots for the winter.

Fig. 13.6 Wimberry picking at Driboeth-wen, near Mainstone in the 1930s.
Left to right: Mrs Ethel Jones (Acton), unknown, Mrs Close, Mrs Nicholls, unknown
and Mrs Cooke. A Cooke's Garage car took the pickers up the hill. Children would walk all the
way up after school to join their mothers, though some remember riding on the running board on
each side of Mr Cooke's car – and he would tie them on with a rope!
(Photograph from S.W.S.H.A.S. Collection)

The collective memory is strong, even nowadays, of their favourite places – Rhadley Hill, the Long Mynd or near Mainstone. Time off for wimberry picking is frequently mentioned in the school log books.

Bishop's Castle – parole town

Occasionally glimpses of the personalities and events of Bishop's Castle's distant past history come to light. During the Napoleonic War between 57 and 80 French prisoners on parole appear to have been billeted in the town.[2] The parish register records at least 11 births, deaths and marriages relating to French prisoners of war in Bishop's Castle. In an issue of *Bye-Gones* in February 1901, Thomas Caswall remembered talking to an old man named Meredith, born in Bishop's Castle in 1805. Meredith recalled that at the age of 10 he had been an odd-job boy at the Six Bells. 'At this time there were a number of French prisoners of war on parole in the town, nine of whom were quartered at The Bells. They cooked their own food and I waited upon them ... They were allowed to walk out by themselves the distance of a mile on either of the principal roads, on each of which a post painted white was put up to mark the distance: if found exceeding the proscribed limit, they were arrested. There was an officer with a few English soldiers quartered in the town who kept an eye on them. They were not short of money, and they behaved very well to me for waiting upon them.'

More recent local memories refer to the road from the Kennels Bank towards the Lea as 'The Frenchman's Mile'. There are various known inscriptions connected with their stay in houses in the town, as well as the well known grave of Louis 'Paces' (now confirmed as Pagès) – 'Lieut Colonel de chevaux legers, chevalier des orders militaires des deux Siciles et de l'Espagne, mort a Bishop's Castle le 1 mai 1814, age de 40 ans'. It has recently been discovered that Louis Pagès was born at Revel, in the south of France, descended from Huguenot stocking makers and was a Protestant. He was captured at the battle of Vittoria (21st June 1813) and had served in the Garde Royale under Joseph Bonaparte, King of Spain and Napoleon's brother.[3]

In 2013 an enquiry to the Six Bells, where another parole prisoner Joseph-Louis Hetet had stayed, came from a family in New Zealand. He had married Mary Morgan, a shopkeeper's daughter; they had a son Louis, who later joined his father in France. Louis had an adventurous life and eventually

Fig. 13.7 Robert and Awhina Hetet from New Zealand visiting the grave of the mother of their ancestor Louis Hetet, born in Bishop's Castle, the son of a Napoleonic parole prisoner. (Photograph [October 2015] by Trevor Chalkley, © Shropshire Star)

landed from a whaling ship in a Maori area of New Zealand, acted as a conciliator between the Maoris and the British government, and married the daughter of a tribal chief. His descendants, John and Sybille Hetet visited Mary Morgan's grave in 2013 and were able to fill in details of his later life. When they posted details on the internet, another descendant of Louis Hetet and Mary Morgan, Robert Hetet and his daughter Awhina decided to visit Bishop's Castle in 2015. They were shown the milestone on 'the Frenchman's Mile' and were deeply moved to see Mary Morgan's grave: 'relict of the late Louis Hetet'. Robert addressed a Maori acknowledgement to his ancestor, giving thanks to the people of Bishop's Castle for preserving and respecting her grave. He presented a carved 'wahorara' depicting his Hetet ancestry to the Heritage Centre and a plaque to the Church. For those who had researched the evidence of the Napoleonic prisoners some years before, it was a thrilling moment to experience the rest of the story.

Bishop's Castle at war

The First World War, 1914-18, had a profound effect on every community. The citizens of Bishop's Castle did their bit in providing for the troops. The Infants School log books record contributions sent 'for soldiers at the Front'. On 'Dec. 3rd 1915 Fruit and vegetables again brought for the Fleet' and on 'Dec. 9th The Mistress received a letter from HMS *Ben Strome* thanking the children for their gifts of fruit and vegetables'.

Parcels were also sent by people of the town to the troops, and Mr E.C. Davies, iron-monger and mayor of Bishop's Castle, preserved some of their letters of thanks. Miss Gladys Radford, born 1919, was very moved to be shown in 2014 one of these letters, written by her father, Gunner F.J. Radford, Royal Garrison Artillery, in 1917.

Many letters from serving soldiers have survived: a series from Fred Green, of Lydham, a private in the Tank Corps, consists mainly of reassuring letters to his mother, but just one to his father that gives a truer picture of the horrors: 'We have been out of the trenches now about 2 months but we are winding our way up towards the High Wood. I wish this War was over its up to your harse [sic] in muck here wet clothes on day after day and covered with lice. I tell you a fact If they only knew in England what the poor Tommies are going through there would be a stink up ...'[4] Fred was killed in action on the 23rd August 1918. He is commemorated on one of three wooden battlefield crosses in Lydham Church.

Thomas Thornley, son of the Congregational minister, lost both his hands in the war (Fig. 13.8), was awarded the Military Medal and was given a

Fig. 13.8 'This is my own writing with an artificial hand': Thomas Thornley, son of the Bishop's Castle Congregational minister, lost both hands in action in the 1914-18 war. (Photograph from S.W.S.H.A.S. Collection)

hero's welcome on his return to Bishop's Castle after convalescence: 'April 10th 1919 Ex-Private Thomas Thornley, who acted as regimental stretcher-bearer with the 1st Cheshires on the Western Front and was deprived of both arms, gave an interesting demonstration including some remarkable feats of dexterity with his artificial limbs, in the Lecture Hall on Friday.'[5]

In 1987 the memories of Mr Jack Davies were recorded, from his apprenticeship with a Bishop's Castle shoemaker to his service in the Great War. By the time he was awarded the Légion d'Honneur by the French he was 102 – the recording confirmed the details of his training and war-record. He was buried at Edgton at the age of 104 in sight of his old home, the Last Post being sounded by a bugler from the Light Infantry.

Those who were children in 1938 still have vivid memories of the arrival of an unexpected visitor from abroad. Haile Selassie, Emperor of Abyssinia, having been exiled from his country when it was invaded by Mussolini, came with his entourage to stay at Walcot Hall near Lydbury North with the Stephens brothers. He paid a visit to Linley Hall, where one of the parlour maids remembered that her employer practised her curtsey beforehand, and the royal standard had to be rushed back to Walcot for the emperor's return. He was also welcomed at Bishop's Castle Town Hall.

Fig. 13.9 Haile Selassie, Emperor of Abyssinia, with his daughter and Foreign Minister, arriving at Craven Arms Station – welcomed by Ronald and Noel Stevens from Walcot Hall, 1938. (Photograph from Mrs A.Humphries)

At the outbreak of the Second World War the young men of Bishop's Castle were again called to serve. In 1993 the Higgins brothers, Cuthbert and Roly, recorded some of their army experiences. Cuthbert joined up before the war and became a P.T. Instructor. He was made up to corporal immediately because he was experienced in drill, having been in the Bishop's Castle Church Lads Brigade. In 1940 he was sent to join the British Expeditionary Force in France, and was caught in the retreat to Dunkirk: 'I was in charge of a detail to fill up spaces in the BEF, and halfway to the destination we met them coming back, so we had to turn round and come back too. I was on the beach for a couple of days, and I got wounded in the leg. It was a funny situation – you didn't know where to go or what to do, and you were in and out of the water, in and out of the water. I think more men got hurt by being pushed off by boathooks – they were trying to get in and tipping the boats – you see only little mini-boats could get in. There were too many trying to get on them, so they were pushing them off with boathooks. But eventually we got organised into columns, 20 or 30 or whatever, and away we went.'

Roly joined up when he was 18, and both brothers went to France a few days after D-Day in June 1944. Roly drove a tank with the Royal Armoured Corps, and Cuthbert was a lorry driver with the Royal Army Service Corps. Both saw action in Normandy, at Arnhem, on the Rhine and in the Teutoberg Forest. Both were at Lüneburg Heath when the Germans surrendered. Cuthbert recalled: 'I was on guard when the Peace was being signed. I saw old 'Doughnuts' [Grand Admiral Dönitz] going in the tent ... I know we got drunk. There was a rum issue!' Roly added: 'We were actually surrounding the building they were collecting in; there were some of the bigger notches there – we rounded all those up!' At the end of the war Cuthbert was demobbed and returned to Aldershot, while Roly was sent to Palestine in an armoured car unit. He did not get home until 1946.

Fig. 13.10 This unique photograph comes from a ten-second piece of cine-film taken by Mr Erskine Roberts, landlord of The Three Tuns in the 1930s. It confirms many childhood memories of seeing an elephant stabled outside the Castle Hotel, left behind by a circus at the outbreak of the Second World War. Mr George Evans (b.1930) remembered as a boy seeing it being taken for walks. Some schoolboys gave it a swede, and it stepped on it to make it easier to eat!

Bishop's Castle had men serving in all three services. The War Memorial in the churchyard records the names of those who did not return – 33 in the First World War and eleven in the Second World War.

On the Home Front reminiscences have been collected from Land Girls, evacuees from Liverpool and London, and German prisoners-of-war who married and settled in the area. Mrs Maura Gough (*née* Cunningham) joined the Women's Land Army and was attached to the Women's Timber Corps, engaged in felling timber on estates such as Linley Hall: 'The town of Bishop's Castle buzzed with busy-ness and there were crowds of soldiers. The roadsides, just over the hedges, were lined with neatly-piled boxes of ammunition covered with shelters of corregated iron. I had a weekly bath at the Three Tuns, Mrs Erskine Roberts charged sixpence for the luxury, and the proceeds went to a Forces fund – we were requested to use no more than four inches of water! The bathroom was warm too, because of the brewing – I had never been in a warm bathroom before!'

When the 1939-45 War ended, the returning servicemen and women took part in a celebratory concert in the Church Room near the Six Bells, and an enterprising band of them went on to found 'The Legionaires', a concert party who entertained crowds of people in Bishop's Castle and surrounding villages for many years. Judging by the photographs, their appearances at the Carnivals (particularly with a home-made life-sized camel at the

Fig. 13.11 The Legionaires, Bishop's Castle Carnival, 1957.
Left to right: (back row) Maxie Weaver, Dot Higgins, Harold Jones, Kath Weaver,
Aubrey Higgs, Tom Woolley and Sid Morris;
(front row) Norman Gwilliam, Rosemary Higgs, Mary Lloyd, Roly Higgins and Ted Powell;
(inside the camel) Doug Williams and Vic Lloyd. (Photograph from S.W.S.H.A.S. Collection)

time of the Suez crisis) were sensational, and those who took part still have many happy memories.

It is salutary to remember that Bishop's Castle played a part in the general anxiety and defence precautions during the time of the stand-off between the Western Allies and Russia, known as 'the Cold War'. In the 1950s a Royal Observer Corps group was formed locally to watch for enemy aircraft and report to Shrewsbury. Colin Millichope joined in 1959: 'The Observer Post we reported from was at Lydbury North – there was a bit above ground for the aircraft recognition, but also an underground post for the nuclear monitoring. There was a gadget above ground which would record a nuclear burst, and there was a pressure-meter which recorded the intensity of the blast, and some kind of monitoring equipment to read the radiation – the fall-out from the blast ... They were tense times, it's easily forgotten. Literally, you went to bed at night seeing the newsreel of Mr Krushchev thumping the desk with his shoe. Were we going to be here in the morning? It was as bad as that.'

Conclusion: 'They prided in what they did'

For those engaged in local history research in the Bishop's Castle area, it has been a privilege to meet so many men and women prepared to share their recollections and treasured photographs and memorabilia. Their detailed reminiscences have helped to convey the experience of living through local and national events, dealing with hardships and emphasizing the aspects and feelings of a strong, close knit, hardworking community, growing up with family and friends, making their own entertainment. Memories such as these evoke a different world, but one which has strengthened and invigorated the identity of this isolated little town.

As Mr Sid Cadwallader (1908-99), son of Tom Cadwallader, guard on the railway, said about the railwaymen 'They always seemed a very happy gang – they prided in what they did'. That seems to capture the spirit of Bishop's Castle then and now.

Bibliography and further reading
D. Beattie, *South Shropshire's First World War* (Logaston Press, 2014)
Shropshire Folk-Lore, ed. C. Burne (1883; repr. EP Publishing Ltd. 1973)
G. Jackson, *A Shropshire Word-Book* (1879; repr. Candle Lane Books, 1982)
The Gale of Life – Two Thousand years in South-West Shropshire, ed. J. Leonard *et al.*
     (S.W.S.H.A.S. and Logaston Press, 2000)
J. Preshous, *Bishop's Castle Well-Remembered: Memories and photographs of a small
     Shropshire market town* (1990; reprinted 1995)

Francis Abell, *Prisoners of War in Great Britain 1756–1814* (Oxford Univ. Press, 1914)
Ronald Blythe, *Akenfield* (Penguin, 1979)
George Ewart Evans, *Spoken History* (Faber & Faber, 1987)
Robin Hill and Paul Stamper, *The Working Countryside 1982-1945* (Swan Hill Press, 1993)
Charles Kightly, *Country Voices: life and lore in farm and village* (Thames & Hudson, 1984)

Two early postcard photographs of Church Street / High Street, Bishop's Castle –
Dora Skillett's 'Streets unpleasant in all weather'!

Not Everyone Loves Us!

Description of Bishop's Castle, Shropshire

Hovels, barns and pigsties mixed together,
Streets unpleasant in all weather.
Gates and stiles, hedges and ditches,
Idle men with hardly any breeches.
Gaudy things enough to tempt you,
Showy outsides, insides empty.
A new Church with an old steeple,
A cursing Parson and drunken people.
Bubbles trades but few mechanic arts,
Coaches, wheelbarrows and carts.
Warrants, bailiffs, bills unpaid,
Ladies of laundresses afraid.
A Rogue that made himself very handy,
That cocked the trigger & killed poor brandy.
Women that often fight with men,
Coachmen, Footmen and two idle Policemen.
Lawyers, Doctors but no Physicians,
Noble and simple in all conditions.
Women brown, red, fair, and gray,
Prudes and such as never pray.
Few handsome, lots ugly, noisy and still
Some that will not and some that will,
Saucy, fat, coarse, and dirty,
Women divorced before they're thirty.
Few good but hundreds bad,
Some joyful and many sad.
Grocers, Drapers, Butchers, Bakers,
Undertakers and mischief makers.
Many a Plain Girl that calls herself pretty,
Many a Fool that thinks himself witty,
Many a Woman not unwilling,
Many a Fop without a shilling.
Many a seeming bargain if you strike it,
This is Bishop's Castle, and I don't like it.

Dora Skillett, *née* Evans, of Plowden, *c.*1860

Fig. 14.1 Bishop's Castle, looking south from above Field Cottage.
(Photo. D. Preshous)

Fig. 14.2 Town Band procession, Remembrance Day, 2011, Paula Middleton leading.
(Photo. D. Preshous)

14   'A Nice Place To Be'

Fortunately, Dora Skillet's extremely dyspeptic view of Bishop's Castle (see page 141) is not widely shared today!

In the early 1900s a short and informative *History of Bishop's Castle* was published by Edward Griffiths, and in 1986 Bishop's Castle Chamber of Trade, wishing to update it, commissioned a *Town Guide*. It was written by one of their members, Maurice Cheesewright, and provided an excellent short account of the history and development of the town. The concluding chapter ended with the author's personal assessment of the town: 'All in all, a nice place to be!' Thirty years later most residents and visitors would endorse that opinion.

Travel writers have given the town a mixed reception. A.G. Bradley[1] described it as 'of no high distinction, either historically or architecturally'. John Betjeman[2] thought that 'it looks like an inland Cornish town such as Helston'. H.T. Timmins[3] waxed lyrical: 'A place, half town, half village … a drowsy little market town, yet proud withal of being the metropolis of an extensive agricultural district, renowned for its great cattle fair, frequented by breeders and "men whose talk is of bullocks".'

Bishop's Castle can make some unusual claims for a small, rural town: its population (1,893 in the 2011 Census) has not greatly increased over hundreds of years; it has retained at its centre the physical shape of the original planted town; and it continues to function as a thriving service centre for a remote and sparsely populated rural area.

The 20th century confronted the countryside with massive challenges – greater mobility and widening horizons, revolutions in agriculture, the impact of two world wars, increasing centralization of government and life-changing developments in every branch of technology. How has Bishop's Castle fared in these times of change?

In 1962 the town lost its municipal borough status (having previously enjoyed being described as the smallest borough in England) and became part of Clun and Bishop's Castle Rural District. Later still it became a component of South Shropshire District before that too was swallowed up by Shropshire Council. Yet its citizens still firmly and proudly correct visitors who refer to it as a 'village'. The mayor and council still meet to debate local issues, and recently the Town Hall was refurbished and modernized. That has enabled the building to retain its council chamber, while extending its use as a centre for a variety of functions and as the town's Tourist Information Centre.

The town council today comprises 12 councillors – elected or co-opted – a voluntary role and one that is undertaken in spare time; for many in addition to a full-time job. Each year in May the council elects its chairman from its members. A short Mayor

Making follows, whereby the chairman takes up the mayoralty for the forthcoming year and publicly declares acceptance of the post.

The mayor chairs all council meetings and is an ex-officio member of any special committees or working parties set up for projects to be undertaken by the town council. At the annual council meeting in May a vice-chairman is also elected, and the council schedules its future meetings. The mayor also convenes and presides over the annual Town Meeting, when residents have the chance to ask questions and put forward suggestions for the town.

Those who have lived a long lifetime in Bishop's Castle will have seen significant fluctuations in the town's fortunes. Many will remember the rather depressed appearance of the streets in the 1950s, before several of the properties were saved from destruction and carefully and sensitively renovated. Today the streets make a pleasing picture, with attractive shop fronts and well maintained houses, some painted with eye-catching designs and colours. In 1973 the 400th anniversary of Queen Elizabeth I's charter was an occasion when the townsfolk celebrated the town's identity – a time of civic pride coupled with a real sense of rejuvenation.

Big changes have taken place since 1900. A new Methodist Church was built in 1904, while other chapels closed, the most intriguing history being that of the Wesleyan Chapel in High Street, which went through adaptation to a cinema (the Plaza), a clothing factory (Walters) and then an office unit. In 1922 a new secondary school, the County High

Fig. 14.3 View up Church Street from the church tower.
(Photo. D. Preshous)

144

School, was opened (the county's first co-educational secondary school). It later became Shropshire's first comprehensive, and finally, in 1987, its first rural community college. A new primary school was opened in Oak Meadow in 1975. In 1965 the Clun Union workhouse was demolished and replaced by Stone House Residential Home and Hospital, a unique combined facility.

Many shops which had been kept by individual families for generations have closed or been taken over for new functions under new management. Strikingly, the streets are now lined with motor vehicles, where, even 50 years ago, one could have looked up and down High Street and seen only pedestrians and the occasional car.

There have been threats to the facilities of the town – in the 1980s the High School successfully fought off attempts to reduce its status, and, in so doing, was redesignated as the Community College, with increased public use of its premises and facilities. There were at the same time threats to the future of the Stone House (by then a Community Hospital and Coverage Care Residential Home). Those dangers too were averted.

In 1996 the town won a £1m Rural Challenge bid, which led to the establishment of Enterprise House – an Information Technology Centre which today, as Enterprise South-West, offers computer and other technical facilities, a conference suite, an equipment hiring service (Village Outreach) and a home to the town's branch library.

Stone House, the hospital and residential home, was again faced with closure in 1995 but saved by a vigorous campaign: *'Don't Take the Heart out of Bishop's Castle!'* Still today, as governments and councils seek to make drastic economies, the community remains constantly on the alert to find ways of fending off the potential downgrading or loss of business, sport and leisure facilities at Enterprise House, the library and the SpArC (Sports and Arts in the Community) complex at the college.

This is an age of rapid change and fluctuating fortunes, and this assessment of the town's existing services and facilities must inevitably be qualified by the words 'at the time of writing'. Nevertheless, as this book goes to publication, the town is buoyant and can offer its residents a remarkable quality of life. Maurice Cheesewright described it as 'workaday, friendly, relaxed and classless', adjectives which can still be comfortably applied to the community.

Consider the services the town still sustains – a mayor and town council, police and fire services, livestock and farmers' markets, a bank, a post office, solicitors, accountants, builders, plumbers and electricians, an IT centre, library, Heritage Resource Centre, two museums (the House on Crutches and the Bishop's Castle Railway and Transport Museum), SpArC leisure centre (swimming-pool, fitness centre, squash courts, sports hall and all-weather sports pitch, and a handsome theatre or lecture hall), garages, motor and cycle services, filling stations, bus services (including a Dial-a-Ride service), several function rooms and cafés, bed and breakfast accommodation, six thriving public houses or hotels, two breweries, a fish and chip shop, and Indian and Chinese cuisine.

There is an industrial estate with a large thriving timber business, an egg-packing station and units housing an agricultural and horticultural machinery firm, building services, and other light industry. In or close to the town, there are businesses offering home and garden services, cycle sales and servicing, cycle building, pest control, publicity, architectural services, camping and caravanning, yurt building, motor engineering, printing and publishing, and musical instrument making. Other small concerns are housed on private premises, some conducting their business entirely on-line.

The educational, medical and spiritual needs of the community are well provided with a pre-school play group, secondary and primary schools, medical and dental practices, a pharmacy, alternative medicine practices, Anglican and Methodist churches and a Quaker meeting, a community hospital, an Abbeyfield House, residential homes (caring for the elderly and adults with learning difficulties) and a funeral service.

A wide range of commodities is still offered in the town's shops and services: three small supermarkets with off-licences, hair-dressing salons, a butcher, a baker, a pet shop, a veterinary surgery, a florist and a delicatessen; others sell textiles, clothing and footwear, televisions and electrical goods, books, CDs and records, gifts, and antiques and 'collectables'. There are charity shops, a regular farmers' market, and food and flea markets in the Town Hall.

The uninitiated town dweller may suggest that there's 'not much to do in the country', especially in winter. But Bishop's Castle can offer a wide range of activities. Most major sports are strongly represented – rugby, soccer, cricket, tennis, hockey, badminton, squash, swimming, snooker and bowls, as well as keep-fit facilities. There is a recreation ground with a children's play area. The United Pack of hounds still meets, there is a race-horse training stable, and trout and coarse fishing can be enjoyed nearby. Walking and cycling are major attractions – this is an 'Area of Outstanding Natural Beauty'. The Shropshire hills are crossed by many well defined routes to suit all abilities and the town is on a National Cycle Route.

The town maintains a civic society, film society, drama group (Castle Players), Historical and Archaeological Society (S.W.S.H.A.S.), art societies, a Poets' Corner (where poetry enthusiasts meet over dinner), a creative writers' group, a philatelic society, bell ringers, two morris dancing teams (Shropshire Bedlams and Martha Rhoden's Tuppenny Dish, launched by the distinguished folk musician John Kirkpatrick), a community choir, classical musicians, an orchestra and a jazz orchestra, rock and pop bands, youth clubs, Young Farmers, a Tai Chi group, and the SpArC theatre offering live shows, regular screening of films, and direct transmissions from the Globe Theatre, the Royal Shakespeare Company,

---

Literary Allusions

Bishop's Castle features as 'Mallard's Keep' in two novels by Mary Webb (1881-1927). In *Seven For A Secret* (1922) she describes a journey from 'the Junction' (Craven Arms) to 'the Keep' (Bishop's Castle) on the celebrated Bishop's Castle Railway.

Nina Bawden (1925-2012) was evacuated to South Wales in World War II and also spent some time at Owlbury Hall, Snead. Her memories of evacuation inspired her best-known children's book *Carrie's War*, with a Welsh setting; but she also wrote *Off the Road* (1998), which is centred at Owlbury Hall Farm, near Bishop's Castle.

Bishop's Castle is on the edge of the country described by Malcolm Saville in his 'Lone Pine' adventures, set mostly in the Long Mynd and Stiperstones area.

the National Theatre, and the Royal Ballet and Opera House. In 2002 Bishop's Castle established a successful twinning arrangement with Saint-Marcel (Eure) in Upper Normandy.

Bishop's Castle is fortunate to have a number of good places to hold social events: the Community College assembly hall, Fletcher and Easthaugh Community Rooms, the Community Hall in Station Street, the top room at the Three Tuns Inn, the Methodist Church hall, the Town Hall, the Church Barn and the SpArC theatre.

Perhaps the most significant development in the life of the town has been the realization of its potential as a centre for outdoor activity and tourism. The words 'remote' and 'sparsely populated' are still applied to south-west Shropshire, and its beautiful and unspoilt hill country has become increasingly popular, in particular with cyclists and walkers. There is a flourishing Walking Group which has a weekly programme with walks of varying length, and a Walking for Health Group, which offers shorter outings. In May there is the Bishop's Castle Walking Festival with an extensive and varied programme of guided walks and associated activities.

Bishop's Castle's main artery, High Street running down to Church Street, provides – despite its steep gradient – an excellent setting for parades and processions throughout the year, and there is a rich programme of events and festivals: Arts Festival, Real Ale Festival, Midsummer Rejoicing and Rush-bearing Procession, Carnival, Party in the Park Music Festival, Tandem Triathlon, Michaelmas Fair and Christmas Lights. The town council and the Town Band also parade to church on Mayor's Sunday and Remembrance Day.

Fig. 14.4 Rushbearing procession, Midsummer Rejoicing, 2008.
(Photo. D. Preshous)

A number of support groups active in the town include the Bishop's Castle and District Community Land Trust, the Community Energy Group, the Wasteless Society and Climate Change Group, the Castle Land Trust, the Just Credit Union, Friends of Bishop's Castle Library and the Friends of Bishop's Castle Community, Care Home, and Community Hospital. Christian Aid, Rural Support Network and Amnesty International are also actively supported, as is the nearby Clun food bank. In 2014 work began on a new Bishop's Castle Community-led Town Plan. Consultations have focused on a number of issues – Parking and Traffic Solutions; Affordable Housing; Job Opportunities and Business Development; Townscape; Community Services; and Economic Sustainability. It is hoped that the plan will set the direction for the town's future development.

Fig. 14.5 Steam engine in New Street, Michaelmas Fair, 2012.
(Photo. D. Preshous)

The town lies at the heart of a deeply rural area, and has for centuries reflected the varying fortunes of the agricultural industry. Forty years ago, the majority of High School pupils were destined, on leaving school, to follow careers in agriculture or allied industries. Mechanization has greatly reduced the number of people working on the land, and farming has struggled with overseas competition, price wars, and new and constricting regulations. South-West Shropshire remains an area of low wages, and many small farms and businesses have disappeared. The sale of the large Garnett-Botfield estate between 1919 and 1921 brought big changes to the pattern of landownership in a wide area around the town.

Sir Albert Howard, Agricultural Pioneer

Albert Howard was born at the Cottage Farm, Colebatch, in 1873, and baptized in St John the Baptist's parish church, Bishop's Castle. He was educated at Wellington (later Wrekin) College and St John's College, Cambridge. His life was devoted to the study of agricultural methods in Britain, the West Indies and India, and in 1914 he was made of a Companion of the Order of the Indian Empire. He supported traditional methods of agriculture and made special study of the care of the soil, earning him the unofficial title 'father of composting'. His publications included *Agricultural Testament* (1940) and *Soil and Health* (1944). He was knighted in 1940 and died in 1947.

The annual Bishop's Castle Agricultural Show, a major event in the calendar, achieved its centenary in 1991, but subsequently had to be discontinued, largely because of the constraints placed upon the movement of livestock following outbreaks of such diseases as foot and mouth. Happily, the livestock market held in the auction yard off Station Street, which was at one time expected to close, has been saved, thanks to vigorous campaigning. Farmers continue to respond positively to the demands made of them.

Many young people have been compelled to look for employment further afield. Although there are still regular bus services to major centres, mobility is restricted for those who do not have their own vehicles.

Coincident with these rural difficulties, there has been, nationally, a population move to the country – by city dwellers looking for second homes or holiday cottages, or wanting to retire to rural locations. Bishop's Castle has welcomed incomers (people 'From Off'!), who have brought new vigour and initiative to the community. Happily, so far there is a healthy balance between old and new.

Although the town has remained small and compact, new housing has been provided: council houses before and after the Second World War and more recent distinctive eco-friendly developments at Bells Court and the Wintles. With small modern estates on the edges of the town, and attractive properties in the main streets, Bishop's Castle offers a

Fig. 14.6 Aerial view over the town from the south.
The church is at the bottom of the photograph. The industrial area bottom right includes the timber yard occupying the former railway station site. On the left, Stone House and the Recreation Ground can be seen. Top centre is the castle site amid trees, and the Wintles recent development is top left (Photo.© Shropshire Council)

decent range of accommodation, although it reflects the national problem of a shortage of affordable properties for first-time buyers and affordable rented properties for those on low incomes.

All these factors suggest a healthy and stimulating environment, but more important are the less easily quantifiable components of 'quality of life'. There is much unanimity among residents and visitors that Bishop's Castle is not only a visually attractive town but a vigorous and friendly community.

As in every community, the role of volunteers is vital in sustaining a wide range of activities and services. Bishop's Castle is fortunate to have a strong, united body of long-term residents as well as many newcomers willing to give their time and talents. Their efforts are warmly appreciated, and in 2015 the mayor instituted the presentation of Civic Awards to recognize the contribution made to community life by voluntary groups and individuals.

For centuries Bishop's Castle had the unsettled history of a border town, and, later, a colourful and chequered career as a parliamentary borough. Its historical significance has inevitably faded, but it has retained its role as a vital centre, serving a wide and remote rural area. More importantly it has preserved its distinctive and positive character, perhaps a little quirky but essentially good-humoured, lively and sociable. It is indeed –

'A Nice Place to Be'.

Fig. 14.7 Bamber Hawes leading the elephant he designed and made for the Michaelmas Fair, 2015. (Photo: D. Preshous)

References & Notes

Chapter 3

1. *Domesday Book: Shropshire*, ed. F. and C. Thorne (Phillimore & Co. Ltd, 1986).
2. Gildas, *On the Ruin of Britain* at http://www.gutenberg.org/ebooks/1949.
3. Bede, *A Hist. of the English Church and People*, ed. L. Sherley-Price (Penguin Classics, 1962).
4. J. Keeling, 'What makes the British?' (2013) at http://www.oxfordtoday.ox.ac.uk/features/what-makes-british#.
5. S. Williams, 'Dig uncovers Wales' first Saxon "palace" ' at http://www.walesonline.co.uk/news/wales-news/dig-uncovers-wales-first-saxon-1902665; and http://ansax.com/gaer-farm-saxon-palace-wales/.
6. *Domesday Bk.: Shropshire*, ed. Thorne.
7. A.T. Bannister, *The Cathedral Church of Hereford: its history and constitution* (S.P.C.K., 1924).
8. 'What is Anglo Saxon Britain?' at http://www.discovershropshire.org.uk/html/search/verb/GetRecord/theme:20061024112010.
9. P. Kessler and E. Dawson, 'The Mercian Tribal Hidage' (2008) at www.historyfiles.co.uk/FeaturesBritain/EnglandMerciaHidage01.htm.
10. Bannister, *Cathedral Church of Hereford*.
11. H.P.R. Finberg, *Early Charters of the West Midlands* (Leicester Univ. Press, 1961).
12. Ibid.
13. Nick Clark at http://www.independent.co.uk/news/science/archaeology/watlington-hoard-reveals-alfred-the-greats-stalin-style-airbrushing-of-history-a67687.html.
14. F.M. Stenton, *Anglo-Saxon England* (1947).
15. S. Zaluckyj, *Mercia: The Anglo-Saxon Kingdom of Central England* (Logaston Press, 2001), chap. 6.
16. M. Wood, 'Penda' at www.bbc.co.uk/programmes/b01ngr45#in=collection:p0144xrk.
17. *The Anglo-Saxon Chronicles*, ed. G.N. Garmonsway (Everyman's Libr. 1955).
18. Stenton, op. cit.
19. *Asser's Life of King Alfred*, ed. W.H. Stevenson (Oxford, 1959).
20. 'When was Offa's Dyke built?' (2014) at http://www.medievalists.net/2014/04/20/offas-dyke-built.
21. 'Æthelflæd's achievements' at http://historysheroes.e2bn.org/hero/achievements/4292/print.

22. Rose Lagram-Taylor, 'Earl Roger of Montgomery and the Norman Colonisation of Shropshire c. 1071-1083' (Oxford Univ. M.St. thesis, 2014).
23. *Domesday Bk.: Shropshire*, ed. Thorne.
24. J. Newman and N. Pevsner, *Shropshire* (The Buildings of England, 2011).
25. P. Ottaway, 'Anglo-Saxon Ironwork' (2015) at http://www.pjoarchaeology.co.uk/academic-consultancy/anglosaxon-ironwork.html.

Sources for the maps: *Britain in the Dark Ages: 410 AD-870 AD* (Ordnance Survey, 2nd edn. 1966); H.P.R. Finberg, *Early Charters of the West Midlands* (Leicester Univ. Press, 1961); D. Hill, *An Atlas of Anglo-Saxon England* (Blackwell, 1981); H.M. and J. Taylor, *Anglo-Saxon Architecture* (Cambridge Univ. Press, 1965); and C. Humphery-Smith, *Phillimore Atlas and Index of Parish Registers* (1948). Border decoration for map 3:1 was inspired by St Chad's Gospel (8th century), Lichfield Cathedral, that for map 3:3 by the New Minster, Winchester, charter (966) – Brit. Libr. Cott. MS. Vesp. A. viii.

Chapter 4

1. Which Harold Godwineson had sworn (though perhaps under duress during captivity in Normandy) to respect and promote. William also had papal blessing for his campaign. Cf. D.C. Douglas, *William the Conqueror* (1969), cap. 7 (for Anglo-Norman relations before 1066) and pp.176-7, 187-8; C. Morris, *The Papal Monarchy: The Western Church from 1050 to 1250* (1991), pp.95, 145-6.
2. Above, Chapter 3; R.W. Eyton, *Antiquities of Shropshire*, **11** (1860), pp.194-6.
3. Eyton, op. cit. **11**, pp.197-8, 203; *The Place-Names of Shropshire*, **1** (Eng. Place-Name Soc. **62-63**), p.49; C. Walmsley, 'The Castle of Bishop's Castle', *Jnl. of S.W.S.H.A.S.* No. **4**, p.7.
4. For comparative plans see L. Butler in *The plans and topography of medieval towns in Eng. and Wales*, ed. M.W. Barley (C.B.A. Research Rep. No. **14**, 1976), pp.32, 36, 38; T. Rowley, *The Shropshire Landscape* (1972), Chapter 10.
5. Eyton, op. cit. **11**, pp.196, 198, 203, 208; F.M. Stenton, *The First Century of Eng. Feudalism 1066-1166* (1932), p.206.

6. Eyton, op. cit. **11**, p.197.

7. M. Salter, *The Castles and Moated Mansions of Shropshire* (Folly Publications, 2001), p.49; below, Chapter 5.

8. Cf. F. Lavender, 'The Castle at Bishop's Castle', *T.S.A.S.* **51**, pp.157-9.

9. *Jnl. of S.W.S.H.A.S.* No. **4**, pp.8-11.

10. Eyton, op. cit. **11**, pp.197-8.

11. For the charter see F. Lavender, 'Charters of the Borough of Bishop's Castle', *T.S.A.S.* **53** (1949-50), pp.252-3.

12. For the general point see Sir G. Pollock and F.W. Maitland, *Hist. of Eng. Law*, **1**, pp. 578-9; N. Denholm-Young, *Seignorial Administration in Eng.* (1963), pp.87 sqq.

13. *V.C.H. Salop.* **3**, p.47. The sheriff thereafter had no routine jurisdiction in the bishop's manors (Eyton, op. cit. **11**, p.198), but during vacancies in the see or royal seizures of the episcopal estate it was a different matter.

14. Pollock and Maitland, op. cit. **1**, p.579.

15. R. Bartlett, *Eng. Under the Norman and Angevin Kings 1075-1225* (2000), pp.165-6.

16. *V.C.H. Salop.* **3**, p.21.

17. S. Painter, *The Reign of King John* (1959), pp.238 sqq.; Bartlett, op. cit. p.30; *Oxf. D.N.B.* **7**, pp.674-7. The family faded out in the early 1230s.

18. *Calendar of Charter Rolls*, 1226-1257, p.257; F. Lavender, 'The Castle at Bishop's Castle', *T.S.A.S.* **49**, pp.247-8. For the Savoyard d'Aigueblanche see *Oxf. D.N.B.* **1**, pp.475-8.

19. *Calendar of Charter Rolls*, 1226-1257, p.340.

20. The *quo warranto* inquiries: cf. Eyton op. cit. **11**, pp.200-1.

21. *T.S.A.S.* **53**, pp.253-4, corrected by Eyton, op. cit. **11**, pp.279-80.

22. Rowley, *Shropshire Landscape*, p.178.

23. Eyton, op. cit. **11**, p.197; *T.S.A.S.* **49**, p.247.

24. Eyton, op. cit. **11**, pp.204-5; M. Prestwich, *Plantagenet Eng. 1225-1360* (2005), pp.112, 148-9.

25. *Oxf. D.N.B.* **1**, p.477.

26. Eyton, op. cit. **11**, pp.205-6.

27. Ibid. p.206; cf. https://www.measuringworth.com/ukcompare/relativevalue.php (accessed Apr. 2016).

28. *A Roll of the Household Expenses of Richard de Swinfield, Bishop of Hereford, during part of the years 1289 and 1290*, ed. J. Webb (Camden Soc. 1854-5) summarized in Eyton, op. cit. **11**, p.206.

29. M. McKisack, *The Fourteenth Century, 1307-1399* (1959), pp. 80-91; Eyton, op. cit. **11**, p.213; *Oxf. D.N.B.* **41**, pp.934-6 (esp. p.935).

30. Eyton, op. cit. **11**, p.207.

31. *Charters and Records of Hereford Cathedral*, ed. W.W. Capes (1908), pp.226-8.

32. *Calendar of Patent Rolls*, 1358-1361, pp. 499, 508, 511; *T.S.A.S.* **49**, p.248 (misdating the appointment).

33. *Calendar of Charter Rolls*, 1341-1417, p.349; *V.C.H. Salop.* **4**, p.70.

34. R.R. Davies, *The Revolt of Owain Glyn Dwr* (Oxford Univ. Press, 2001), pp.115-16, 118, 250-1; A.J. Pollard, *John Talbot and the War in France 1427-1453* (2005), pp.8-9.

35. *The Register of Robert Mascall, Bishop of Hereford, A.D. 1404-1416*, ed. J.H. Parry (Cantilupe Soc. 1916), pp. 20-22; *The Shropshire Peace Roll, 1400-1414*, ed. E.G. Kimball (Salop County Council, 1959), pp.72, 91.

36. P. Minton-Beddoes, 'The Murder in Mersh Lane', *Documents Relating to Crime and Punishment in Shropshire From the Records and Research Unit, Local Studies Library, Castle Gates, Shrewsbury* (copy in S.A.).

37. *The Itinerary of John Leland ... 1535-1542*, ed. L. Toulmin Smith (1964 edn.), **3**, p.50; **5**, p.15.

38. *V.C.H. Salop.* **4**, p.130; *T.S.A.S.* **49**, p.246.

39. For this and the next five paragraphs see *Calendar of Patent Rolls*, 1572-1575, pp.14-15; *T.S.A.S.* **53**, pp.255-6; and for Plowden see *Oxf. D.N.B.* **44**, pp.596-7; *Hist. of Parliament, Commons*, 1509-1558; G. de C. Parmiter, *Edmund Plowden: an Elizabethan recusant lawyer* (Catholic Record Soc., monograph **4**, 1987).

40. Cf. below, Chapter 6.

41. B.C.H.R.C., Borough minute book.

Chapter 6

1. *Calendar of Patent Rolls* 1572-1575, pp.14-15, 181, 272; *Dict. Welsh Biography, s.v.* Herbert family, of Montgomery [etc.] at http://yba.llgc.org.uk/en/s-HERB-TRE-0000.html (accessed June 2016); *V.C.H. Salop.* **3**, pp.248, 359. Pembroke later became ld. president of Wales and ld. lieut. of Shropshire. Except where otherwise stated, this chapter is based on the sources listed for further reading.

2. As at Wenlock: *V.C.H. Salop.* **3**, p.247.

3. Cf. A.D.K. Hawkyard, 'The Enfranchisement of Constituencies 1509-1558', *Parliamentary History*, **10** (1991), pp.1-26 (especially p.11,

noting that in the early 16th century it was generally 'assumed' that enfranchisement was 'implicit' in the grant of charters of incorporation not specifying it); E. de Villiers, 'Parliamentary Boroughs Restored by the House of Commons 1621-41', *Eng. Hist. Rev.* **67**, pp.175-202 (especially pp.177-8, 200-1). Manoeuvring between king and Commons 1673-7 resulted in the fossilization of the English and Welsh constituency list until 1832 – except for Grampound's statutory disfranchisement in 1821: B. Kemp, *King and Commons 1660-1832* (1965), pp.11–14.

4. P. Hutton, 'The First Members of Parliament for Bishop's Castle', *Jnl. of S.W.S.H.A.S.* **22**, pp.8-16, gives much useful background and personal information about Jukes and Cole. Lack of parliamentary enfranchisement in the 1573 charter prompted the suggestion ibid. pp.9-10, 12-16, that, coached by Plowden, they gained unauthorized entry to the Commons on 23 Nov. 1584 (like the London skinner Richard Robinson), so creating the parliamentary borough by subterfuge. But the Crown's prerogative power of enfranchising by means other than charters makes the suggestion unnecessary.

5. A.F. Pollard and M. Blatcher, 'Hayward Townshend's Journals', *Bulletin of Inst. of Historical Research*, **12-15**.

6. M. Moran and H. Hand, *A Jacobean 'Market Hall', Bishop's Castle, Shropshire* (S.W.S.H.A.S. and Logaston Press 2009), pp.10-12.

7. The Long Parliament M.P.s were recalled in 1659-60, at first (May 1659) as the Rump, later (Feb. 1660) with the excluded members: G. Davies, *The Early Stuarts 1603-1660* (1963), pp.243 sqq.; A. Woolrych, *Britain in Revolution: 1625-1660* (illustr. reprint edn. 2004), pp.765 sqq. Corbet and Thomas both lived to see the Restoration, but it is not known whether they took part in the events of 1659-60.

8. D. Underdown, *Pride's Purge: Politics in the Puritan Revolution* (1985), pp.210-11, 220; B. Worden, *The Rump Parliament* (1974), pp.23, 391-2; Woolrych, op. cit. pp.427-8.

9. He commanded Bridgnorth castle garrison for three weeks until its surrender to the Parliamentarians in Apr. 1646: J.F.A. Mason, *The Borough of Bridgnorth 1157-1957* (1957), p.25.

10. Cf. Worden, op. cit. pp.30, 389.

11. H.R. Trevor-Roper, 'Oliver Cromwell and his Parliaments', *Essays Presented to Sir Lewis Namier*, ed. R. Pares and A.J.P. Taylor (1956), pp.1-48.

12. *V.C.H. Salop.* **3**, p.112.

13. Moran and Hand, '*Market Hall*', pp.13-14.

14. Pious and Parliamentarian. D.F. Harris, 'The More Children of the *Mayflower* Part III', *The Mayflower Descendant*, **44** (**2**) (1994), pp.113-16, discusses the 'firm, if not radical, puritan sympathies' of Richard's grandfather (d.1643) and namesake.

15. R.J. More represented S. Shropshire as a Liberal 1865-8 and 1885-6 and a Liberal Unionist 1886-1903, but his grandson Jasper (kt.1979) sat for Ludlow division as a Conservative 1960-79.

16. See e.g. *T.S.A.S.* **10**, pp.128-9.

17. The Commons had jurisdiction over such petitions until it was passed to an initially reluctant judiciary by the Parliamentary Elections Act, 1868, 31 & 32 Vic. c. 125: C. O'Leary, *The Elimination of Corrupt Practices in British Elections 1868-1911* (1962), cap. I (pp.27-57). Mr Mark Hutton is thanked for help with this point.

18. The first couple divorced by Act of Parliament without prior sentence in a church court: Sir H. Nicolas, *A Treatise on the Law of Adulterine Bastardy, with a report of the Banbury Case, and of all other cases bearing upon the subject* (London, 1836), pp.118-20; L. Stone, *Road to Divorce: England, 1530-1987* (1995), p.317. The Act 10 Wm. III, c. 23 (Private), bastardized Anne's issue but restored most of her fortune on account of her husband's 'profligacy'. The poet Ric. Savage – championed by Sam. Johnson in his *Life of Mr Richard Savage* (1744) – claimed to be her son by Earl Rivers, which Anne denied and is not now believed: cf. *Boswell's Life of Johnson*, ed. G.B. Hill, revised and enlarged by L.F. Powell, **1** (1934), pp.161-74; R. Holmes, *Dr Johnson & Mr Savage* (1994), pp.57-61 (treating Anne sympathetically).

19. Moran and Hand, '*Market Hall*', p.14.

20. The 'atheist' was John Toland, a deist – but contemporaries regarded deism as proximate to atheism: J. Redwood, *Reason, Ridicule and Religion: The Age of Enlightenment in England 1660-1750* (1996), pp.166, 205. The 'murderers' were Macclesfield who, in drink, had killed a footboy in 1676, and his psychopathic nephew (and eventual heir) Lord Mohun, who appears as an evil character in Thackeray's *Henry Esmond*.

21. *Britain in the First Age of Party, 1680-1750: Essays Presented to Geoffrey Holmes*, ed. C. Jones (1987), pp.30-1.

22. *Avant la lettre*: A. McInnes, *Robert Harley, Puritan Politician* (1970), p.124.

23. Sir L. Namier, *The Structure of Politics at the Accession of Geo. III* (2nd edn. 1961), pp.235-6.

24. To whom Clive was about to make himself acceptable, the by-election out of the way: R. Harvey, *Clive: The Life and Death of a British Emperor* (1999), p.277.

25. *The Visitation Records of Archdeacon Joseph Plymley 1792-1838*, ed. S. Watts, **1** (Shropshire Record Series, **11**, 2010), p.39.

26. Namier's words: *Hist. of Parliament, House of Commons 1754-1790*, **1**, p.362.

27. Solicitor-general 1771-8, attorney-general 1778-80, cr. Ld. Loughborough in 1780 and Earl of Rosslyn in 1801, he was Chief Justice of Common Pleas 1780-93 and Ld. Chancellor 1793-1801.

28. Making it the Great Reform Act, 1832, 2 & 3 Wm. IV, c. 45.

Chapter 7

1. A.G. Bradley, *In the Borderland of Wales, Shropshire, Herefordshire and Monmouth* (Constable, 1911), p.257.

2. R.W. Eyton, *Antiquities of Shropshire*, **11** (1860), pp.194-5; R. Palmer, *Folklore of Shropshire* (Logaston Press, 2004), p.88.

3. S. Chappell and A. Lawrence in *The Gale of Life*, ed. J. Leonard (S.W.S.H.A.S. and Logaston Press, 2000), p.112.

4. M. Prestwich, *Plantagenet Eng. 1225-1360* (2005), pp.216-17.

5. *Charters and Records of Hereford Cathedral*, ed. W.W. Capes (1908), pp.226-9.

6. J. Lawson, 'Later Medieval Piety in the Parish of Bishop's Castle', *T.S.A.S.* **76**, pp.79-80.

7. H.B. Walters, 'Church Bells of Shropshire, III', *T.S.A.S.* 3rd ser. **5**, p.14.

8. A.T. Bannister, *Diocese of Hereford: Institutions A.D. 1539-1900* (1923); *The Visitation Records of Archdeacon Joseph Plymley 1792-1838*, ed. S. Watts, **1** (Shropshire Record Series, **11**), pp.39, 49.

9. *Shropshire Parish Registers, Diocese of Hereford*, **24** (**1**), p.53.

10. Information and research by Malcolm Redgrave.

11. J. Lawson, ' "A Second Solomon" – Walter Stephens, vicar of Bishop's Castle 1576-1629; an anonymous biographical sketch', *Jnl. of S.W.S.H.A.S.* **14**, pp.22-26.

12. In 1974 Mrs Barbara Bradbury from California, visited Bishop's Castle and revealed the chequered career of her ancestor, Nathaniel Eaton. *Oxf. D.N.B.* **17**, pp.609-10; Shropshire Par. Regs. Heref. Dioc. **24** (**1**): Bp.'s Castle, Pt. **1**, p. [ix]; G. Ormerod, *Hist. Co. Palatine of Chester*, ed. T. Helsby (1882), **1**, p.611.

13. B.C.H.R.C., *Richard Mason's Sermons* (1741).

14. D. Grounds, *Son and Servant of Shropshire* (Logaston Press, 2009).

15. *Visitation Records of Archdeacon Plymley 1792-1838*, pp.38-49.

16. They were later pencilled on the parish register endpaper: *Shropshire Parish Registers, Diocese of Hereford*, **24** (**4**), p.435.

17. *Visitation Records of Archdeacon Plymley*, pp.39-40, 49; Grounds, *Son and Servant of Shropshire*, p.93.

18. *T.S.A.S.* 3rd ser. **5**, pp.13-14.

19. *Shropshire Par. Regs., Dioc. of Heref.* **24** (**5**), p.457.

20. Ibid. p.526.

21. E.G. Griffiths, *History of Bishop's Castle* (Hughes, Bp.'s Castle, 1901), p.24.

22. B. Trinder, *A History of Shropshire* (Chichester, 2008).

23. G. Milburn, *Exploring Methodism: Primitive Methodism* (Epworth Press, 2002), p.13.

24. B.C.H.R.C., T. Evans's letter 1864 (NM 2138/239).

25. *1st Rep. Com. to inquire into Municipal Corporations of Eng. and Wales*, H.C. 116, *Appendix* Pt. IV, p.2691 (1835), xxvi.

26. *Sir Stephen Glynne's Church Notes for Shropshire*, ed. D.C. Cox (Shropshire Record Series, **1**, 1997), pp.14-15.

27. *Church and Chapel in Early Victorian Shropshire*, ed. C.D. Field (Shropshire Record Series, **8**, 2004).

28. A. Jenkinson, 'The Building Stones of Bishop's Castle', *Jnl. of S.W.S.H.A.S.* **25**, pp.41-9.

29. *Glynne's Church Notes*, pp.14-15.

30. A. Mee, *The King's England: Shropshire: County of the Western Hills* (Hodder & Stoughton, 1948).

31. The church bells were not the only summoning bells in the town: *c.*1900 the town clerk remembered a Town Hall bell being rung to call burgesses to their Saturday meetings; by then, however, its two bells (Mears, 1860) were used only for the clock. See *T.S.A.S.* 3rd ser. **5**, pp.14-15.

32. Ibid. p.14.
33. J. Leonard, *The Churches of Shropshire and their Treasures* (Logaston Press, 2013), p.289. Cf. D.H.S. Cranage, *An Architectural Account of the Churches of Shropshire*, **1** (1901), pp.378-80; J. Newman and N. Pevsner, *Shropshire* (The Buildings of Eng. 2006), pp.150-1.
34. *Kelly's Dir.* (1909).
35. J. Preshous, *Bishop's Castle Well-Remembered* (Hillman Printers, Frome, 1990).
36. *V.C.H. Shropshire*, **4**, p.210.
37. For this paragraph see *Jnl. of S.W.S.H.A.S.* **21**.

Chapter 8
1. B.S. Trinder, *History of Shropshire* (Phillimore, 1983), cap. XV.
2. J. Bennett, 'On the Buses in Wartime', *Omnibus Magazine*, July 1996. Much detailed information and photographs of Bishop's Castle bus companies were gathered by Charles Klapper who travelled many of the routes. In 1996 John Bennett contributed material to a Michaelmas Fair exhibition '*On the Buses*' organized by the South-West Shropshire Historical and Archaeological Society.
3. For an excellent (illustrated) description of his operations see *Buses and Trams*, ed. C.F. Klapper (Ian Allen, 1949), pp.93-96.
4. S.A., deposited plan 291.

Chapter 9
1. Selwyn Pearce Higgins, a schoolmaster and railway enthusiast, took many pictures of the railway before and during the demolition. He bought *Carlisle's* chimney and brass safety valve cover from the demolition contractors. He was given a receipt at the time signed by Brocklebank. This and all his other railway papers ended up at the National Railway Museum, where they may still be found.

Chapter 10
1. E. Vale, *Shropshire* (1949), p.41
2. M. Moran, *Vernacular Buildings of Shropshire* (Logaston Press, 2003); M. Moran & P. Theobald, *A Tudor Home* (Insight Guide, B.C.H.R.C., 2016).
3. K. Davies, *Artisan Art: Vernacular wall paintings in the Welsh Marches, 1550-1650* (Logaston Press, 2008), pp.157, 162, 172.
4. Moran, *Vernacular Buildings*, pp.339-40.
5. M. Moran and H. Hand, *A Jacobean 'Market Hall' Bishop's Castle, Shropshire* (S.W.S.H.A.S. and Logaston Press, 2009).

6. Ibid. pp.12-13; M.C. Hill, 'A Common Market in the 17th Century', *T.S.A.S.* **57**, pp.17-19; *V.C.H. Salop.* **10**, p.101.
7. S. Lewis, *A Topographical Dictionary of Eng.* **1** (1840), pp.228-9.
8. Ibid.
9. *V.C.H. Salop.* **3**, p.157.
10. *Universal British Dir.* (1791).
11. *The Visitation Records of Archdeacon Joseph Plymley 1792-1838*, ed. S. Watts, **1** (Shropshire Record Series, **11**, 2010), pp.40-1.
12. For this paragraph see *Kelly's Dir. Salop.* (1905), pp.33-5.
13. Ibid. (1937), pp. 36-9; C. Robinson, 'Bishop's Castle Clocks and Clockmakers' (B.C.H.R.C. 'Insight Guide', 2016).
14. Transcripts by Bishop's Castle Historical Research Group (under the direction of Dr Barrie Trinder) in the Group's possession.
15. By Lewis Bayly (d.1631), the Puritan bishop of Bangor. It was a best seller and widely translated for over two centuries.
16. Indentures studied by the late Mrs Ivy Evans, a member of Bp.'s Castle Historical Research Group.
17. Lewis, *Topographical Dictionary*, p.228.
18. *V.C.H. Salop.* **4**, p.230.
19. See above, chapter 9.
20. Cf. B.C.H.R.C. website: lostpubsofbishopscastle.co.uk.
21. See below, chapter 11.
22. Lewis, *Topog. Dict.* p.228.
23. A.H.S. Waters, *Rep. on Water Supplies within the County, with Recommendations* (Salop County Council, 1946), p.11.
24. Gordon Tucker's detailed study of the mills of S.-W. Shropshire (1991).
25. Lewis, *Topog. Dict.* p.229.

Chapter 11
1. *The Visitation Records of Archdeacon Joseph Plymley 1792-1838*, ed. S. Watts, **1** (Shropshire Record Series, **11**, 2010), p.38.
2. J. Colson and R. Ralley, 'Medical Practice, Urban Politics and Patronage: The London "Commonalty" of Physicians and Surgeons of the 1420's', *Eng. Hist. Rev.* **130**, pp.1102-31.
3. A. Chaplin, 'Medical Education in Oxford and Cambridge, 1500-1800', *Proceedings of the Royal Soc. of Medicine*, **12** (*Supplement*, 1919), pp.83-107.
4. R. Moore, *Shropshire Doctors and Quacks* (Amberley, 2001), p.63.

5. S.A., DA 1/100/1.
6. L.G. Matthews, *Antiques of Pharmacy* (Bell, London, 1971).
7. *Shropshire Parish Registers, Diocese of Hereford*, **24** (**7**) (Bp.'s Castle Index), p.725.
8. In S.A.
9. *Visitation of Archdeacon Plymley*, p.41.
10. Pigot, *Salop. Dir.* (1828).
11. N. Culpeper, *The English Physician* (1652); idem, *The Complete Herbal* (1653).
12. Pigot, *Salop. Dir.* (1823, 1828).
13. See tabulated list of chemists, druggists, and pharmacists 1823-2011 in B.C.H.R.C.
14. A spell from Woodbatch, written in the early 20th cent., is a mixture of religious and dog Latin words and phrases: *S.W.S.H.A.S. Jnl.* **6**, p.12.
15. See tabulated list of veterinary surgeons 1841-1917 in B.C.H.R.C.
16. See tabulated list of medical practitioners 1661-1941 in B.C.H.R.C.
17. *Shropshire Parish Registers, Dioc. of Hereford*, **24** (**1**), p.53.
18. B.C.H.R.C., BCB/B/1 (Boro. Min. Bk. 1598-1649).
19. Ibid.
20. B.C.H.R.C., BCB/E/1-2 (Boro. Chamberlains' Acct. Bks. 1727-1737; 1758-1844).
21. Mrs I. Evans, private memoir (via Mrs Janet Preshous).
22. Mrs Belinda Penney, private communication.
23. Private corresp., reproduced with permission. Dr Puckle, having just taken up his first appointment in the town, sent his impressions of it to his fiancée, Annie Bremner, in Edinburgh.
24. Two volumes of Bp.'s Castle Boro. nuisance notices 1886-1902 (in B.C.H.R.C. but destined to become S.A., DA 1/819/1-2).
25. Ibid. notices 1886-94, 19 Nov. 1891.
26. B.C.H.R.C., 30-yr. loan at 3½% p.a. sanctioned by the Public Works Loan Board (Town Chest document destined to become S.A., DA 1/151/3/11).
27. S. Watts, *Shropshire Almshouses* (Logaston Press, 2010).
28. *24th Rep. Com. Char.* H.C. 231, pp.461-5 (1831), xi – in *Charities of the County of Salop.* (Jas. Newman, London, 1839) in S.A., accession 252/1 (qC 37.2).
29. For 39 Eliz. I, c. 3, and 43 Eliz I, c. 2, see W.E. Tate, *The Parish Chest* (3rd edn. 1974), pp.191-2.
30. Over 82% of the parishioners lived in the borough.

31. *Visitation of Archdeacon Plymley*, pp.41, 48.
32. S.A., P 33/L/2/4.
33. Sir F. Morton Eden, *The State of the Poor: or, An History of the Labouring Classes in England ... 2* (London, 1797).
34. B.C.H.R.C., BCB/D/1 (Town Chest docs., Boro. Reg. of Apprentices).
35. S.A., P 33/L/3/1.
36. S.A., P 33/L/1/2.
37. S.A., P 33/L/1/1.
38. *V.C.H. Salop.* **3**, p.170. Campaigners against the 1834 Poor Law included Radicals, who hated its inhumanity, and Tories, who resented the Commission's centralizing power, and the Commissioners were derided as cruel oriental despots – pashas ('Bashaws').
39. *T.S.A.S.* **82**, pp.94-9.
40. Prescription Bk. 1855-99 from Martha Cam Bills's pharmacy, on loan from Alan H. Screen.
41. House on Crutches Museum, Collection OE0318, wedding dress from Stone House Hosp.
42. J. Preshous, *Bishop's Castle Well-Remembered* (privately published, 1990).
43. D.C. Cox, *Shropshire County Council: A Centenary History* (Shropshire County Council, 1989), pp.48-9.
44. S.A. 5461/1.
45. *Kelly's Dir.* (1885).
46. I. Evans, 'The Bishop's Castle & Lydbury North Female Friendly Soc.' *Jnl. of S.W.S.H.A.S.* **1**, pp.19-20.

Chapter 12
1. S. Curtis and M. Boultwood, *An Introductory Hist. of Eng. Education Since 1800* (University Tutorial Press, 1966).
2. F. Lavender, *Hist. of Bishop's Castle* (3rd edn. 1955), p.3.
3. R. Hume, 'Voluntary Education 1660-1833: The Shropshire Evidence', *T.S.A.S.* **74**, p.51.
4. *P.O. Dir.* (1870).
5. *The Visitation Records of Archdeacon Joseph Plymley, 1792-1838*, **1** (Shropshire Record Series, **11**, 2010), p.48.
6. *24th Rep. Com. Char.* H.C. 231, pp.461-3 (1831), xi – in *Charities of the County of Salop.* (Jas. Newman, London, 1839; S.A., accession 252/1, qC 37.2). Cf. *1st Rep. Com. to inquire into Municipal Corporations of Eng. and Wales*, H.C. 116, Appendix Pt. IV, p.2690 (1835), xxvi. Cf. the tabulated list of masters of Wright's Charity (or 'free') School 1828-80 in B.C.H.R.C.

7. Bp.'s Castle Elementary Schools, Wright's Charity. Notice of Scholarships, 28 Sept. 1928.

8. Benefaction table, Bp.'s Castle Primary Sch.

9. Sampler, silk work on linen by Sarah Morris, Sarah Pearson governess, Bp.'s Castle, 1804.

10. See the tabulated list of teachers or proprietors of private schools and academies 1835-79 in B.C.H.R.C.

11. See Chapter 11.

12. B.C.H.R.C., TS. memoir by Mrs Ivy Evans.

13. Earl of Powis to Trustees, Conveyance of a piece of Land and newly erected School therein situate in Bp.'s Castle in the County of Salop for the purposes mentioned, 26 Oct. 1843 (Town Chest papers, uncatalogued document).

14. *Shrews. Chron.* Nov. 1839 – S.A. 1037/92/7.

15. S.A. 552/8/121, Partics. of the Earl of Powis's Bp.'s Castle Survey, 1809 (Stephens & Sayce).

16. M. Daniel, 'The Old Boys School, Bishop's Castle', *Jnl. of S.W.S.H.A.S.* **4**, pp.21-4, citing A.J. Owen's 'Hist. of Bishop's Castle' (TS. in possession of Bishop's Castle Civic Soc.).

17. Census, 1851, *Education. England and Wales. Report and tables.*

18. Elementary Education Act, 1891, 54 & 55 Vic. c. 56.

19. *V.C.H. Salop.* **3**, p.175.

20. This and following refs. are from uncatalogued material in the Town Chest.

21. Uncatalogued material ibid.

22. See the tabulated list of teachers at National and Board schools 1841-1931 in B.C.H.R.C.

23. P. Theobald, *The Bowling Club, Bishop's Castle* (2009; copy in B.C.H.R.C.).

24. Boys Sch. log bk.

25. The Education Act, 1902, 2 Edw. VII, c. 42, s.1, provided that councils of non-county boroughs with over 10,000 inhabitants and of urban districts with over 20,000 should be local education authorities for the purposes of Part III of the Act. Wenlock was one such 1903-12: *V.C.H. Salop.* **10**, p.210.

26. Education Act, 1918, 8 & 9 Geo. V, c. 39.

27. Log bk.; private inf. from Mrs J. Preshous.

28. S.A., ED 441/1.

29. Log bk. 1914-44.

30. Girls County Sch. log bk. 1922-45.

31. Education (Provision of Meals) Act, 1906, 6 Edw. VII, c. 57.

32. 7 & 8 Geo. VI, c. 31.

33. B.C.H.R.C., School Prospectus, 1922 (Community Coll. deposit, uncatalogued material).

34. E. Humphries and K. Baker, 'Hockey Sticks and Bicycles', *The Gale of Life*, ed. J. Leonard *et al.* (Logaston Press, 2000), p.238. Cf. the tabulated list of head teachers of the High School and the Community College in B.C.H.R.C.

35. B.C.H.R.C., Community Coll. deposit, uncatalogued material.

36. S.A., ED 2782/1.

37. B.C.H.R.C., Sykes Foundation Trust Min. Bk. (Community Coll. deposit, uncatalogued material).

38. Ibid. Governors Mins.

39. B.C.H.R.C., Admissions Reg. (Community Coll. deposit, uncatalogued material).

40. *School & Community: Bishop's Castle & District Community College* – copy in S.A. 16561 (S25.5 v.f.).

41. A Research Project for the National Development Centre for School Management Training, Bristol, 1985.

Chapter 13

1. Much material in this chapter is based on digital recordings and transcripts of oral tapes in B.C.H.R.C.

2. The late Richard Rose's unpublished talk to S.W.S.H.A.S., Mar. 2011.

3. Mr and Mrs J. Hetet, New Zealand: research on Hetet and Pagès families.

4. Fred Green's letters are used by permission of Mrs Gwynneth Evans.

5. Mr Alan Brisbourne's cuttings from the *Church Stretton Advertiser*.

Chapter 14

1. A.G. Bradley, *In the March and Borderland of Wales* (1911; reprinted 1994, Lapridge Publications, Hereford).

2. J. Piper and J. Betjeman, *Shropshire: a Shell Guide* (Faber, 1951).

3. H.T. Timmins, *Nooks and Corners of Shropshire* (1899; reprinted 1993, Lapridge Publications, Hereford.)

INDEX

Place-names are in Shropshire unless stated otherwise

Griffiths, Edward, author of *BC Railway* 143
Groom, Thomas, carrier 75
Gwilliam, Norman, bus driver 78

Hadrian, Roman emperor 17
Haile Selassie, Emperor of Abyssinia 136
Hailstone, Bill, bus operator 78
Hardwick 31
Hare, Revd Sarah 72
Harley family of Brampton Bryan, Herefordshire 57
Harley, Lady Brilliana 45
Harley, Sir Robert, Lord Treasurer 57
Harley, Sir Robert, MP, Parliamentarian 45
Harnage, Richard, MP 56
Harold, king of England 31
Harp House 93
Harrington, Thomas, burgess 40
Harris, Francis, leader of clubmen 51
Hastings, battle of 26
Hawes, Bamber, designer 150
Hawking, R.H., head teacher 124
Haycock, Edward sen., architect and surveyor 111
Hayward, Mary, head teacher 120
Heath, Revd Richard, curate at Clunbury 51
Hemmings, Lucy 130, 131
Hen Domen, Powys 31
Henry III, king of England 34, 35
Henry IV, king of England 39
Henry VI, king of England 39
Henry VIII, king of England 39, 64
Herbalists 103
Herbert, H. A., Whig politician 57
Hereford, cathedral and diocese of 19, 21, 34, 63
Hereford, city of 29, 74
Hereward the Wake 26
Heritage Resource Centre, Bishop's Castle 145
Hetet, Joseph Louis and family 134, 135
Hidage, Tribal 20, 26
Higgins, Cuthbert and Roly 137
High Ercall 45
Hillforts 13, 14
Hinksman, Eva 128
Holiday, Henry, stained glass artist 70
Holmes, William, MP 61
Holocene era 9
Hope valley 75
Hopesay 29, 51
Hopton Castle 34, 49
Horderley 77, 82

Hotspur, Harry *see* Percy, Sir Henry
House on Crutches 93, 127
Howard, Sir Albert CIE, agricultural pioneer 148
Howard, Sir Henry, earl of Northampton 54
Howard, Sir Robert MP, Royalist commander 46, 54
Howell, William ap, tenant of the king 37
Hughes, Annie and Christopher, printer and stationer 117, 13
Hunt, Terry, head teacher 125
Hut, the, Colebatch 98
Hwicce 20, 21, 23
Hyssington, Powys 13, 75

Iapetus Ocean 4
Icel/Icil, ?king of Mercia 23
Iclingas 23
Ieuan, tenant of Bishop's Castle 37
Independents (later Congregationalists) 67, 69
Iron Age 14, 16
Isabella, queen of England 37

Jackson, Georgina, author *A Shropshire Word-Book* 127 128
James I, king of England 40, 41, 44
James II, king of England 55
John, king of England 34, 35
Jones, Charles, coachbuilder 76
Jones, Edward, burgess 40
Jones, John, carrier 75
Jones, Tom, photographer 133
Jukes, Thomas, MP 53
Jurassic limestone 5

Keble, Revd John 69
Keenan, James, teacher 119
Kekewich, Mr Justice 87
Kemp valley and river 9, 10, 14, 102
Kempton 68, 77
Kenchester, Herefordshire 73
Kerry ridgeway 2, 4, 31, 73, 102
Kettle holes 6
Kidderminster, Worcestershire 74
Kinchant, Francis 61
Kinchant, J.C. 61
King, Alexander, MP 53
King, Ambrose, burgess 48
King, John Dashwood MP 58
King's Head, pub 100
Kinnaird, the Hon. Douglas, MP 61